THE
SOVEREIGN
TRICKSTER

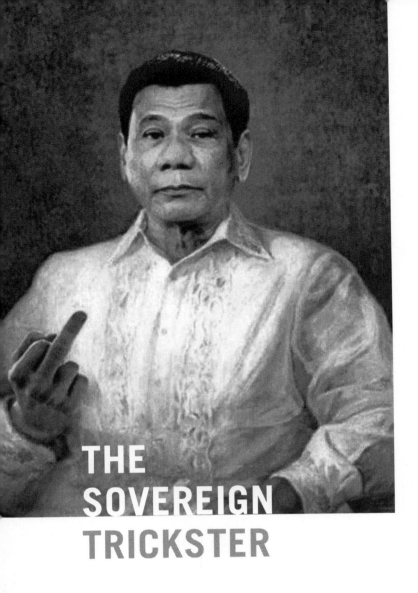

THE
SOVEREIGN
TRICKSTER

Vicente L. Rafael

DEATH AND LAUGHTER IN THE AGE OF DUTERTE

Duke University Press   *Durham and London*   2022

Frontispiece. Internet meme from a Twitter parody account illustrating Duterte as a sovereign trickster, combining the traditional rendering of presidential figures with a universal image of vulgarity. From "Rodrigo Duterte @DigongDU3o, 16th President of the Philippines, The Punisher, Master of Profanity, Great Leader, Parody Account." https://twitter.com/DigongDU3O.

© 2022 Duke University Press. All rights reserved.
Printed and bound by CPI Group (UK) Ltd, Croydon, CR0 4YY
Designed by Courtney Leigh Richardson
Typeset in Whitman and Trade Gothic by Copperline Book Services

Library of Congress Cataloging-in-Publication Data
Names: Rafael, Vicente L., author.
Title: The sovereign trickster: death and laughter in the age
of Duterte / Vincente L. Rafael.
Description: Durham: Duke University Press, 2022. |
Includes bibliographical references and index.
Identifiers: LCCN 2021015724 (print)
LCCN 2021015725 (ebook)
ISBN 9781478015185 (hardcover)
ISBN 9781478017790 (paperback)
ISBN 9781478022411 (ebook)
Subjects: LCSH: Duterte, Rodrigo Roa, 1945– | Presidents—
Philippines—Biography. | Extrajudicial executions—Philippines. |
Philippines—Politics and government—21st century. | BISAC:
HISTORY / Asia / Southeast Asia
Classification: LCC DS686.616. D88 R343 2022 (print) |
LCC DS686.616. D88 (ebook) | DDC 959.905/3092 [B]—dc23
LC record available at https: //lccn.loc.gov/2021015724
LC ebook record available at https: //lccn.loc.gov/2021015725

COVER ART: An alleged drug dealer—and Duterte supporter—
arrested after a buy-bust operation in a slum area in Manila,
September 28, 2017. Courtesy Noel Celis/AFP via Getty Images.

For Lila

CONTENTS

Acknowledgments · ix

INTRODUCTION. Prismatic Histories · 1

1. ELECTORAL DYSTOPIAS · 6

SKETCHES I: *The Dream of Benevolent Dictatorship* · 18

2. MARCOS, DUTERTE, AND THE PREDICAMENTS OF NEOLIBERAL CITIZENSHIP · 21

SKETCHES II: Motherland *and the Biopolitics of Reproductive Health* · 36

3. DUTERTE'S PHALLUS · 42
On the Aesthetics of Authoritarian Vulgarity

SKETCHES III: *Duterte's Hobbesian World* · 57

Duterte's Sense of Time · 60

4. THE SOVEREIGN TRICKSTER · 63

SKETCHES IV: *Comparing Extrajudicial Killings* · 87

Death Squads · 89

On Duterte's Matrix · 94

Fecal Politics · 98

5. PHOTOGRAPHY AND THE BIOPOLITICS OF FEAR · 103
Witnessing the Philippine Drug War

CONCLUSION. Intimacy and the Autoimmune Community · 131

Notes · 147

References · 151

Index · 169

ACKNOWLEDGMENTS

In an ideal world, there should be no need for acknowledgments. One could simply say, "To all those who helped with this book, you know who you are. You know the joys and the hardships you put me through," and then leave it at that. Of course, we live in a world that is far from ideal, where gifts are given but left unreciprocated, obligations are neglected, kindnesses unrecognized, disagreements unresolved, friendships done and undone. A book, like all things made, emerges from these exhilarating but difficult conditions, a repository of ongoing collaborations and unfinished torment. Acknowledgments as a genre for recording the coming of a particular book thus remains unavoidable and necessary. It is also a source of pleasure as it allows one to think back to those times of openness and uncertainty, when ideas were not yet well formed, and, thanks to the unintended intervention of others, anything seemed possible. So here goes.

There was no way I could have written this book without the courageous coverage of Duterte and the drug war by a number of dedicated journalists, photographers, and filmmakers. I am especially grateful for the generous friendship and insightful accounts of Sheila Coronel. Ramona Diaz furnished me with much food for thought regarding the biopolitics of reproductive health in her closely observed film *Motherland*. Many others provided me with rich sources for writing this book. Their stories and images have been indispensable for compiling an archive of many facets of Duterte's regime. Given the current political conditions of fear and the repression of journalists, I have decided not to mention them by name lest their association with this book prove awkward. Rather I have cited them in the notes and references that follow. I do not know what they will think of this work, but I hope they will find in it some vindication of their difficult task of witnessing the crimes of this administration.

I am also indebted to many friends and colleagues in the Philippines, North America, and Europe who shared materials, invited me to talk about parts of this work, and offered lots of useful criticisms and comments along the way, both offline and on. They include Jamela Alindogan, Fr. Albert Allejo, SJ, Arjun Appadurai, Clara Balaguer, Rick Baldoz, Tani Barlow, Remmon Barbaza, John Bengan, Karina Bolasco, Boom Buencamino, Fenella Cannell, Ruben Carranaz, Rosa Cordillera Castillo, Leloy Claudio, Nancy Amelia Collins, Tina Cuyugan, Cathy Davidson, Adrian de Leon, Deirdre de la Cruz, Edilberto J. de Jesus, Al Dingwall, Nuelle Duterte, Luis Francia, Tak Fujitani, Erik Harms, Donna Harraway, Caroline Hau, Janet Hoskins, Cristina Juan, Webb Kean, Ralph Litzinger, Mac McCarty, Alfred McCoy, Mahar, Thetis, and Maria Mangahas, the late Sylvia Mayuga, Erik Mueggler, Yoshiko Nagano, Matthew Nicdao, Ambeth Ocampo, Johanna Poethig, Kerry Poethig, Mary Louise Pratt, Michael Purugganan, Sharon Quinsaat, Rachel A. G. Reyes, Marian Pastor Roces, Renato Rosaldo, Joel Pablo Salue, James Scott, Vincent Serrano, Howie Severino, Shu-mei Shih, John Sidel, Cheryll Ruth Soriano, Megan Thomas, Ashley Thompson, Karen Tongson, Von Totanes, Nhung Tuyet Tranh, Anna Tsing, Tony La Viña, Laura Wexler, Jenifer Wofford, Lisa Yoneyama, Krip Yuson, and James Zarsadiaz.

The ethnographic work of several anthropologists was absolutely essential for putting flesh on the bones of my arguments, especially regarding the cultural and material basis of Duterte's popularity. I am particularly grateful to Nicole Curato, Wataru Kusaka, Steffen Jensen, Karl Hapal, Gideon Lasco, Jonathan Ong, Koki Seki, and Anna Warburg. The political commentary and scholarship of writers such as Carmela Abao, Jojo Abinales, Cleve Arguelles, Walden Bello, Randy David, Richard Heydarian, Pete Lacaba, Ronald Mendoza, Antonio Montalvan, J. P. Punongbayan, Ninotchka Rosca, Julio Teehankee, and Mark Thompson were also very useful.

My colleagues and students, past and present, at the University of Washington were always supportive throughout many stages of this project, and I am deeply appreciative of their help and hospitality: Andrea Arai, Jorge Bayona, Jordana Balkian, Joe Bernardo, Davinder Bhowmik, Rick Bonus, Shannon Bush, Ana Mari Cauce, Purnima Dhavan, Christoph Giebel, Jenna Grant, Danny Hoffman, Lin Hongxuan, Arthit Jiamratanyoo, Moon-Ho Jung, Resat Kasaba, Roneva Keel, Mehmet Kendil, Jesse Kindig, Selim Kuru, Symbol Lai, Celia Lowe, Tony Lucero, Allan Lumba, Ted Mack, Laurie Marhoefer, Arzoo Ozanloo, James Pangilinan, Ileana Rodriguez-Silva, Laurie Sears, Balbir Singh, Lynn Thomas, Jack Turner, Adam Warren, Anand Yang,

Glennys Young, and Kathy Woodward. I especially thank Sandra Joshel for indulging my questions during many of our memorable Costco seminars.

In writing this book, I found myself revisiting the works of James T. Siegel. His writings on violence and the sublime provided me with ways to think about encounters with death and defacement. His books on the Suharto regime prodded me to consider the authoritarian imagination in relation to extrajudicial killings, trauma, corpses, photography, and what he calls the "nationalization of death." While Indonesia and the Philippines differ in many important respects, they share a history of colonial and postcolonial dictatorships reliant on the technologies of mass killings, deep-seated corruption, and counterinsurgency that sustain the biopolitics of fear.

Ken Wissoker, as always, offered valuable advice, unstinting support, and generous friendship. Like all my previous books, this one would have been impossible without his help and encouragement. I was fortunate to have two enthusiastic anonymous readers who convinced me that there was something much more interesting in the manuscript than I had originally seen. Their patient and informed engagement were valuable in shaping the final form of this book. In particular, I owe Ralph Litzinger a special *utang na loob* for carefully reading various versions of the manuscript. I also thank Ryan Kendall and Susan Albury for their unflagging editorial assistance in helping me prepare the manuscript for publication.

Portions of this work were presented in several venues: Columbia University, Ateneo de Manila University, De La Salle University, London School of Economics, School of African and Asian Studies, University of Copenhagen, University of Amsterdam, Humboldt University, University of British Columbia, Virginia Tech, Yale University, University of Southern California, UCLA, University of San Francisco, University of Toronto, NYU, University of Washington, University of Michigan, University of California–Berkeley, and University of California–Santa Cruz. I thank the organizers for their generous invitations.

Manila was a far more welcoming place to do research thanks to the unfailing hospitality of the Rafaels, especially my brothers Joey, David, and Ricky (when he was visiting from Vancouver) and my various cousins, nieces, and nephews. I am deeply grateful to the late Senator Leticia Ramos Shahani, who offered me her home, her friendship, and inspiring conversation. I also thank her son, Chanda Shahani.

Lila Ramos Shahani's contribution to this work has been manifold and difficult to enumerate. She provided both intellectual and emotional support while offering many sharp observations and timely corrections. Long conversations with her and her mom disabused me of my state-phobia and provoked me to reconsider many of my assumptions about the Philippine government. Lila never failed to push back so I could push forward, and it is to her that I dedicate this book.

Shorter versions of chapters 4 and 5 were published, respectively, in the *Journal of Asian Studies* 78, no. 1, February 2019, and *positions: asia critique* 28, no. 4, November 2020. The versions that appear here have been substantially revised and expanded. Some of the pieces that make up the section "Sketches" first appeared in the *Philippine Daily Inquirer* ("The Dream of Benevolent Dictatorship" and "Duterte's Hobbesian World"), *Rappler* ("Death Squads," "Comparing Extrajudicial Killings"), and in *Bulatlat* ("Fecal Politics"). They have also been extensively revised and expanded for this book. The rest of the shorter pieces are published here for the first time.

If you lose your job, I'll give you one. Kill all the drug addicts. . . . Help me kill addicts. . . . Let's kill addicts every day. —PRESIDENT DUTERTE, addressing returning overseas Filipino workers, 2017

Crime is glorified because it is one of the fine arts, because it can be the work only of exceptional natures, because it reveals the monstrousness of the strong and powerful, because villainy is yet another mode of privilege. —MICHEL FOUCAULT, *Discipline and Punish*, 1977

Duterte and Me

The one and only time I ever met President Rodrigo Roa Duterte was at a funeral in Manila on March 22, 2017. It was not, fortunately, for one of the victims of his drug war but for the late Senator Leticia Ramos Shahani, sister of former President Fidel V. Ramos and mother of my partner, Lila Ramos Shahani (see Jett 2018 for an account of her remarkable career). During the wake, we were told that he would drop by at around 10 p.m. But his return from a trip to Bangkok was delayed, and we got word that he wouldn't be there till midnight. At 1 a.m., we saw him on a live TV broadcast on the airport tarmac holding forth. This was typical of the president, who was always hours late for his appointments. Finally, at around 4 a.m., he began to arrive. His arrival was long and drawn out, signaled by a sudden flurry of activity among his entourage (consisting mostly of cabinet members) that woke us up from our sleepy vigil. About a dozen security personnel in white barong shirts with walkie-talkies did a sweep of the funeral home. A caravan of vehicles followed, and he emerged from one of them, flanked by his assistants and assorted flunkies. Finally, the king had arrived.

He strode in slowly, waving at those who remained at the wake and shaking hands with the family. Noticeably subdued, he approached the coffin, looking at the corpse with quiet respect. His mother had been a friend of Senator Shahani. The latter was among those who had been appointed by former President Cory Aquino to oversee the transition from the dictatorship to democracy in 1986 after the overthrow of Ferdinand Marcos. Cory Aquino had asked Soledad Duterte, a staunch opponent of Marcos, to serve as mayor of Davao during the transition. Soledad demurred, suggesting instead someone else, while her son Rodrigo or "Rody" became vice mayor and eventually mayor. Later, he briefly served as a congressman, then vice mayor and mayor once again for the next two decades, before finally becoming president in 2016. Thus did the overthrow of one dictator pave the way for the rise of another.

During his visit, I stayed outside the circle of family and friends that had formed around him, engaged in quiet conversation. I was reluctant to get drawn in. As he was about to leave, there was the usual call for a group photograph. I tried to hide in the back so as not to be part of the picture. Too late: Lila's uncle, who had earlier endorsed and later criticized Duterte, called for me to join them. Reluctantly, I posed in the back of the pack. In every photograph with Duterte, everyone is expected to do the "fist salute," a symbol of his campaign and his supposed strength. It always seemed to me like a warmed-over fascist salute. I refused to raise my fist, distancing myself from him. But, like all slight gestures of resistance, it was easy to overlook and largely ineffectual. Inevitably, I was folded into the scene, unable to extract myself from the grip of his authority. Remaining silent, and then compelled to shake his hand out of politeness at the end, I felt as if I had become complicit in the crimes of his regime. Despite several articles I had written criticizing his policies, especially his drug war, I reluctantly grasped his hand and felt contaminated by the bloody history of its brutal commands.

As he walked out of the chapel where Senator Shahani was laid out, he was greeted by resounding cheers in the lobby of the funeral home. Like a celebrity, he was approached for selfies. While I was deeply reluctant to shake his hand or even be pictured with him, everyone else seemed agog at his presence and wanted a photographic souvenir of their encounter. Watching all this put me in a quandary: How to explain the wide gulf between them and me? Knowing what we all knew about his drug war and penchant for violating human rights, especially those of the poor, why would so many celebrate him, or at least willingly accept his authority, while I would remain critical and disdainful—indeed, afraid—of him? Did my fear bear any relationship to the majority's approval of him? Or could it be that it was this widespread fear that was the basis of his power and therefore popularity? Given his eagerness to kill and imprison all those he perceived to be his enemies, could his remarkable popularity—last polled at over 91 percent in October of 2020—as well as the relative fecklessness of the opposition, be an outgrowth of this government by fear?

These are some of the questions I have been asking myself, and what follows is a modest attempt to address them. Like my refusal to raise my fist in the picture, I hope these pages will allow me to distance myself from Duterte's hold, even as I admit to being infected by his rule.

The Authoritarian Imaginary

This book offers a kind of prismatic view of the age of Duterte, and so, as with a prism, it is "a medium which distorts, slants, or colors whatever is viewed through it" (Merriam-Webster). Rather than provide a clear, unified account of his regime and its historical precedents and global variants, it weaves together a set of topics ranging from the drug war to neoliberal citizenship, from the presidential phallus to the photographs of corpses killed by the police, for example, distancing these, then bringing them up close for scrutiny. I am much less interested in determining what Duterte is—a fascist, a populist, a warlord, a *trapo* (traditional politician), or all of the above— as what he does—the technics of his rule, the rhetoric of his humor, his administration of fear, and the projection of his masculinity and misogyny. And if there is a thematic thread that runs through the book, it is a series of recurring questions: What is the relationship between life and death under Duterte? How does he, like all modern rulers, use one to contain, exploit, and deploy the other? In other words, how does he manage to instrumentalize life to allay death, and how does he weaponize death to control life? What are the conditions that allow him to succeed, as well as fail? How does Duterte's authoritarian imaginary[1] feed off, even as it disrupts, the vernacular articulations of community and intimacy, especially among the poor? What is the role of obscenity in the making of his grotesque persona, and how does it feed the formation of fear among those he governs? How is an "intimate tyranny," to use the phrase of Achille Mbembe (2001), produced by the play of conviviality and coercion between the ruler and the ruled? Or, to put it on a slightly different register, how do the technics of what Michel Foucault calls "biopower" (Foucault 2010)—the control and management of all aspects of life to ensure and foster more than life—inextricably combine with what Mbembe refers to as "necropower" (Mbembe 2019)— the power to control death, to decide upon who must die so that others might live—in the age of Duterte?

Along with this introduction, five chapters plus a brief conclusion make up this book, interrupted and reconnected by a series of shorter pieces, which I refer to as sketches. They deal with a series of related topics such as the biopolitics of reproductive health, Duterte's view of history, his abilities as a storyteller, incomplete histories of extrajudicial killings, death squads, fecal politics, and more. The longer essays—touching on the history of electoral dystopia, the rise of neoliberal citizenship, Duterte's phallic power, the hybrid figure of the absolute sovereign and wily trickster as a defining feature of Duterte's persona, photography, trauma, and the biopolitics of fear in the context of witnessing the drug war, and intimacy and the autoimmunity of community—extend and elaborate upon the sketches. The sketches were written mostly on the fly in response to the events of the day, most of them appearing as social media posts or opinion pieces in Philippine newspapers. We can think of the sketches as rehearsals or drafts for the chapters. While the latter are meant for an academic audience, the former seek to reach an informed "general reader"—whatever that fictional construct might mean. Unlike the sustained arguments of the longer essays, the sketches function as a kind of decalage, marking the temporal and spatial differences between the minor and major pieces (Edwards 2003). They set things out of alignment, forcing one to see the gaps between and within the arguments of the essays, showing their hesitations, overlaps, revisions, and repetitions, thereby inviting further interpretation, correction, and critique. Thus do the longer essays begin to feel like displacements of the shorter pieces, even as the latter anticipate and defer to the former. Both come across as bits and pieces of an assemblage whose parts do not necessarily amount to a unified whole. Rather, they are more like shards awaiting excavation in the future to help puzzle through this current moment.

This book, then, is far from being a definitive history of the age of Duterte. It is impossible to write such a work given the fact that Duterte is still in power as of this writing and, barring a coup or his falling ill to cancer or the COVID-19 virus currently raging across the planet, he will likely remain in place until the next election in 2022. Barred by the Constitution from running for a second term, he will have been on his way to retirement by the time this book reaches print, even as elements of his governing style, what some have called "Dutertismo," will continue to be emulated by his followers. Anachronism will thus be unavoidable. Neither does the book offer policy alternatives or pathways toward reform and revolution. It is diagnostic rather than prescriptive, and even then is far from being an exhaustive examination of the state of play. It registers a history of the present that is already past even as its traces continue to survive, exercising effects on the future as far-reaching as they are contingent.

Still, readers might find something useful here, whether they are primarily interested in the Philippines or in comparing authoritarian forms in other parts of the world. In the pages that follow, I try to recast Duterte from the unforgiving authoritarian and over-masculinized figure that many see him as into a more complex, fragile, and ambiguous character in a political drama he cannot fully control. The journalist Sheila Coronel gets at these multifaceted, one might say prismatic, aspects of Duterte. She relates one of the stories he often told on the campaign trail about shooting one of his classmates in law school who kept making fun of his provincial accent. "I waited for him," Duterte recalled some forty-five years later. "I told myself, I'll teach him a lesson." The classmate survived, but no one ever messed with Duterte again. And then the punch line: "The truth is, I am used to shooting people." The audience, as they invariably do, laughed. Coronel observed that "it was a typical Duterte story, with Duterte cast not as the aggressor but as the aggrieved. . . . He took the law into his own hands, but by doing so, he earned the grudging respect of his tormentor. The telling, too, was classic Duterte: boastful while also being self-deprecating. It was crass, hyperbolic, transgressive. And its conclusion—'I am used to shooting people'—could be construed as a joke, a fact, or a threat. Its power and its beauty lay in its ambiguity" (Coronel 2012; see also Rosca 2018).

It is precisely the "power and the beauty," which is to say the political aesthetic of Duterte's rule, that interest me the most. Seen in the context of post-Marcos history characterized by the conjunction of counterinsurgency and neoliberalism, the formal qualities of his discourse can provide a key to understanding the brutal logic and deadly effects of his rule. By appreciating the tendentious ambiguity that allows him to dominate his listeners, we can begin to map the contours of his authoritarian imagination that at once repels and attracts his followers and detractors alike.

1. ELECTORAL DYSTOPIAS

While many in the United States were thunderstruck by the election of Donald Trump in November 2016, people in the Philippines were not entirely surprised. Along with many other people outside the US, they had been swept by the recent storms of authoritarianism that had been blowing, like the warming winds of the Arctic, across the world. The US election was significant in many ways, not least of all because of the fact that from a global perspective it retired the myth of American exceptionalism.

Seen from this perspective, the election of Rodrigo Duterte in May of 2016 seems to have been part of a global trend. Thanks to his tough-guy talk, his unapologetic misogyny, his unmitigated hostility to human rights, his taunting of President Obama and the United States, along with his warming relations with China's Xi Jinping and Russia's Vladimir Putin, and most of all his unremitting war on drugs waged by way of extrajudicial killings, Duterte has become a global sensation. There isn't a major media outlet in the world that hasn't featured him, and the comparisons to Trump have been plentiful, if often inaccurate. The temptation to compare the two has been unavoidable. However, rather than resort to glib comparisons, I want to step back and ask about the historical context and the conditions of possibility that allowed for someone like Duterte to become president. Such conditions have a lot to do with the history of colonialism in the Philippines under Spain, the United States, and Japan, and the postcolonial republic that continued to be under the spell of the US. To understand such conditions, we can begin with a few observations about the role of elections in liberal democracies generally, and in the Philippines more specifically.

The Colonial Roots of Elections

In most liberal democracies, elections tend to be Janus-faced. On the one hand, they are essential to the ongoing democratization of society insofar as they are expressions of popular sovereignty. The act of voting is an indispensable ritual, performed privately, yet counted publicly: a solitary act with collective consequences meant to ensure the peaceful and legitimate transfer of power and the legislation of social change. On the other hand, elections, by mobilizing people, set them against one another into a state of civil strife. Not for nothing are electoral contests, like wars, called "campaigns." Unleashing long-held social antagonisms, elections also act to contain them. Just as they drive one to become political, elections also set about domesticating politics, draining it of its potential insurgency. Voting rechannels the boisterous energies let loose by the street and arena campaigns into the orderly halls of Congress, presided over by political professionals. In this way, elections tend to turn movements into moments managed by elected representatives (Anderson 1998).

This dual character of elections can also be seen in formerly colonized countries but with important variations. In a place like the Philippines, where liberal democracy came by way of the most illiberal means such as wars of conquest and colonization, the history of elections traces a different path. Voting was a colonial practice introduced by the Spaniards in the later seventeenth to eighteenth centuries. The lowest ranks of the colonial bureaucracy had been opened to natives and mestizo elites to aid in the administration of the colony. Members of the local elites and their surrogates could choose among themselves who would fill the positions of *cabezas de barangay*, or village headmen, and *gobernadorcillo*, or municipal governor. They sent the names of their top three choices to the governor general, who made the final choice. These highly localized electoral exercises were strictly controlled by Spanish friars, who had veto power over any of the winners. The franchise, as one might imagine, was extremely limited: only current and former officials and the male members of their families could vote. In some provinces, surrogates of elite families rather than elites themselves ran for office (Abinales and Amoroso 2017; Copurz 1957; de Llobet 2011; Fradera 1999; May 1987; Robles 1969). Elections, then, were instruments for regularizing elite collaboration. They reproduced the colonial hierarchy by preserving the social positions and privileges of local leaders—especially their exemption from tribute and forced labor—and thereby secured the power of Spanish rulers.

In the wake of the Napoleonic invasion of Spain, Spanish colonial rule entered a period of liberalization after 1812. Representation to the Spanish parliament, or Cortes, was extended to the colonies to keep them within the empire. While briefly granted representation, such a right was eventually withheld from *las islas Filipinas*—the only colony to be wholly without representation in the parliament. Such was due mainly to the fact that Spaniards regarded the Filipinos as too racially mixed and therefore inferior (de Llobet 2011; Fradera 1999; Mojares 2006; Schumacher 1997; Simbulan 2005). Filipino exclusion from political representation on racial grounds was resented especially by the Hispanized Filipino elites, who, given their education and wealth, regarded themselves as more Spaniard that the average Spaniard. It became a major bone of contention in the emergent nationalist movement starting in the 1860s, triggered by the racist exclusion of highly competent Filipino priests from being assigned to parishes. Separatist sentiments gradually emerged from this experience of electoral exclusion and other acts of Spanish injustice, boiling over into the Revolution in 1896.

Initial successes against Spain led to the formation of the Filipino Revolutionary Government in March of 1897. Elections were held to determine its leadership. Participants were drawn mainly from a small number of male revolutionary leaders, many of them hailing from the ranks of the provincial elites who had earlier served in the colonial bureaucracy. Plagued by rumors, ad hominem attacks, and voter fraud, the very first presidential election was won by the Chinese mestizo General Emilio Aguinaldo over the so-called "father" of the Revolution, Andrés Bonifacio. Denouncing the results, Bonifacio and his supporters decided to plot a coup. Hearing of this plot, Aguinaldo ordered the arrest and execution of Bonifacio. In this state of revolutionary emergency, the first Filipino election was thus marked by fraud, contested results, aggrieved candidates, coup attempts, and the violent elimination of political rivals. This pattern of intra-elite factional rivalries exploding into violence would figure prominently in the history of succeeding elections (Agoncillo 1956, 1960).

We can see this pattern in the second Filipino elections, in 1898. As Filipino revolutionary forces proved victorious over Spain, and as they sought to deal with the growing presence of American troops in the archipelago, they retreated to the town of Malolos in Bulacan, north of Manila. There they crafted a constitution and formed the First Republic by calling for elections. The franchise was limited to the wealthiest and most educated men, who unapologetically referred to themselves as the "brains of the nation" and an "oligarchy of the intellect." The conservative makeup of Congress was such that it retained many of the Spanish laws and restored the hated poll taxes and forced labor to support the new government. The First Republic eventually proved unpopular among many in the lower classes, and resistance to its authority emerged. The masses had expected not merely regime change but a real social revolution that would restore true *kalayaan*, or freedom, understood as a moral society of mutual caring and compassion. But before such class tensions could escalate into a civil war, the US invasion plunged the country into a protracted and brutal guerrilla war between 1899 and 1902 (Agoncillo 1960; Guerrero 2015; Ileto 1979; Mabini 2007).

The US invasion eventually overwhelmed the Filipino Republic after a long, protracted battle. However, insurgencies continued to break out all throughout US colonial occupation till the 1930s. Anxious to end the fighting, the United States set up elections as a counterinsurgency measure. Elections were seen as a means to co-opt local elites, many of whom were leaders of the Filipino forces, and ensure their local basis of power. Local elections were held in places deemed "pacified" by the US military between 1901 and 1903, followed by national elections for representatives to the first Filipino colonial assembly in 1907. The franchise, not surprisingly, was limited to those who were wealthy, educated, and male. Only about 1.7 percent of the population was qualified to vote in 1907—educated male property owners with a degree of fluency in Spanish or English—a number that would rise gradually through the period of American rule (Corpuz 1957; Cullinane 2005; Kramer 2006; May 1980; Stanley 1974).

Electoral Counterinsurgency

Intended to be a counterinsurgency measure, elections not surprisingly produced largely conservative results. As in the Spanish colonial era, elections under US rule were meant to organize and regularize collaboration. They also had the effect of reproducing and protecting class and gender hierarchy in the face of an ongoing insurgency and the popular demand for social revolution. However, elections by themselves could not accomplish these twin goals, and thus were joined to an ensemble of other measures. These included setting up a network of public schools, parks, a public health system, and new communication and transportation infrastructures designed to "pacify" and "reconcile" the population while suturing class divisions (Abinales and Amoroso 2017; Cullinane 2005; Foster and Go 2006; May 1980; McCoy 2009b; McKenna 2017).

Colonial biopower, however, was sustainable only if the colonial state could assert its unwavering sovereignty and quell challenges to its rule. This entailed setting up paramilitary forces such as the Philippine Scouts and police forces to replace the departing American troops. Harking back to the colonial militias established by the Spanish regime, such native colonial forces were then assigned to provinces and attached to local elites who supported them in exchange for their services. Such services included intimidating rival elites, especially during elections, putting down dissident peasants and workers, and so on. In short, elections by the first half of the twentieth century were part of an ensemble of governing practices designed to regulate political participation in ways that would ensure colonial order while preserving the social inequality essential to that order. Once again, democratic institutions were calculated to produce undemocratic ends. Key to this colonial paradox was the use of violence, not just by agents of the state but also by loose, informally organized militias acting often as paramilitary forces and private bodyguards to politicians. The relative strength of such local forces was further highlighted by the weak central apparatus of the colonial state and, as in the case of the US, the absence of a professional colonial civil service to carry out federal mandates (Abinales and Amoroso 2017; Kramer 2006; McCoy 2009b).

The nature of colonial electoralism—that is, elections as a form of counterinsurgency productive of social hierarchy, the maintenance of which depended on highly localized paramilitary violence—continued in the wake of independence in 1946. However, it went through some important mutations. Chief among these changes was the expansion of the franchise. Such an expansion had been going on since the 1930s, when literacy and property qualifications were modified and when women were given the vote in 1938. With independence, near universal voting rights were established, with the goal of democratizing society. Of course, things didn't quite work out as planned. Expanding the franchise gave the vote to the majority, many of whom were poor people. Politically empowered, they remained socially marginalized and economically impoverished. Ruling elites, many of whom had collaborated with both the US and, during the Pacific war, with Japan, had to find novel ways to persuade and coerce this new electorate to vote for them under changed conditions (Abinales and Amoroso 2017; Hedman and Sidel 2000; McCoy 1993). They did so in three ways.

First, they changed the style of campaigning. In the past, presidential candidates had campaigned mostly from their homes, making limited appearances and rarely mixing with crowds. The presidential campaign of Ramon Magsaysay in 1953 changed all that. Directed by the legendary CIA operative and former advertising executive Edward Landsdale, Magsaysay turned campaigning into a series of public spectacles. A political upstart who banked on his close ties with the American military forces and his reputation as an anti-communist populist, Magsaysay toured the country, engaging in highly theatricalized campaigns, often photographed eating with his hands. Future candidates would follow his example, projecting themselves as "men of the people" by posing with farmers planting rice, barnstorming across the archipelago, and dazzling audiences with bombastic rhetoric and the singing and dancing of popular movie stars (Kerkvliet 2002).

The second thing candidates did in the face of an expanded electorate was to resort to massive vote buying. Earlier, they could rely on provincial ties of patronage to compel clients to vote for them. Now, they were faced with anonymous voters. In the absence of personal connections built over long histories of exchanging favors, candidates resorted to giving cash to gain their vote. This, in turn, made it imperative for candidates to raise huge sums of money to buy their way into office. Old-money oligarchs could rely on their inheritances and earnings from their lands and other businesses. However, newer politicians, such as Ferdinand Marcos, and local warlords who were outside the established oligarchy had to find ways to raise money quickly and massively. Aside from plundering state coffers, politicians supplemented their incomes by turning to a variety of criminal activities, such as smuggling, gambling, especially *jueteng* (an illegal numbers game), a variety of protection rackets, and more recently drug dealing, especially crystal meth, called *shabu*. Today, the cost of elections has become so steep that one would have to be many times a millionaire, or enjoy the patronage of one or several, to run even for local offices, much less the presidency (Abinales and Amoroso 2017; Hedman and Sidel 2000; McCoy 2009a; Mojares 1986).

Finally, the third way that ruling elites dealt with the expansion of the franchise was to intensify the use of violence, intimidating and often assassinating their rivals. For this, they relied on their bodyguards and private armies recruited from former guerrillas who fought the Japanese, local police forces, lumpen proletariats, criminal gang members, former communist fighters, and other assorted thugs.

Postwar elections were thus characterized by the widespread use of "guns, goons, and gold." Rather than peaceful transitions to power, elections increasingly unleashed as much money as blood. And winners were invariably tainted with charges of corruption as they assumed office, even as they would turn around and accuse their opponents of being similarly corrupt. Corruption was normalized both as a means to win elections and as a major electoral issue to hurl at one's opponents. Once again, the irony: candidates railed against corruption even as they relied on corrupt practices in order to win.

From Martial Law to Elite Democracy

Ferdinand Marcos came into office precisely by promising to do away with corruption. At the same time, he proved to be the most corrupt politician in order to win the election of 1965 and win reelection in 1969. Allied with certain elements of the Stalinist Communist Party, Marcos sought to "revolutionize" Philippine society (Scalice 2017). He did so principally by declaring martial law in 1972 and proceeding to rob the country blind in order to maintain his power. Along the way, he rewrote the constitution to his liking, ruled largely by executive order, abolished Congress, and installed a rubber-stamp parliament and Supreme Court. At the same time, he ordered the disarming of an array of private armies to neutralize his elite rivals on the right even as he unleashed the armed forces of the Philippines against student activists, workers, peasants, and communists on the left. In a bid to monopolize the use of violence, Marcos turned the Philippine military and the Constabulary into his own private army to do his bidding (Abinales and Amoroso 2017; Hedman and Sidel 2000; McCoy 2009b; Mojares 2016; Wurfel 1988).

After twenty years in power, Marcos was finally overthrown by a nonviolent uprising called "People Power" in Manila. This civilian-led uprising came on the heels of a failed military coup. It was initially provoked, however, by Marcos's rash decision to hold snap elections, which he declared on American TV in order to prove to his Washington critics that he was still popular. But he vastly underestimated the necrological aura that surrounded Cory Aquino, widowed after her husband and chief challenger of Marcos, Ninoy Aquino, was assassinated on the airport tarmac as he returned from exile in Boston in August 1983. Marcos did what he had always done: he tried to steal the election by rigging the computer tabulation of the results. The public exposure of manual and electronic ballot stuffing by disheartened computer tabulators and by the media further contributed to triggering the uprising that overthrew Marcos. Just as rigging elections allowed him to seize power, so did its exposure bring him down (Manzanilla and Hau 2016; Thompson 1995).

With the end of martial law, electoral practices in the post-Marcos era resumed much of their pre-Marcosian patterns. This was not surprising since the end of Marcos marked not a revolution but a restoration of the old oligarchy side by side with the new rich presiding over a divided society where over a third of the population lived below the poverty line. Elections continued to be marked by fraud and violence. Yet there was also something different (Anderson 1988; David 2013; Kerkvliet and Mojares 1992; McCoy 2009b). Aside from their rampant brutality and mind-boggling thievery, the Marcos years left behind three related legacies.

One was the spectacular growth of the Maoist Communist Party and their armed wing, the New People's Army, led by former English professor and teacher of Rodrigo Duterte, Jose Maria Sison. The communists offered the best, and often the only, organized resistance movement during the dark days of martial law, and Marcos was often referred to as their single best recruiter. At the same time, the Stalinist leadership of the party had long worked to hasten the coming of martial law in order to intensify oppression and thereby drive people to join the party. Indeed, toward the end of martial law, the communists had managed to control over 20 percent of the countryside and had extensive networks of allies above ground, organized into an urban coalition called the National Democratic Front. Holding fast, against all odds, to their strategy of PPW, or protracted people's war, designed to take the cities by controlling the surrounding countryside, the Maoist insurgency continues to operate on a smaller scale, with far less support in several areas of the country, especially in northern Mindanao (Abinales and Amoroso 2017; Quimpo and Quimpo 2012; Scalice 2017).

A second legacy was the spread of organized Muslim separatist movements led by Nur Misuari, who founded the Moro National Liberation Front, or MNLF, in 1972 in the wake of the infamous and controversial Jabidah Massacre, wherein Muslim military recruits were allegedly killed by their military trainers for reasons that remain vague to this day. This massacre came on the heels of centuries-long tensions between Muslim peoples and Christian settlers in Mindanao, whereby the latter were largely seen to be favored by the Christian government in Manila while the former were woefully neglected and marginalized. Since Marcos, the government response has alternated between diplomacy and scorched-earth policy. The latest attempt to pass a Bangsa Moro Law that would grant greater political, economic, and religious autonomy to the predominantly Muslim areas came with relentless military attacks in areas like Marawi in western Mindanao, where ISIS-inspired groups have sought to take control. The separatist movement thus continues to this day, albeit splintered into several factions. Younger members, aided by a few foreign fighters, are daily radicalized by both global jihadist movements and the continuing conditions of violence and poverty widely blamed on both local Muslim elites and the Manila government. To counter these so-called terrorist activities, Duterte has declared martial law in Mindanao (appropriately, while on a visit to Putin's Russia) with the approval of both the Congress and the Supreme Court. In Mindanao, the history of electoral politics has come full circle, returning to the authoritarianism of the Marcos years (Hutchcroft 2016; Lara 2014).

The third legacy of the Marcos years was the fracturing of the military. Racked by corruption and favoritism, the officer corps was split between Marcos cronies who benefited from his wealth and power, and disillusioned and highly professional soldiers who held the latter in contempt and had sought to overthrow Marcos. Divided, demoralized, and politicized, the military found itself fighting a two-front war: the communists and the Muslim separatist rebellion in the south. To remedy their weakness they began to rely on paramilitary groups and volunteer militias that they armed and paid for. Let loose on the population, such undisciplined forces terrorized towns and preyed upon their residents, quickly devolving into death squads and vigilantes. In addition, the faction in the military who called themselves RAM, or the Reformed Armed Forces Movement, had triggered the coup attempt against Marcos that led to the People Power uprising. In the wake of the Marcos dictatorship, they would launch a series of coups seeking to topple Aquino's government between 1987 and 1989.

Under Cory Aquino, there was an initial attempt to get rid of these armed groups and negotiate with the Communist Party. However, beset by coup attempts from a military hostile to the left, peace talks eventually broke down, and fighting resumed. Supplementing an emboldened military, Cory tolerated the formation of right-wing civilian volunteers, many of whom were drawn from overlapping social groups: lumpens, former rebels, and gang members. They were formed and funded with the aid and protection of local police and the military. Anti-communist death squads proliferated in areas where the communists were strongest, and the rate of extrajudicial killings rivaled those of Marcos's time (Abinales and Amoroso 2017; Coronel 1993).

Thus can we see the intertwined histories of elections, money, and violence in the postwar Philippines. Rooted in colonial and postcolonial history, all three are essential elements in the formation of the state and the making of civil society. During the transition from Marcos to Aquino—that is, from the end of authoritarian rule to the restoration of elite democracy— the post–martial law oligarchy turned to civilian volunteers, organized and sponsored by the police and the military into anti-communist vigilantes. Such death squads were the other side, the dark side if you will, of People Power.

Originally directed against Marcos, populist violence was now aimed at the communists and assorted criminal gangs. Under succeeding presidents, the police and their volunteers were tacitly empowered to carry out summary executions of suspected communist leaders, while local elites subcontracted death squads to deal with labor leaders, journalists, and rival elites. Gruesome displays of violence—severed heads and mutilated corpses displayed on roadways—were the signature of vigilante groups like Alsa Masa in places like Davao, where the mayor then was none other than Rodrigo Duterte (Coronel 1993).

President Duterte made his reputation as the tough-talking mayor of Davao by negotiating with both vigilantes and communists, absorbing elements of both into his regime. According to various reports, he, or at least those around him, recruited former NPAs and other lumpen types to serve as paramilitary forces in dealing with a new enemy: drug lords and drug users. After having served as prosecutor, he became vice mayor of Davao. Duterte's mother had been a strident opponent of Marcos (even as his father served in his cabinet). He subsequently ran for mayor and has won every election since then, including a brief stint in Congress. Coming from the ranks of provincial elites, Duterte's father, Vicente, was also the governor of Davao province and was a prominent cabinet member of Marcos's government. Now that he is president, Rodrigo's daughter, Sarah, serves as the mayor of Davao, his youngest son Sebastian as vice mayor, and his eldest son Paolo serves in Congress. Such family ties, always crucial in Philippine politics, clearly situate Duterte as part of a political dynasty—and thus part of the very oligarchy that he is given to condemn in his speeches. His reputation as "the Punisher" emerged at the crossroads of democratic transition and counterinsurgency, when People Power was taken to mean that ordinary people would be empowered to act on behalf of the state and kill its designated enemies. In a way, death squads have become the perverse doubles of NGOs, or nongovernmental organizations, since both share a parallel history in the outsourcing of state functions (Curato 2017a; Heyderian 2018; Miller 2018; Paddock 2017).

Spanish and American colonialism, followed by the postcolonial Republic, thus established the historical conditions for Philippine elections. By intensifying the circulation of money, elections have called for, as much as they have enabled, the mass mobilization of voters. But they also intensify the proliferation of armed vigilantes and death squads to coerce political rivals and run rackets for the accumulation of money. Regarded in the late 1980s as a much-needed supplement to the military's counterinsurgency war, they have now morphed into the death squads serving as essential supplements to the police in Duterte's war against drugs. Accompanying electoral contests, especially after World War II, death squads, vigilantes, and paramilitary volunteers of all sorts have long been an integral, though disavowed, feature of the state.

As with other modern states, the Philippine state has pursued what seems like a contradictory course: it has simultaneously sought to monopolize the use of violence even as it outsources it, using uncivil means to secure civil society. The legal and the illegal constantly blur into one other, as the language of the president, both during and after the elections, often sounds like the rhetoric of a gangster. As we shall see in chapter 4, the police often double as vigilantes when they are not moonlighting as racketeers, working both within and outside the cover of law. Extrajudicial killings, sold to the public as a remedy for the inefficient and corrupt legal system, normalize mass murder, especially of the poor, even as they foreground fear as a primary technique of governing. Public resources are used to forge private armies—a kind of PPP, or public–private partnership, for the efficient delivery of justice in the form of assassinations. Exercising a kind of biopower, the state seeks to secure the life of its citizens. But as the following chapters will seek to show, it does so by way of a necropower, whereby the state designates accursed others as social enemies destined for abjection and disposal.

To conclude, I want to return to the idea I began with: of elections as Janus-faced, especially visible in countries like the Philippines that bear the deep traces of a history of colonialism. Taking place amid conditions of socioeconomic inequality, a culture of impunity, and deeply entrenched practices of political patronage and routine fraud, elections unsurprisingly produce conservative results. At the same time, elections are also moments of intense popular mobilizations that stimulate expectations. Such expectations vary. From the perspective of the ordinary people, who are often regarded as passive objects to be exploited and set aside rather than active participants in the political process, elections arouse the possibility that things may be different.

Such expectations were stimulated in the last election that swept Rodrigo Duterte into the presidency by a plurality of votes. He continues to be popular—the latest polls as of October 2020 set his approval rating at an astronomical 91 percent—despite and because of his gruesome war on drugs and, as of this writing, the economic and social devastation brought about by the global pandemic (Tuquero 2020). His "colorful language" and anti-American tirades also continue to endear him to his supporters. He is able to pass himself off as an agent of revolutionary change marking a decisive break from earlier ruling elites and from the United States, even as he appears to be unconditionally subservient to rising Chinese ambitions, especially in the South China Sea. At the same time, he is very much in the tradition of provincial elites, combining the talents of an engaging storyteller with the grim and murderous disposition of an authoritarian ruler. Whether or not this popularity will hold, given his obsessive war on drugs, only time—measured in the grim harvest of corpses that nightly populate the city streets—will tell.

SKETCHES I. THE DREAM OF
BENEVOLENT DICTATORSHIP

As the elections of 2016 approached, there reemerged the dream of a benevolent dictatorship. We saw this not only among the younger generation, who may be ignorant of the brutal excesses of the Marcos regime, but even among older citizens who longed for a leadership that was at once decisive and compassionate—features that they think were sorely lacking in the administration of President Benigno "PNoy" Aquino. The keen interest in a Duterte candidacy was, of course, emblematic of this wishfulness.

Why this enduring fantasy that associates authoritarianism with benevolence?

This dream is not new. It lies at the foundation of the Philippine nation-state, rooted in the history of colonialism. From the Spanish to the Revolutionary Republic to the United States and Commonwealth periods, the Philippines was ruled by a succession of dictatorial regimes, headed respectively by the Spanish king, Emilio Aguinaldo, the US president (via his representative in the colony, the governor general), and Commonwealth President Manuel L. Quezon (subject to American rule). During World War II, the Japanese imposed the "East Asia Co-Prosperity Sphere," installing Jose P. Laurel as the agent of Japanese dictatorship.

The Marcos regime occurred during the springtime of Third World dictatorships. Decolonization brought about the regimes of Duvalier, Mugabe, Yew, Pinochet, Suharto, Mao, and others. In geopolitical terms, martial law was not an aberration but part of a global trend during the Cold War that sought to either foster or counter communism with whatever means were necessary. Seeking to save Philippine society, the Marcoses and their cronies, of course, became the chief perpetrators of the very ills they claimed to cure.

What are some of the features of this discourse of benevolent dictatorship?

First, there is the notion of the sovereign as savior who comes to redeem the country and punish the evildoers. He—for the dictator is invariably a patriarchal figure—will then return the nation to a state of grace. He will restore laws and, just as important, suspend them when he thinks it necessary. His sovereignty is thus premised upon his ability to take exception to the law—especially in a coup d'état—in the name of restoring order and preserving his rule.

Second, the actions of a benevolent dictator are seen to be unfailingly just, combining brutality and compassion. He does not hesitate to use whatever means are necessary to pursue justice, including the most unjust measures, so long as these are aimed at criminals, who, to begin with, are already considered to be enemies from within, and thus bereft of any rights.

Third, the benevolent dictator is invested with magical powers. He rules as if he knows everything about everybody, deciding without delay or hesitation. Results are instantaneous, progress is always already at hand. Furthermore, his magical powers are seen to be contagious, infusing officials and citizens alike with virtue, bringing them to dwell in a moral community.

Finally, such dreams always turn into nightmares. The fantasy of benevolent dictatorship is exactly that, a fantasy. Those who indulge in this dream often think that the solution to the nation's problems can only come from a heroic figure willing to risk everything for them. In exchange, he asks only for their unquestioning obedience.

But it is precisely this demand for unconditional submission that threatens to dash the fantasy of benevolent dictatorship. A dictator succeeds only by extracting compliance from those he rules, brooking neither dissent nor debate.

For this reason, dictators are wholly dependent on force. Might makes right, and those who are most righteous are also those who do not hesitate to murder designated enemies. Attempts to call dictators and their henchmen to account put one in the position of the enemy, subject to the same rough justice. Steeped in violence, dictators stimulate resistance, and thus more violence, sending any semblance of benevolence crashing to the ground.

In short, benevolent dictatorships are not benevolent at all. As the violent negation of democracy, they subsist on an ethos of barbarism. What is this ethos? It says: freedom belongs only to me and those I choose to grant it to. The measure and assurance of this freedom lies in my capacity to take away your freedom, whoever you are, whenever I want to. You have no choice but to obey. If you resist and take exception to my right to take exception, you will become my enemy and you will be brought to justice—silenced, imprisoned, and killed.

Democracy, history shows us, is the better dream. It speaks not in the accents of the barbarian, but in the words of the world citizen; not as an exclusive "I" jealous of its prerogatives and privileges, but as an inclusive "we," schooled in the difficulties of sharing and the necessity of deliberation and debate. It is ethically egalitarian, while keenly skeptical of the claims of power, benevolent or otherwise. It is a dream that one can have only by being fully awake.

—*Philippine Daily Inquirer*, November 15, 2015

2. MARCOS, DUTERTE, AND THE PREDICAMENTS OF NEOLIBERAL CITIZENSHIP

Authoritarian Modernities

One way of situating Duterte is to see his rise to power as part of a long historical arc that begins with the downfall of the Marcos dictatorship in 1986. After ruling for nearly two decades, Marcos was overthrown by a civilian-backed coup supported by the United States, encouraged by the Catholic Church, and with the massive participation of Filipinos from all classes, led by elites, mostly in Metro Manila. The early accounts of what came to be known as "People Power" or the EDSA uprising (named after the main highway, Epifanio de los Santos Avenue, where it occurred) stated that it marked the toppling of a brutal dictatorship that had used the instruments of the state to plunder the economy while repressing dissent. By forcing Marcos and his family to flee, the Filipino people, through nonviolent means, restored liberal democracy.

This narrative, however, is only partly true. As other scholars have pointed out, People Power, while succeeding in ending the dictatorship, left many of the institutions and personalities of the Marcos years in place. There was never any reckoning with the military and the police responsible for torturing and tormenting the opposition during martial law nor with the massive plunder during those years (Davis 2016). Despite partial and uneven attempts to recover the Marcos loot, the practice of cronyism as the Philippine manifestation of what Caroline Hau has called "authoritarian developmentalism" continued.[1] And while a new liberal constitution was drawn up in 1987 emphasizing human rights, succeeding administrations have routinely resorted to extrajudicial killings and state terrorism to deal with criminal gangs, leftist insurgencies, journalists and human rights workers, labor and peasant advocates, and various Muslim separatist groups.

People Power thus had many faces. On the one hand, it sought to "enlarge the democratic space," in the common parlance of activists and analysts of the time, restoring long-repressed freedoms—of speech, of the press, of assembly. It thus held out hope not just for regime change but also for social transformations that would address historic injustices and inequities. On the other hand, it also amounted to the return of the old oligarchy that Marcos had sought to control and whose holdings he had confiscated. Starting with the return and assassination of Marcos's nemesis, Benigno "Ninoy" Aquino Jr., from his Boston exile in August 21, 1983, to the rise of his widow, Cory Aquino, in February of 1986, the aftermath of the EDSA coup quickly resulted in the restoration of many of the elites from the old order who had flourished under martial law, now joined by new elites. The people who most benefited from People Power were therefore from the class that had long ruled the country. It was their rights that were privileged and their wealth that continued to be protected, beginning with the landowning Aquino family. Indeed, one of the ironies of People Power was that, while the Cory Aquino administration released political prisoners en masse, it also fostered the formation of paramilitary death squads to deal with the communist insurgency. Such death squads, from which Duterte's own Davao Death Squad would emerge, were the other, more malevolent face of People Power—vigilantes made up of unemployed lumpen, former communist rebels, and police, led and funded by military commanders and local politicians—many of whom engaged in assassinations and extrajudicial killings (Manzanilla and Hau 2016).

Duterte's connections to Marcos are varied. His father, Vicente, was part of a Cebuano political dynasty and served in the cabinet of the first Marcos administration until his death in 1968. But his mother, Soledad, became a fierce opponent of the dictatorship, organizing regular protests against Marcos in Davao. As I mentioned earlier, it was precisely because of his mother's ties to the anti-Marcos movement that Cory Aquino offered to appoint her as mayor of Davao, an offer she turned down but which would later lead to her son's election as vice mayor and then mayor. During the presidential campaign of 2016, Rodrigo received what appears to have been a generous campaign contribution from the Marcoses. In exchange, he pushed for the election of Ferdinand "Bongbong" Marcos Jr. for the vice presidency (which he lost). He also arranged for a hero's burial of the desiccated corpse of Ferdinand, a wax figure that had long been on display in his hometown in Ilocos Norte, at the Libingan ng mga Bayani (Cemetery of Heroes) in Manila. Despite much opposition, the burial took place on October 18, 2016, within months of Duterte assuming the presidency (Arguelles 2017; Paddock 2016; Reyes 2019).

Despite these connections and sympathies, Duterte differs from Marcos in significant ways. Walter Benjamin famously wrote that the artifacts of civilization are founded on a long train of barbarisms. The aesthetic of the former conceals, just as it articulates, the latter. In Duterte's regime, the distinction between civilization and barbarism tends to be obscured. There is only the shameless display of brutality and loud pride in ignorance in order to instill a government of fear. Under Marcos, Imelda sought to "beautify" the country and aestheticize the dictatorship. She used "culture"—from the restoration of heritage sites like the Spanish colonial walled city of Intramuros; the building of the Cultural Center, the Film Center, and the Folk Arts Center; the patronage of artists and writers; the sponsorship of film festivals and beauty pageants; along with the remorseless removal of slum areas seen as "eyesores," and much more—to build what she called the "City of Man." In this sense, she was resorting to the colonial tradition of "benevolent assimilation" introduced by the United States by claiming to uplift and civilize people in and through the extravagant displays of Marcosian modernity. Ferdinand and Imelda, for all their avarice and relentless self-promotion, easily grasped the need to project an aristocratic façade in order to impress the world and stupefy the masses. The Marcos dictatorship combined urbanity with cruelty, a particularistic narcissism with pretentions of cosmopolitanism (Rafael 2000).

Duterte has none of these pretentions. His aesthetic priorities and geopolitical orientations are quite different. He stresses the "simplicity" of his life, the humbleness of his house and food, the striped shirts and jeans he dons, the mosquito netting that shrouds his bed, and the rough language he uses to address those both high and low. Unlike Marcos, Duterte appears to have little interest in cultural heritage, among other "soft" concerns. He remains adamantly parochial in his outlook, preferring to be called "mayor" rather than president. Emphasizing his local attachments over his national title, the president spends much of his time in the familiar surroundings of his Davao home, rather than in the fancier digs of Malacañang Palace (Heydarian 2018; Paddock 2016). Born in 1917 and 1929, respectively, Ferdinand and Imelda Marcos were very much products of the US colonial educational system. They came of age during World War II and came to power during the Cold War. Their fluency in English, their Hollywood cultural references, their steadfast devotion to US presidents and the United Nations arguably led them to seek a larger role on the world stage of the Second and Third Worlds. They forged diplomatic ties with communist countries like China, Russia, and Cuba, and opened diplomatic missions in Eastern Europe and the Arab world, evincing an eagerness to buttress their national dominance with international legitimacy. In contrast, Duterte, born in 1945, at the end of World War II and at the dawn of Philippine independence, cared little for the international stage. Unlike the academically accomplished Marcos, Duterte brags about being a bad student, academically below average and forced to leave several schools for his unruly behavior. He begrudgingly attends ASEAN conferences, often going home early or declining to go at all. Marcos admired Americans even as he sought to play them to his advantage, and he and Imelda felt genuinely close to certain figures like the Reagans. Duterte, by contrast, detests the United States for reasons both personal (he was once questioned about his visa while visiting there years ago) and political (memories of the American massacres of Moro people, experiences with CIA interventions, and what he took to be insulting criticisms of his human rights record by Obama and the State Department).

Duterte's only real international attachment is to China under Xi Jinping. He has virtually ceded some of the Philippine islands (and the seas around them that belong to the country's Exclusive Economic Zone) in the South China Sea to China, and has allowed hundreds upon hundreds of Chinese workers to come into the Philippines to operate online gambling operations, colonizing many of the real estate spaces in the Metro Manila area in the process. During one of his state visits to China, he openly declared his "divorce" from the United States while, on another occasion, he half-jokingly suggested to the Chinese ambassador that China should just annex the Philippines as one of its provinces. Duterte's rejection of the United States (along with the European Union and the United Nations— both very critical of his drug war) and turn to China for aid is thus not an anti-imperialist move, as many of his supporters claim but a strategic replacement of one imperialist power with another. This is precisely the kind of bilateral diplomacy that would have been alien to the Marcoses, who were essentially multilateralists. They not only gloried in international recognition but also used these ties to plunder the loans from transnational institutions such as the World Bank, the IMF, and the ADB (Bello, Kinley, and Elinson 1982; Wurfel 1988). While Duterte does not openly court these institutions, his economic team nonetheless has continued to engage with them.

At the onset of martial law, Marcos adopted the slogan "*Sa ikauunlad ng bayan, disiplina ang kailangan*" (for the progress of the nation, discipline is needed). By yoking discipline to national progress, Marcos put forth martial law—which he would also refer to as a "revolution from the center"—as a modernizing project designed to produce new subject-citizens who, above all, were obedient to the dictates of the state. We could think of this modernist authoritarianism as a kind of biopolitical governance, that is, as a mode of governance designed, as with Imelda's colonizing cultural projects, to "uplift" and improve the lives of the people. But to do so required securing the state against its enemies. Such enemies were internal to society, made up of left-wing rebels and right-wing oligarchs, both of whom were armed, thus impinging upon the ability of the state to monopolize the exercise of violence. What was needed was the other side of *disiplina*: not simply a demand for obedience but the concerted use of violence to neutralize the state's enemies. Alongside biopolitics, the state also exercised necropolitics— the right to kill those it deemed to be threats to its existence. The call for discipline was also a call to annihilate the agents of subversion by way of a complex technology of counterinsurgency: surveillance, co-optation, spying, incarceration, torture, and assassination. The necropolitical imperative for extrajudicial killings was thus integral to the biopolitical call for discipline. Obedient citizenship entailed the rejection of insurgency. Yet, without the reality of insurgency and its spectral invocations by the state, biopolitical discipline would make no sense. The need for discipline required security, which, in turn, required the creation of insecurity in order to justify its operations. It was this dialectic of security and insecurity, of a politics of life and a politics of death, that characterized the governing logic of martial law.[2]

Marcosian modernity was supposed to uplift the people and improve the country, with Imelda's Westernized notion of high culture providing the civilizational scaffolding for the disciplinary regime of development and counterinsurgency. Instead, it devolved into a series of lucrative rackets that benefited Marcos's family and their cronies (Aquino 1987; Salonga 2000). The biopolitical promise of progress failed to materialize for the majority, while discipline itself was hollowed out into an empty shell. Counterinsurgency operations did not lead to state victories over insurgents but to the reverse. Communist and Muslim rebels grew to numbers that would alarm the United States to the point where they would start to seriously consider finding alternatives to Marcos in the interests of protecting their military bases—the largest in the Asia-Pacific region. Meanwhile, Marcos's own military became embroiled in factional strife between Marcos loyalists and those who were unhappy about his favoritism and corruption (McCoy 1999). By the last years of the Marcos regime, the necropolitical had subsumed the biopolitical, as the economy went into a tailspin and people who were not killed were left to die, starved and neglected by a state now run by the ailing body of a dictator. With the assassination of his nemesis, former Senator Benigno "Ninoy" Aquino, as he returned from exile in 1983, Marcos's downfall began. It was only a matter of time before Marcos would be ousted by a conjunction of forces from the middle class, marginalized oligarchs, the Catholic Church, and dissident military forces.

The Biopolitics of Neoliberal Citizenship

In the wake of the EDSA coup, the state was left in shambles, looted by the Marcoses and weakened in its capacity to govern. Authoritarian developmentalism under Marcos led not only to the country's deep indebtedness to international lenders but also to a host of other social and economic problems. Chief among them was the increase in income inequality. While the GDP grew steadily under successive post-EDSA administrations—at one point, between 6 and 7 percent annually under the Ninoy Aquino administration— the Gini coefficient measuring income inequality had barely budged, hovering between 44 and 49 percent from 2000 to 2018. Poverty incidence also worsened to about 21–25 percent through 2019. And in "self-rated poverty" surveys—highly selective but no less influential surveys conducted by the Social Weather Station—45–50 percent of families rated themselves as *mahirap* (poor), while 33–35 percent rated themselves as "food insecure" during the same years (SWS 2018). Aided by various civil society groups and international lending institutions such as the World Bank, IMF, and the Asian Development Bank, the state launched a series of "poverty alleviation programs," not only to improve people's lives but also to blunt the raging insurgencies among communist and Moro groups, which was largely borne by a long history of material deprivation and political and social oppression.

Under Cory Aquino, there were attempts to institute a comprehensive land reform program that, like many attempts at land reform in the past, were stymied by a landlord-dominated Congress in addition to a series of failed coup attempts. The administration of Fidel V. Ramos, with its social reform agenda, was particularly committed to addressing the connection between poverty alleviation and counterinsurgency, realizing that solving one would also promote the other. In 2007, under President Gloria Macapagal Arroyo, the state launched one of its more ambitious programs: that of conditional cash transfers patterned after those of Brazil and Mexico. Renamed the 4PS, or *Pantatawid Pamilya Pilipino Program*, it was expanded under the presidency of Benigno "PNoy" Aquino. It consisted of providing 1,400 pesos ($28) a month for five years to poor families with three children. These funds were to be used to cover health and educational expenses of the children. The cash transfers were given mainly to the mothers, on the assumption that they were more responsible for the well-being of the family. However, fathers were allowed to take the cash if their wives were indisposed or took jobs abroad (Shahani 2012). Under Duterte, the 4PS was signed into law and the amount of cash increased to 1,700 pesos ($34) a month to cover the education of children through high school (World Bank 2017). Over the years, the 4PS has proven to be a boon to the lives of poor people, improving health outcomes and literacy rates (Shahani 2013; Tabuga and Reyes 2012). But, as we shall see, such improvements came at a cost.

The post-EDSA state thus sought to resume the project of biopolitics that had given way to the brutalities of necropolitics in the Marcos years. Through their highly specific targeting of families in such programs as 4PS, state programs, from poverty alleviation to the Cultural Center of the Philippines, were characteristically localized, decentralized, and in some cases outsourced—in part as a reaction to the highly centralizing tendencies of the Marcos dictatorship. At the same time, by focusing on reaching individual and family recipients, such state programs tended to skirt around larger structural sources of inequality and poverty, resorting to developmental practices guided by the logic of capitalist markets, or what today is more commonly referred to as neoliberalism.

As Michel Foucault and Wendy Brown have pointed out, neoliberalism is not simply a variation of liberalism, nor is it merely an economic system. It is, rather, a mode of governance that establishes relations of power based on the "conduct of conduct." It seeks to alter behavior by working through the agency of the individual—"empowering" them, as the cliché goes—and indeed, individualizing rather than collectivizing social agency by stressing the need to assume responsibility for one's life and "accountability" for one's actions. In this way, neoliberalism transforms the individual into a kind of entrepreneurial subject engaged in the accumulation of his or her "human capital"—through education, for example, business enterprises and self-help projects, and so on. Families themselves are seen as "enterprises" and child-rearing as "investment" in the future of the child. Framing everything in terms of the logic of the marketplace, neoliberalism stresses competition over cooperation, identifies freedom with deregulation, and seeks the ceaseless instrumentalization of lifeworlds into calculable aggregates of profit and loss. The neoliberal subject is thus the capitalized subject: one whose conduct is conducted by the larger workings of the market. As such, their labor power is seen not as the raw material extracted by capital to produce surplus value but as a form of capital itself that the individual invests to further him/herself. Neoliberalism, therefore, seeks to abolish the antagonism between capital and labor, reconceptualizing everyone as essentially a capitalist competing with other capitalists (Brown 2019; Foucault 2010).

In the Philippines, it is worth noting that recent neoliberal styles of governance have been amalgamated with older methods, especially those associated with moral education dating back to the discourse of late nineteenth-century nationalists like José Rizal to the Protestant public school system of the American colonial era and the "moral recovery program" of the post-EDSA period. Neoliberalism wedded to moral education is meant to produce citizen-subjects who are at once entrepreneurial and responsible for their own actions, market-driven in their aspirations, while socially disciplined in their behavior. Such discipline was less about obedience to state authorities, as in the Marcos era, than it was about the rejection of dissipation, "laziness," and other behaviors considered excessive and nonproductive such as social drinking, gambling, adultery, and drug use, as well as criminal acts such as drug dealing, human trafficking, prostitution, and theft. Such "immoral behaviors" were seen as a drag on the development of the individual's potential and prevented them from participating fully in the market.

Crucial to the biopolitical cultivation of the neoliberal citizen is the colonization of urban space. "Urban development" amounted to the relentless commodification of space through an ongoing process of gentrification. The latter entails a range of strategies, including building walled residential villages, climate-controlled shopping malls, imposing business towers, pricey tourist destinations, and so on, all highly fortified and selective about who is allowed in and who is kept out (Ortega 2018). Gentrification reorganizes space to maximize the flow of capital and minimize the friction from labor. For this reason, the practice of contractualization, whereby employers, both at home and abroad, hire workers on a temporary basis to curtail extending benefits and discourage unionization, has become increasingly common. The state has also mandated the use of cctvs by local governments to police movements in and around neighborhoods, offices, malls, and streets. Along with the omnipresence of private security guards inspecting bags and cars at the entrances of buildings, cctvs have had the effect of normalizing the surveillance of everyday life (Arcangel 2019). Finally, infrastructure such as streets, waterways, electricity, public transportation, and so on are designed to create zones of suburbanization enforced through the segregation of "undesirable" populations.

To this extent, the Hausmannization, as it were, of urban space (Benjamin 1968; Harvey 2005) also requires the relocation of slum dwellers away from squatter areas deemed "danger zones," prone to criminality and natural disasters such as frequent flooding, to newly developed "clusters," which resemble suburban townhouses. The new settlements are designated by the state and its NGO partners as "social enterprise zones" where residents are encouraged to be personally responsible for their upkeep. To qualify for such housing, residents are expected to adhere to all sorts of prohibitions that amount to leaving behind their former, more informal communities for a newer, more disciplined life. For instance, one resident complained "it is forbidden to keep pets . . . to hang laundry in front of your house, to stroll without a shirt on, to gossip with your neighbors, to sit in the corner picking lice from your neighbor's hair. . . . You cannot bring to the relocation site the things you are accustomed to. . . . Don't bring your 'squatterness.' Your way of thinking, your mindset, should be formal . . . you cannot be lazy, you cannot be without a job. You cannot waste your time idling; you should learn how to succeed" (Seki 2020b, 35). Shedding your "squatterness" is akin to the colonial project of conversion, whereby you are compelled to transform yourself from an uncivilized and backward native to an upright bourgeois individual invested in propriety and property. One must go from picking lice to picking products, as it were.

We can further understand this process of inducing neoliberal transformation if we return to the case of conditional cash transfers, or 4ps. Through ccts the state seeks to alleviate poverty by "investing in the country's human capital" (Shahani 2013). Such a program requires the cultivation of morally disciplined, neoliberalized subjects. Qualified families are determined by a government data collection agency with the rather kilometric name of National Household Targeting System for Poverty Reduction, partially funded by the World Bank and administered by the Department of Social Welfare and Development (DSWD). Collecting information on over 5.2 million families, the NHTS-PR is designated as a "data management office" that surveys potential and current recipients of government aid. It thus forms part of an elaborate network of surveillance that allows the state to reach down to individuals through the 4Ps program to conduct their conduct (Shahani 2013; Velarde 2018). As a former assistant secretary explained, "The receipt of cash is based upon the behavior of recipients. In effect, CCTs are designed to discipline parents in assuming direct responsibility for the welfare of their children. The state acts simply to monitor (and, if necessary, mediate in order to protect) the welfare of the child, rather than to intervene directly" (Shahani 2013). Other studies have also shown the counterinsurgent effects of CCTs. Dependent on cash transfers, recipients are less likely to join insurgent movements since that would deprive them of access to aid. Furthermore, the state assumes that the recipients of aid will be more prone to collaborate with the government by providing information on rebel activities (Shahani 2013).

To receive government cash transfers—targeted, as I mentioned above, primarily at women, who are regarded as being more responsible than men—one is required to attend "values formation classes" such as "Family Discussion Sessions" that monitor their behavior (Seki 2015, 2020b). They must make sure that their children attend school and visit doctors for regular checkups. These disciplinary practices are meant to turn people into "model citizens" deserving of state protections and thus continued cash support. Those who refuse these disciplinary demands run the risk of being cut off from aid and face all sorts of social sanctions (Curato 2016, 2017b; Kusaka 2017b, 2020; Seki 2015).

Recent ethnographies of neoliberalism in the Philippines illustrate this point. For example, in the wake of super-typhoon Haiyan (or Yolanda, as it is locally known) in the southern province of Leyte in 2013, the anthropologist Wataru Kusaka writes about the changes among participants in a microfinance group.

[The typhoon] opened people's eyes. "Being lazy is no longer allowed [Bawal na magtapulan]," one of them said. This change entailed a moral dimension. Previously, those who were willing to share their resources with others were "good," while those who refused to do so were frowned upon by neighbors as misers. Nowadays, on the contrary, those who skillfully make profits, ascetically live a decent life, and patiently work are regarded as disciplined "good citizens," while those who adhere to the previous laid-back lifestyle that prioritizes the sharing of joy and the decency of hard work have come to represent immorality. Resentment against an "undisciplined" lifestyle has developed at three layers under the neoliberal governmentality. At the individual and household level, the more people are pressed to work hard under disciplined conditions with great stress, the more they are likely to resent those whom they regard lazy and vicious. At the community level, the grouping system installed by microfinance and the conditional cash transfer program has strengthened mutual surveillance among villagers against problematic behaviors that may lead to default or suspension of cash release. At the structural level, the blame for poverty has shifted to immorality of individuals, depoliticizing structural factors of inequality. Thus, people who failed or rejected embracing neoliberal discipline have come to be legitimately abandoned as "undeserving of rescue." (Kusaka 2020, 81–82)

Starting with the later Marcos years and increasingly during the post-EDSA era, the economy has moved from the more cooperative and collective demands of agricultural work to the more individualized and largely contractual service jobs such as overseas work, tourism, construction, and call centers. During this transition, biopolitics has been articulated along the matrix of neoliberal discipline. It has created not only new kinds of entrepreneurial subjects who feel entitled to state protection. It has also created new social cleavages that cut across classes, forging divisions between the "deserving" and morally responsible population, on the one hand, as against those who, for whatever reason, fail to make the changes demanded of them, on the other. The latter are seen as less than full citizens, "undeserving" and therefore alien to the emergent neoliberal society. Excluded from rights and protection, those considered immoral and undisciplined face not only neglect but also abjection. Regarded as dissipators, drunks, drug addicts, or criminals, they are liable to be ostracized, arrested, jailed, and in some cases, killed.

The biopolitics of neoliberalism thus requires a necropolitics of moral cleansing, as those unable or unwilling to conduct themselves properly are treated as somehow "inferior" and granted few, if any, rights. They are racialized, as it were, their bodies inscribed with signs of their incivility and moral lack. Seen as disruptive, they potentially become subversive. Biopolitics governs life as a whole so that it can become more than life, ensuring not just the existence and affordances (social and biological) for deserving citizens. It also requires their division into, and separation from, those who refuse to be disciplined. Seen as threats to the neoliberal conduct of life, they are faced with all sorts of sanctions, from being marginalized by neighbors to arrest and incarceration by the police. More commonly, they are unable to access government programs and so are subjected to gross neglect and mired in pervasive poverty. In place of recognition and support, they are deprived of basic services, and face disease, violence, and displacement, most acutely during natural disasters that frequently hit the country, from super-typhoons to earthquakes to volcanic eruptions. In short, they are relegated to a precarious existence and chronic neglect that amount to a kind of social death.

This dichotomy between "deserving" and "undeserving" citizens, however, is not hard and fast. Among many communities, the pre-neoliberal ethos of cooperation and compassion continues to be practiced, albeit fitfully. Even the "undeserving" and "lazy" can often count on finding some help, especially during times of great need or natural disasters. But surveys showing the frequent spikes in food insecurity by the Social Weather Station over the last decade suggest that people are not only living more precariously because of their destitute circumstances; they are living more precariously because the sort of mutual aid they could count on in the past, where those with more resources are given to sharing with those who have less, is fast disappearing. Indeed, it is not uncommon for some mothers, when asked, "What is your ultimate desire?" to respond with "having three meals a day" (Kusaka 2020; Seki 2020b; SWS 2018).

With the onset of the drug war starting in July 2016, neoliberal programs such as CCTs have been thrown into disarray. Many of those killed by the police or vigilantes have been male heads of households who often were gunned down inside or near their homes, depriving families of their main breadwinner. A recent study has shown that many of the widows tended to move out of the house and seek support from another man, leaving behind their children in the care of grandparents, who were then forced to take on low-paid work. With families severely traumatized and broken up, CCTs have stopped coming, as conditions for receiving cash payments could no longer be met. Children found themselves harassed in schools, stigmatized for their association with drug addicts, and in many cases forced to drop out altogether, and in the case of older children, look for jobs to support their families. As one study of the effects of the drug war on CCTs pointed out, "Drug-related killings are often bookended by other hazards such as flooding, fires and home demolitions. The direct effects of these killings, compounded with disaster and other socio-economic shocks, traumatizes CCT families, erodes social cohesion and pushes them further into poverty" (Fernandez, Quijano, and Pangilinan 2019, 1),

Subtending the biopolitical, the necropolitical is precisely the zone of never-ending catastrophe. But given the uncertainties of the market, frequency of natural disasters, and more recently the violence of the drug war, anyone can fall into this zone, even putatively "responsible citizens": you can lose your job, you can run out of food, get flooded out of your home by the next typhoon, get seriously sick or have someone close to you become ill, get hooked on meth trying to stay awake at work or stave off your hunger pangs, you can get pregnant with your fifth child at twenty then contract sepsis after childbirth, you can get robbed, get raped, get beaten up by local thugs, picked up and jailed or even killed by the police, targeted by police or vigilantes, and who knows what else. In the context of neoliberalism, the boundary between the "good" and the "bad" subject can easily blur, precisely because of the very conditionality of social protections held captive to the marketplace. What emerges, in the view of the sociologist Nicole Curato, is a "politics of anxiety," an ongoing sense of dread arising from the material uncertainties that underlie everyday life. In the post-EDSA era, the spread of capitalist markets and capitalist logics has eroded traditional sources of authority and sociality. Even as material living conditions might have improved for some, they are built on the ineluctable flux of the market, which offers no guarantees of stability and is lately aggravated by the effects of the war on drugs. Social protection gives way to criminal prosecution and extrajudicial killings. Ironically, individual "empowerment" within set conditions and the demand for discipline has only intensified a general feeling of precarity (Curato 2016).

It was precisely these conflicted and unsettled conditions that accompanied the rise of Rodrigo Duterte into national prominence. One place where we can see the dramatization of precarity is in a short antidrug film produced by the Presidential Communications Office shortly after Duterte's election, made by the noted director Brilliante Mendoza. In a series of clever montages, the film shifts between a mother working abroad as a domestic and her son left at home in Manila. While she scrubs bathrooms, picks up the children from school, bathes the dog, and feeds the elderly, he gets high on meth, parties hard, and gets into serious trouble. She is virtuous and hardworking, while he persists in being unruly and spoiled. The last scene shows him sitting exhausted, shaken up after a fight, unable to answer his mother's call as she tearfully waits for him to pick up his phone, unable to do anything more than send him money. It is a telling scene. Overseas work forces mothers to leave their children and earn money by taking care of other people's families. The market logic that drives the mother overseas is the very logic that drives her son to extremes of dissipation. The biopolitics of neoliberalism produces a painful condition: the disciplined mother, by substituting money for love, ends up with undisciplined children. What is missing, the film suggests, is a strong paternal figure who would suture this neoliberal wound (Mendoza 2016).[3]

Watching this ad, it is easy enough to imagine a figure like Duterte, depicted in his campaign ads astride a large black motorcycle, coming to the rescue with his slogan *Tapang at Malasakit* (Bravery and Compassion).[4] Reframing the generalized anxiety coursing through neoliberal citizenship, Duterte not only gave a name to the problem—"drugs"—but also provided a method for its expeditious eradication—the extrajudicial killing of dealers and users. Duterte's restoration of familial order in his version of discipline and punish would consist of seizing upon death as a way of advancing life. Regardless of the fact that drug addiction was far from being the most serious problem in the country, Duterte demarcated it as the source of generalized disorder. Hence, in his State of the Nation Address in 2018, he could say, "When illegal drug operations turn nasty and bloody, advocates of human rights mock our law enforcers and this administration to no end. . . . Your concern is human rights. Mine is human lives" (Villamor 2018b).

Where liberalism might affirm the link between rights and lives, Duterte separates the two, seeing the former as an impediment to securing the latter. Declaring a state of emergency by launching a "war on drugs," he sets rights aside, pursuing death as a means of securing life. In doing so, he makes explicit what otherwise tends to remain implicit or disavowed in all modern states: that social life requires the administration of social death. With Duterte, then, necropower supersedes biopower as the means of rescuing all the displaced mothers and their abandoned children. Referred to by his supporters as *tatay*, or father, as well as "the Punisher," or what we can take to mean "the disciplinarian," Duterte is invested with a kind of phallic power with which to counter the crisis brought about by neoliberalism. We'll take a closer look at the nature of this power in chapter 3.

SKETCHES II. *MOTHERLAND* AND THE
BIOPOLITICS OF REPRODUCTIVE HEALTH

Another area where we can see the entanglement of the politics of life with the politics of death is in reproductive health (Danguilan 2018). The 2017 documentary *Motherland*, by Ramona Diaz, gives us an immersive view of the biopolitics of reproductive health that combines pastoral care with disciplinary technologies within a neoliberal matrix (Diaz 2017). The film focuses on José Fabella Memorial Hospital in Metro Manila, the largest maternity hospital in the country, where women, particularly those who are poor, can deliver their babies and avail themselves of state-subsidized postnatal care. In a predominantly Catholic country where maternal and infant mortality rates remain high[1] and where birth control devices are met with suspicion if not outright rejection, Fabella Hospital offers a kind of social safety net for women with few resources to care for themselves and their newborns. Housed under the Department of Health and supported by the government insurance system, Phil Health, and the Department of Social Work and Development, with supplemental funds from the Philippine Charity Sweepstake Office, the hospital has been described as a "baby factory," where over a hundred births occur in a space that has seven hundred beds but is occupied by twice that number of women. Rather than chaos, however, the film shows how such crowded conditions in fact produce a certain order, as health care workers patiently look after mothers and children, and where men visit during regularly scheduled hours.

Indeed, the doctors, nurses, and midwives, along with the social workers, exercise what we might think of as a kind of pastoral power (Foucault 2009). Like a small army of clergy, they look after the patients and attend patiently to their needs. As much as they are concerned with the entire population of the hospital, they nonetheless need to look after each and every one of the flock, so to speak, adjusting their medication and meals,

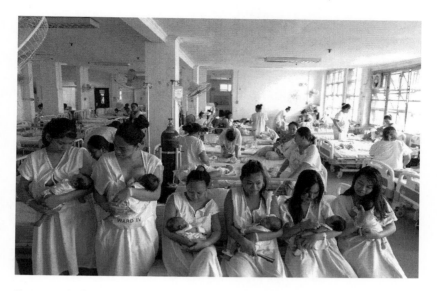

Figure II.1. The biopolitics of reproductive health: teenage mothers at the José Fabella Memorial Hospital. Photo by Hannah Reyes Morales/NPR.

accommodating their individual conditions, listening to their problems, and advising them on the proper care of themselves and their babies. In regular consultations with patients and their male partners, they offer access to birth control such as IUDs and tubal ligation, as well as working with them to find supplemental funding to pay for their medicine. The tone of these conversations is generally empathetic yet straightforward, and an ethics of personal care pervades their relationship.

Pastoral care, however, is also joined to disciplinary practices. The film lingers on the scenes of patient intake, when they are asked information about their medical history, number of children, age, occupation, as well as information on their husbands or partners, and so forth. We learn that many are teenage mothers and by their early twenties may have had as many as three or four children. Their babies are often born prematurely, and in the absence of incubators, the mothers and the visiting fathers are required to put on tube tops and insert the infants to draw them close to their bodies for heat and comfort. They are asked to do so 24/7, or as often as they can, despite the sweltering heat of the hospital wards. Meals, medications, and checkups are administered according to the temporal order of clock and calendar; the babies' health is calculated according to their weight gain, while patients have to deal with reams of paperwork indicating layers of bureaucratic mediation. Pastoral care is thus sustained through disciplinary technologies. Finally, in one of the most telling scenes of the film, a press conference is held to announce the birth of the one hundred millionth Filipino at the hospital. Over cake and balloons, one of the doctors says, "Over time, we will look at the situation of this baby . . . in terms of health services, education, employment opportunities. What we're after is the development of the population. . . . Inclusive growth, that's what we want to achieve." Regarded as part of the country's ever-expanding "human capital," the baby's significance is primarily statistical: its birth will be tracked according to the categories of growth and development. Reproduced by the mother's body, subject to pastoral care and disciplinary technologies, the infant is given a public identity as a statistic already set to enter the marketplace of education and employment. In this way, the Fabella Hospital becomes the site of a biopolitics for the reproduction of neoliberal subjects (*Motherland* 2017).

In the film, there is a sense of communal belonging and cooperation among the women, as they find themselves sharing beds and stories, helping with breastfeeding each other's babies, looking out for each and every other. But in the conversations with health workers, the mood changes. In these one-on-one meetings, the women are encouraged to use birth control, and nearly all refuse, thinking that it would mean disobeying the Catholic Church—which considers contraception as corruption—or contravening the authority of their parents and their male partners.[2] It is not uncommon, for example, for boyfriends to insist that their girlfriends bear their child to keep away other possible suitors. Parents regularly dissuade their daughters from getting IUDs, imagining these as invasive and hurtful, and tubal ligation is seen as wholly unnatural. Even the use of condoms remains in many cases a mystery as teachers are often ill equipped or simply too embarrassed to talk about sex (Almendral 2017, 2020). Thus the intractability of poverty and patriarchy compels women to forgo family planning. Pregnancies and births continue to endanger their lives. Their babies are invariably born into conditions of inequality, often premature and underweight, putting them at a decided disadvantage compared to wealthier babies.

Mothers in the film jokingly refer to their hospital stay as a kind of vacation from the immiseration of their daily lives, where they are taken care of rather than having to cook, clean, and provide for their families at home. Yet they also appear to be anxious to get home to their communities and escape the daily policing of the medical staff. But once released from the hospital (on the condition that they settle whatever bills they've incurred — so health itself is still treated as a commodity), they return to their homes, most of which are in very poor slum areas. At home, they live under conditions of near homelessness in densely populated areas with no regular services such as clean water and electricity. They have no ready access to health care and can barely afford the medicine for themselves and their children without having to go into heavy debt. Cared for at the hospital, they are neglected by the state once they leave. Chronically hungry and ill, they face the prospect of an early death. And while they might receive assistance in the form of conditional cash transfers, the amounts are so small as to barely make ends meet.

Attempts to continue their disciplinary formations beyond the hospital are uneven and largely inadequate. Conditional cash transfers, for example, have been touted as altering the lives of families across generations. Following the examples of Latin American countries, they have in fact reduced infant mortality rates while expanding literacy (see chapter 2 of this book). Such aid, however, is directed mainly at the women, who are then required to submit themselves to "values education," take their children for regular medical checkups, and make sure they stay in school. Men, as I mentioned earlier, are largely excluded from receiving cash assistance since they are seen as largely irresponsible and morally dubious. Only in the absence of the women, for example in cases where they go abroad to work, are the male partners allowed access to the cash. Otherwise, the men try to find jobs. Most of the work available is limited to various kinds of low-level contractual labor in construction, driving pedicabs or jeepneys, and other temporary employment. Others who have skills and resources find jobs overseas, forced to leave their families to the care of their wives. Unable to make ends meet, some are drawn to supplement their income with illegal work such as drug dealing. Moral citizenship thus tends to establish a gender divide, setting women on the side of the "good, responsible" subjects entitled to conditional support, and men on the opposite side as undeserving, driving them further toward dissipation and illegal acts in a kind of self-fulfilling prophecy.

From the example of the Fabella Hospital, we see how neoliberal citizenship looks two ways. It not only sustains life, it also sustains conditions that threaten it and hasten its end. Empowering women, reproductive health at the same time marginalizes men. But given the vast institutional power of the Church and the conservatism of parental authority, the repressive influence of patriarchy and religion do not go away. Many women tend to follow the Church's teachings and refuse family planning even as they cede control of their bodies to men and their parents. However, given changing conditions, such modes of authority enter into a permanent crisis that neoliberalism can only intensify. Biopolitics seeks to regulate reproduction by caring for maternal and infant health. But given the persistent conditions of poverty and patriarchy, women are repeatedly condemned to the necropolitical state of abjection and neglect. Letting live is thus imbricated with letting die. The same people who are cared for at the hospital become, once they leave, subjects who have little choice but to live precariously under the most unlivable of conditions.

We thus have to revise our earlier argument. Neoliberal citizenship not only creates a distinction between the deserving because disciplined, mostly female, subject versus the undeserving and undisciplined, mostly male; it also conflates the two given the contingent and meager support from the state and the crisis of gender hierarchy in the family. Women, for example, who leave to take on overseas domestic work remit cash and so upend the traditional male role of being the breadwinner. By overturning traditional gender roles, they are often blamed for abandoning their children as their roles are reduced to providing money in place of love. For their part, men who are cut off from government programs such as conditional cash transfers or reproductive health care feel emasculated, as it were, even as they seek to assert their claims to paternal authority and women's bodies. Similarly, the Catholic Church seeks to perform its traditional role of caring for its flock by providing spiritual succor and moral guidance. But the biopolitics of reproductive health care, the neoliberal notions of individual responsibility, and the drive to convert all social relations into market calculations detract from the authority of the priests to shape the lives of their flock. What emerges, in the view of the sociologist Nicole Curato, is a "politics of anxiety," an ongoing sense of dread arising from the material uncertainties that underlie everyday life. In the post-EDSA era, the spread of capitalist markets and capitalist logics has weakened traditional sources of authority while intensifying conditions of precarity (Curato 2016).

Motherland closes by showing some of the women back home, posing with their children and, when they are around, their male partners. They hold their newborn and smile for the camera, re-creating the image of the heteronormative family. But it is an image that feels frayed, like the torn cardboard and peeling paint on the walls hinting at the vulnerability of the lives within. In the age of Duterte, these are precisely the neighborhoods where most of the extrajudicial killings take place. Thus are newborn lives always already shadowed by death, both sudden and arbitrary.

3. DUTERTE'S PHALLUS

ON THE AESTHETICS OF AUTHORITARIAN VULGARITY

Obscenity is an integral part of the stylistics of power. . . . The penis [is] a historical phenomenon in its own right. . . . The [autocrat] thinks and expresses himself through his phallus. . . . Without a phallus, the [autocrat] is nothing, has no fixed identity. Thanks to his phallus, the [autocrat's] cruelty can stand quite naked: erect.
—ACHILLE MBEMBE, *Necropolitics*

Controlling the Phallus

What are some of the sources of Duterte's symbolic authority? How has he managed to occupy such a central place in the imaginative life of Filipinos, both supporters and critics alike, at home as well as abroad? One of the ways in which the president lays claim to both national and global attention is through his stories and jokes. Duterte is widely known for his irreverence and bawdy humor, which constitute important elements of his governing style. His stories reveal a reliance on invective and an obsession with obscenity. He is given to generously sprinkling his speeches with cuss words such as *putang ina*, or son of a bitch, which can also be translated as "motherfucker" and "fuck you," at times accompanied with a middle finger directed at his critics. He also makes frequent references to genitalia—his own as well those of his critics—to the delight of his listeners. He revels in what Achille Mbembe calls an aesthetic of vulgarity, which has the effect of establishing a relationship of "conviviality" between himself and his audience. What results is an "intimate tyranny," much of it centered on the tales of his phallus as it encounters the world (Mbembe 2019).

For example, in one of his campaign events in April 2016, Duterte addressed the Makati Business Club, made up of the wealthiest businessmen in the country. Rather than talk about his economic policies, he regaled the predominantly older male audience with stories of using Viagra: "Well, I'm separated from my wife, annulled. So, I'm not useless. I'm not paralyzed. What am I supposed to do with my goddam thing down there? Let it hang forever? Well, there's no drama going on. I drank Viagra and then it stood up. Oh, let's not kid ourselves. I am giving it to you raw. I thought we were all the same age here" (my translation from the original Taglish) ("Duterte Jokes about Viagra" 2016).

Here, Duterte shares with men of a certain age and considerable influence a story about his experience of emasculation followed by rejuvenation. Thanks to a pill, he regains his hard-on, the material evidence of a phallic power that he thought he had lost. Laughter ensues as he discursively shows to the men a part of himself that should have been hidden. His obscenity consists of making the private public, reaching below to connect with those above. It is this sexual politics from below that binds Duterte to these men along with the sprinkling of women who join in the laughter. Together, they share a common fantasy about the authoritarian phallus as something they can imaginatively access, and the prospective pleasures of a drug-induced erection, beginning with Duterte's. But, as we shall see in the other examples below, the presidential phallus comes across not only as an instrument of pleasure, but also as a menacing sign of terror.

In another campaign stop at a large sports complex in Quezon City around the same time, Duterte tells a story that reverberated around the world. While he was mayor of Davao in 1989, there occurred a bloody prison siege in Davao City in 1989. Among the dead was one of the hostages taken by the prisoners, a thirty-six-year-old Australian missionary, Jacqueline Hamill. According to Duterte, she along with the other women hostages was repeatedly raped by the prisoners before being killed. But rather than evoke pathos, the sight of the Hamill's corpse stirs the mayor's desire:

All the women were raped so during the first assault, because they retreated, the bodies they used as shields, one of them was the corpse of the Australian woman lay minister. Tsk, this was a problem. When the bodies were brought out, they were wrapped. I looked at her face, son of a bitch, she looked like a beautiful American actress. Son of a bitch, what a waste. What came to mind was, they raped her, they took turns. I was angry because she was raped, that's one thing. But she was so beautiful, the mayor should have gone first. Son of a bitch, what a waste [*sayang*]. (in Taglish, my translation) (Ranada 2016c)

Hamill's rape and death are used by Duterte as a setup for a joke about himself, more specifically, about the arousal and frustration of his lust. He sees her dead body and her beautiful face, and he feels that he should have been the first in line to assault her. Instead, he comes too late and so isn't able to come at all. It is his failure to assert his claim on the woman's body that is presumably taken by his audience as the object of hilarity. Seeing her dead body fills him with neither rage nor grief, but with a desire that cannot be fulfilled. He is blocked from discharging his authority, as it were. The horror of the scene is thus displaced onto a story about a mayor lamenting the failure of his phallic power. Rather than the erectile victory celebrated in the first story, the second ends with the punch line, "sayang" (what a pity), preceded by the cuss word, "putang ina."

But all is not lost. Duterte's disclosure of desire left unfulfilled and phallic authority undercut produces a payback. The audience laughs, and their laughter compensates him for his lost power. It returns to him both the pleasure and the authority that the dead prisoners and the woman's corpse had deprived him of. Unable to pull rank, the mayor is nonetheless rewarded with the people's recognition of his narrative performance. Reports of the story drew sharp rebukes from feminists, human rights advocates, the Australian and US embassies, and many other quarters. But among most of the electorate, his popularity soared. Horrifying his critics but delighting his supporters with his pungent shamelessness, Duterte's bad language and obscene stories were crucial in propelling him to the presidency.

In tracking his jokes, we can see a set of obsessions built around the question: Who gets to own the phallus? Who gets to wield it and for what purpose? Here, the phallus should be understood less as a biological thing synonymous with the penis than as a symbolic weapon for asserting autocratic authority and patriarchal prerogatives over women and men alike. Like guns, cars, or wealth, the phallus can be used to impress and to threaten, to unify and to disperse, to induce pleasure but also to coerce submission (Rine 2011). Duterte routinely threatens to castrate his opponents, even as he repeatedly reveals his generous endowment. Used to avenge imagined hurts and shore up a fragile ego, Duterte's phallus proved effective in shutting down his opposition.

The presidential phallus, however, is far from being an unassailable force. As we saw in the rape story above, it can also be blunted by other men and the woman whose deaths frustrated Duterte's assertion of his privileges. Indeed, Duterte is notorious for joking about rape as a way of reasserting his ability to police women's behavior and enlist men into affirming the sexism that buttresses his authoritarian imagination. Hence, when critics point out that, contrary to his claims, crime in Davao while he was a mayor had gone up, especially rape, he retorts that wherever there are beautiful women, there will be plenty of rape. Along the same lines, he also spoke approvingly of men who had "the balls" to rape candidates for Miss Universe in exchange for facing certain punishment ("After Drawing Flak" 2017; Villamor 2018). Women are raped not simply because they are women for Duterte; it is because they are "beautiful." It is as if their beauty is a challenge that has to be faced down, a provocation that must be put in its proper place, under the rule and in the service of the phallus.

The philosopher Kate Manne's description of misogyny is useful in understanding Duterte:

> Misogyny is what happens when women break ranks or roles and disrupt the patriarchal order: they tend to be perceived as uppity, unruly, out of line, or insubordinate. . . . Misogyny isn't simply hateful; it imposes social costs on noncompliant women. . . . Think of misogyny, then, as the law enforcement branch of a patriarchal order. This makes for a useful if rough contrast between misogyny and sexism. Whereas misogyny upholds the social norms of patriarchies by patrolling and policing them, sexism serves to *justify* these norms, largely via an ideology of supposedly natural differences between men and women with respect to their talents, interests, proclivities, and appetites. Sexism is bookish; misogyny is combative. Sexism is complacent; misogyny is anxious. Sexism has a theory; misogyny wields a cudgel. (Manne 2016)

In joking about rape, Duterte upholds patriarchal norms and sexist attitudes by wielding the "cudgel" of misogyny. And that cudgel is the phallus, at once "combative" and "anxious," always wary of challenges and eager to assert itself. One particularly disturbing story that illustrates the "law enforcement" role of misogyny involves Duterte encouraging soldiers, when confronted with communist female fighters, to spare their lives but to shoot them in the vagina: "There's a new order coming from the mayor. We won't kill you. We will just shoot your vagina. So that . . . if she has no vagina she would be useless" (Presidential Communication Office 2018b). Shooting them in their vagina was, in a way, taking away what made them "women." It was the punishment for taking up arms and defying the state.

It amounted to "castrating" those who challenged the patriarchal norms integral to the exercise of its authority. Hence, we see how Duterte's misogyny is directed not at every woman, but at particular women who attempt to seize the phallus for themselves, daring to go against his political and sexual authority.

One such woman who has felt the brunt of his wrath is Senator Leila de Lima. Her original sin, as it were, was investigating Duterte while she was head of the Commission of Human Rights for killings he was alleged to have ordered in Davao while he was mayor. Once in the Senate, she held hearings on the president's role in conducting extrajudicial killings that included the testimonies of two former hit men about their involvement in Duterte's Davao Death Squad. Furious at her for challenging his authority, he went about setting her up on charges of being involved in drug trafficking herself. By putting pressure on his Senate allies and the courts, he had her arrested and imprisoned in 2017. As of this writing, she has yet to have her case heard in court ("Philippines: Duterte Critic" 2017).

De Lima's punishment included her public humiliation. The president and his cabinet circulated salacious stories about her affair with her driver, claiming to have sex tapes of the two. De Lima's guilt is thus less about drug dealing—which the administration is hard pressed to prove—than it is about acting upon her desire. She not only defied the authority of the president, she also dared to transgress sexual and class lines in taking up with a member of the lower class. In other words, she disrupted the patriarchal and elite order of things, poaching upon traditional male entitlements. And for that she had to be punished severely. Duterte and the rest of his male cabinet mercilessly ridiculed her, at one point offering to show the fake sex tapes to Pope Francis, who had sent de Lima a rosary in support. From Duterte's perspective, de Lima acted out of line, taking the power of the phallus for herself. He had to retaliate, holding her in prison without benefit of a trial, effectively silencing her (Romero 2017).

Duterte's phallic power is directed, however, not just at women but, as we saw above, at other men, to make sure they, too, fall in line. For example, while campaigning for senatorial candidates during the midterm elections of 2018, Duterte extolled the size of his penis in order to set him apart from the "ugly" candidates running in the opposition. While one's character is important, penis size, he claimed, was crucial. Had God given him a small penis, he continued, he would have gone to the church altar and cut it off saying, "Son of a bitch, is this all you have given me?" Encouraged by the crowd's laughter, he then recalled how he would walk around naked in the hallways at the YWCA as a young man. While everyone else covered up with a towel, he went about proudly displaying his junk. The other residents would look on in admiration: "[They'd tell me] 'Son of a bitch, Duterte, you're so hard!' . . . When I was young, [my penis] almost looked up to the sky," moving the microphone upward to make the point. "Its head would almost reach my belly button. . . . I'm very thankful to my father. At least he let me out into the world highly equipped." He finishes by recalling how women at a local bordello were shocked at the sight of his member. "They ran away. [They said, referring to me] 'We don't like him. That skinny guy. He won't stop [having sex]'" ("Dick Move" 2019).

In his youth, Duterte claims, he literally stood out, creating a vivid impression among both men and women. While men envied his penis, women, however, ran away in fright. Wishing to have a phallus like his, the other men acknowledged Duterte's possession of this power precisely for the respect it arouses in other men and the fear of sexual violence it stirs among women. Merging masculinity with misogyny, Duterte's phallocentric politics is central to his authoritarian imagination, using the image of his penis to put both men and women in their putative places. This brings to mind Hélène Cixous: "Within the 'phallocratic' apparatus, women are subordinated and defined by lack, while men are given the grotesque and unenviable fate of being reduced to a single idol with balls of clay" (Cixous 1976, 884).

We can further see Duterte's phallocentric politics at work in the following example. In a speech in 2019, Duterte reacted to the rumors that he had had a kidney transplant and was dying from colon cancer. The target of his ire was Kit Tatad, a former cabinet minister during the Marcos regime and a major figure in the ultraconservative Catholic sect, Opus Dei. In his newspaper columns, he had written about Duterte's illnesses and frequent absences from public view, suggesting that he was on the verge of dying (Placido 2019). Duterte responded by saying:

> This Tatad, he said my day is coming. That I was confined, serious, in and out of the hospital, with colon cancer. Nearly everyday he was going on and on. . . . You read the newspaper. I mean, how unfair can you get? Everyday . . . even I started to believe him (laughter). So one day, as I undressed to take a shower, I held my, without my underwear, I held my anus, I smelled it (laughter). Smelled like shit, and not some other . . . (laughter).

He said I was already dead. So I hit back. I said, this Tatad, you Tatad, son of a bitch. I would admit it if I were sick. You, son of a bitch, you have a serious case for 30 years of diabetes. You, your dick can no longer (raises microphone to laughter and applause). When you have diabetes, 30 years (drops microphone. Laughter). No more. So I said—let me borrow your wife for one night, I'll let her hold my body, go on. Eh, your insult hurt a lot. Eh, you son of a bitch, you're asking for it. You said I was rude, well son of a bitch, that's true. You said I was no statesman, well that's true. (in Taglish, my translation) (Presidential Communications Operations 2019a)

The president has always been particularly sensitive about rumors regarding his health, despite the fact that his various illnesses have been widely reported, and he takes particular umbrage at those who suggest that he is close to death's door. Duterte takes his revenge in the form of returning Tatad's putative insults with interest. But he takes his time getting there. He recaps the rumor, acknowledging its power to compel belief through its repeated circulation. To make sure that he doesn't have colon cancer, he talks about poking around his anus and smelling his fingers, reassuring himself that it smelled of shit rather than some other cancerous odor. Discursively exposing his anus, he also exposes himself not only to the possibility of being sick but also to the possibility of being duped. Assured that his anal stink is nothing out of the ordinary, he goes on the attack.

Punctuating his remarks with crisp invectives, he points out that it is in fact Tatad who has been ill with diabetes for many years and as a result can no longer get his dick (*otin*) up. Consummate performer that he is, Duterte makes a point of illustrating this with the use of the microphone as a prop. He lifts it up and down to show the contrast between what he can do with his penis and what Tatad can no longer do with his. He goes from exploring his anus to scrutinizing his penis, linking the two as signs of his good health. And to clinch his case, he asks to borrow Tatad's wife so she can verify the hardness of his erection as compared to the flaccidness of Tatad's. His mouth and anus come to the aid of the presidential phallus. Together they marshal a barrage of obscenities that meet with the laughter and applause of the audience. In this way, Duterte effectively unmans his opponent. Tatad's stories depicted Duterte in a state of bodily crisis. Feeling aggrieved, the president hits back, showing that in fact he remains in command, beginning with his control of the narrative and his ability to reverse its target. Returning the insult with interest, Duterte draws a third person into the scene: Tatad's wife, who is pictured as complicit in Duterte's revenge, in effect cuckolding her husband with the invitation for her to grasp his thing (Corrales 2019).

Erectile Confessions

One last, and perhaps most revealing instance of Duterte's power of storytelling: his story of being sexually abused at the age of fourteen by an American Jesuit priest during confession. He often returns to this story as a way of casting aspersions at the Catholic Church, which had been critical of his human rights abuses. Folded into this story, however, is another: his sexual abuse of their household help (which he later confesses was fabricated). Here what we see is a double confession—Duterte to the priest and to the audience—and a double assault: the priest's on Duterte and Duterte's on the maid. The two acts of violation turn out to be intimately related, whereby the priest's assault of Duterte becomes a means for the latter's domination of his audience. He has frequently told these stories on various occasions, usually in a mix of Taglish, Bisaya, and English. Below is my translation of a composite version:

> Now, in Ateneo—who is from Ateneo here? If you are from Ateneo, on Friday, it's communion, confession. That's automatic. And during confession, "Bless me father for I have sinned."
>
> "And what is your sin?"
>
> "Well, it is standing up because you are fondling my goddamn prick. . . ."
>
> While confessing, the priests would fondle our balls. So when you confess, they ask you, "What are your sins, my son?" Eh, I was a freshman. Eh, what was the sin of a freshman? . . .
>
> "I, I . . ."
>
> "Come on."
>
> "I, I . . ."
>
> "I, I is not a sin. We do not have the whole day. Speak up."
>
> "I went to the . . ."
>
> "What?"
>
> "I went to the room of the maid."
>
> "Why?"

"I lifted the blanket."

"And?"

"I tried to touch what was inside the panty."

"And?"

"I was touching. She woke up. So I left the room."

"Where did you go after?"

"To the bathroom."

"Why?"

"*Kuwan*, Father *'yung* the usual." [Well, Father, the, uh, the usual.]

"What is the usual?"

"*Alam mo . . .*" [You know . . .]

"Okay. So you went back? And?"

"I tried to insert my finger, Father."

"Then?"

"I—there was hair and . . ."

"And?"

"It was wet."

"And? Did she wake up?"

"No, Father. She was closing her eyes. Fast asleep."

"Oh," *sabi ng pari* [the priest said]. "And?"

"I went to the bathroom again, Father."

"Again!?"

"Yes, Father. Twice."

"Oh my, God. Say five Our Fathers, five Hail Marys because you will go to hell." (laughter)

That is the explanation behind the finger story. The priests would urge you to tell more sins. What sins could first, second, and third year students commit? Other than spying on women and other stuff. Wolf-whistling women was the only sin that we committed. But Father Falvey, he was always urging you to tell more sins. "Come on, come on, give me your sins." Do you know why? Because the longer you stay there, the more he can fondle your balls. And there were many priests. They would just divide the students among them. If you believed the story that I fingered a woman, you're crazy. I only said it because the priest was insistent that we tell him more sins so we would stay kneeling while he squeezed our balls. Son of a bitch, that's the truth. (laughter) (Presidential Communications Operations 2019b)

Many of Duterte's stories are arguably confessional to the extent that they are about exposing what usually stays hidden, bringing to light what otherwise remains in darkness. The subject who speaks is also the subject who is spoken about as s/he reveals the history of their sinful acts to a priest, who in turn dispenses penance in the name of God. As the mediator of divine forgiveness, the priest exercises an inordinate power over the penitent, registering the penitent's debts and prescribing the penance with which to cancel these (Rafael 1993). However, in Duterte's telling, the very act of confession is subverted. It is no longer meant to seek forgiveness and acknowledge the priest's authority but precisely to ridicule it. Duterte reveals the priest's concupiscence, showing how confession becomes a vehicle not for forgiveness but for clerical abuse. Confession breeds obscenity rather than divine dispensation, making for an uncanny encounter between priest and penitent. What emerges in the experience of confession for the penitent—here a young boy—is the return of the repressed in familiar form: the predator as father. From the perspective of the boy, the father's demands appear autocratic. He cannot be refused. His lust for the boy requires that the latter must stay longer in the confessional, making up sins in order to satisfy the priest.

To comply with the priest's demands, Duterte fabricates a story about "fingering" their housemaid, then masturbating in the bathroom. He evokes a circle of touching: while the priest fondles his genitals, Duterte talks about foisting himself on the genitals of the woman as she sleeps, then subsequently fondling himself. His story connects these improper connections into a sequence of submission and mastery that yields pleasure and laughter. The trauma of sexual abuse for Duterte at the hands of the priest is transmuted into the excitement of probing the maid's genitals, then mastering, as it were, his own. This mixture of fear, shame, and excitement is registered in Duterte's stuttering reply to the priest's insistence that he tell him more and more. "I . . . I . . . ," he says, as the priest, holding his balls, fishes for more, demanding "And . . . Then . . . And?" Duterte's confession climaxes, as it were, with two trips to the bathroom to relieve himself. In the end, the priest waves him off with a few feckless prayers, assuring him of eternal damnation. Rather than a site for contrition and divine forgiveness, confession here is converted into a kind of pornographic machine for the reproduction of sadistic male pleasures. Duterte submits to clerical abuse but turns that submission into a story about his mastery over the maid, who, he claims, remains innocent of her violation. His exposure and disempowerment by someone above become the conditions for overpowering someone below. He thus reverses his position from being abused to being the abuser, from a position of submission to one of domination, from one of fear to one of satisfaction and release. But only at the expense and through the exploitation of a subordinate other.

And what of his audience? Feminists, human rights advocates, the Church hierarchy, and other critics of Duterte reacted with anger. They decried his misogyny at making light of sexual abuse as consistent with his disregard for human rights. Others were scandalized by his "indecency" and filthy language, his lack of *delicadeza*, or civilized behavior. In other words, they read Duterte's obscenity in the way that he had meant it: as an unremitting assault on moral conventions ("Duterte: Outrage" 2018).

Judging from the transcripts and the videos, however, those who were present at his speeches reacted differently. They applauded his stories and laughed at his jokes. Why? Freud once posed this question. When we laugh at jokes, what are we laughing at? Are we responding to the technique of joke-telling or to the content of the joke, or to both? It is never clear, he says, the extent to which jokes, like dreams, are fulfillments of the same wish: to evade repression. "The joke will evade restrictions and open sources of pleasure that have become inaccessible. It will further bribe the hearer with its yield of pleasure into taking sides with us without very close investigation. . . . Reason, critical judgment, suppression—these are the forces against which [a joke] fights in succession" (Freud 1960, 72, 105). The political significance of jokes, the fact that they go against the grain of the reasonable and the normal, would seem to make them valuable resources for the oppressed seeking to overthrow the weight of authority. Mikhail Bakhtin further argues that medieval celebrations like the carnival and modern literary forms like the novel were sites for this upending of hierarchy through satire, disguise, and social inversions. The high is brought down low and the low is elevated, especially parts of the body and their functions (Bakhtin 1968, 1981).

But with Duterte, the subversive potential of humor is put to counter-subversive uses. Bribing his audience, Duterte is like a smuggler of illicit goods, promising forbidden pleasures and overturning repressive strictures. He says what they would have wanted to say but could not. Their laughter could thus be read as a sign of their identification with Duterte's efforts to find a way out of his suffering at the hands of the priest with a tale about abusing the maid who nonetheless remains, or so he claims, unaware of her violation. They delight in his resistance and at his bumbling attempts at mastery that lead to some sort of self-recovery—one that is buttressed by his tendentious disavowal of his own violence. Decades later, when he tells this story, he is no longer a boy but the president of the country. Occupying the heights of power, he is capable of commanding attention wherever he goes, with whatever he says. Duterte's obscenities feel subversive, but subversion in this context is in the service of an autocratic end where laughter produces an intimacy between ruler and ruled. The vulgarity of his language positions him as a kind of rebel inviting others to join him in his assault on bourgeois sensibilities and norms. But it comes with the condition that the audience must submit to his narrative. Only he can tell the stories and expect their laughter. The reverse is never possible as no one, as far as I know, jokes with Duterte in public. He expects no narrative reciprocity, no return with interest, but only a kind of passive acceptance of the surplus of stories he gives you. There is thus nothing democratic in Duterte's humor. Instead, the pleasure that the audience gets from his jokes is intrinsically linked to their willingness to participate in the imaginative violation of others, especially women. Whether he seeks revenge or release, Duterte's tales seek to assert his phallic power over his enemies while simultaneously subordinating and overpowering his audience.

In looking at the narrative structure of his jokes, we see how it hinges not only on classic techniques of joke-telling—those of condensation and displacement, as in dreams (Freud 2010). It is also productive of a hierarchy of listening whereby Duterte as the teller monopolizes the time and the language of telling. As part of the audience, you have no choice but to wait for him—and he is always late—then listen to him take his time unspooling his tales. Unable to leave without drawing his ire, you remain a captive audience. Jokes then become a way of establishing his authority. He exposes himself, renders himself vulnerable, and risks dissolving his authority, but only to recover and reassert his mastery over the scene of exposure. This dialectic of disclosure and domination allows him to forge a tyranny of intimacy, extracting your consent, registered by your laughter. Humor is thus a means of playing out his anxiety while assuaging his fear. Vulgarity is stylized and obscenity performed to release the audience's inhibitions at defying conventions. But this defiance is bogus and deeply conservative since it always comes with the price of submission to Duterte's authoritarian imagination.

While laughter creates conviviality and community, it is always shadowed by violence and fear. Duterte re-creates in every story something of the tone and texture of his primal scene: the dark confessional where he is held captive by the hands of the American priest. Indeed, his performative shamelessness today may be read as the unfinished struggle to master his fear of the father-predator as he attempts to take on the latter's power for himself. It is precisely that same phallic power that he seeks to grasp and wield when he addresses those he considers critical of him such as women and "lesser" men, and especially abject figures of criminality like drug dealers and users. Recklessly cussing at them, he lusts after their deaths, brooking neither dissent nor opposition. "And . . . And . . . Then . . . And?"

Duterte and Death

Closely related to Duterte's exaltation of the phallus is his ambivalent relationship to death. By now, the story is well known. He grew up a skinny, underachieving, lazy student, one who "was kicked out" of several schools. He was a mama's boy who chafed under his mother's discipline. His misogyny is countered by his deference to women around him, especially his mother and elder sister, and now his daughter, Sarah. And the political opponents he fears most are mostly women: Senator Leila de Lima, the journalist Maria Ressa, among others (Miller 2018; Paddock 2017; Sykes 2018).

His putative toughness is also belied by his fragile health. Duterte suffers from several medical conditions: Buerger's disease; Barrett's esophagus, which may have graduated into cancer; myasthenia gravis; chronic back pain from a motorcycle accident for which he has taken fentanyl; vertigo; intense migraine; and perhaps more that we don't know about (Kabiling 2020; Ranada 2016b). It remains unclear what his precise health condition is since we never hear directly from his doctors. And he takes any attempt to question his medical condition as a grave insult, a challenge to his bodily integrity. At the same time, he is given to confessing his physical ailments and weaknesses. Publicly, he will go on at length about his fatigue on the job, his need to sleep late and to take frequent naps. He has never been enthusiastic about national holidays, often skipping ceremonial wreath-layings, parades, and speeches. He has ducked out of international meetings, avoided dinners, and kept to his room because of exhaustion. Indeed, Duterte usually stays in bed till midafternoon and often avoids getting up for morning meetings. He would disappear for days, and remain gone from public view. In one week-long stretch when he was wholly absent from the public eye, he tweeted a photo of himself in bed in his Davao home, wearing shorts and watching *Django Unchained* on Netflix (De Vera 2019). While he never misses an occasion to pronounce his hatred of drugs and disdain for addicts, he has waxed wistful about the pleasures of fentanyl, the relaxing effects of pot, and, he claims, the relatively harmless effects of cocaine (Corrales 2018).

The president frequently talks about dying. He often speculates how much time he has left and what hell will look like when he gets there, saying he would prefer the latter to heaven, where the women will be more beautiful. He is not shy about inviting the military to take over in a coup if they are unhappy with his rule and put an end to his life (Mangosing 2019). This proximity to death is constantly evoked, even cultivated. Duterte's evident glee in murdering his enemies is well documented. He is less interested in penal solutions to illegalities than he is in talking about extreme measures. In part, this has to do with his distrust of the criminal justice system, which he shares with his supporters. The corruption among cops and judges, the criminality that's normal within precincts and jails—all of this makes him skeptical about institutional solutions to crime. Law itself can become an instrument of criminality, as well as a weapon for unjustly pursuing his enemies. For Duterte, it is better to take the law into your own hands. Killing criminals solves the problem of a corrupt justice system and it provides a bonus of pleasure, a heightened affective charge from delivering justice directly. No question: Duterte has a special relationship with death, his own as well as others'. He will tell you how many people he has personally killed, and he has even admitted to being behind the Davao Death Squad ("Duterte: Am I the Death Squad?" 2015). But he will also readily talk about his own bodily frailties and intimations of mortality.

For Duterte, this relationship with death by way of disease and murder sets him apart from other politicians. His putative authenticity comes precisely from admitting his joy in killing, on the one hand, and his professed vulnerability to death, on the other

His toughness is of a piece with his fragility. His frequent admission of murdering people is calculated to impress his interlocutors. He says, in effect, "Yes, I've killed," to journalists interviewing him. I admit it. I risked my life and looked death in the face and was not afraid to kill.[1] At one point in the presidential debates, he proclaimed that only he who was prepared to kill could become president. And at another point, he said that he so despised drug dealers and users that he would kill his own son if he found out he was into drugs.[2]

This intimacy with death, like his skill at storytelling, lies at the basis of what some have called his "charisma." It is not an attraction that is built on the promise of glorious sacrifice or the coming of a utopian future. Neither does it come from the generosity of patronage or the compassion of a bountiful donor. Rather, it is built on his claim of conquering death by controlling his fear of it. He may be dying, his body may already be failing. But just as he is still capable of erections, aided by Viagra, he is still capable of killing, and certainly ordering killings. In other words, he demonstrates his capacity to govern life by administering death. He confronts his own weaknesses by projecting those onto others: his critics, addicts, world leaders, and so on. Killing them literally or symbolically, Duterte makes a show of conquering his own fear of death. He takes exception to death's dominion by turning it into an instrument of his rule. Duterte shows that his phallus, despite everything else, can still rise to the occasion and that he is capable of cutting down anyone who threatens to take it away from him.

We see again a familiar pattern: the biopolitical is subsumed and structured by the necropolitical. Just as his humor is predicated on the monopoly of narrative reciprocity in the economy of joke-telling—he alone can tell the story, not his audience—so his charisma, if that is what it is, is erected on the basis of his proximity to and claims of controlling death. Wielding the autocrat's phallus, he rules by way of fear and laughter, by his capacity to belittle death and dying even as he intimates death's power over him. Similarly, as we saw, he converts his experience of sexual abuse at the hands of a foreign priest into a series of jokes that amount to a kind of counter-confession. He discloses his trauma, displacing his pain by joking about his abuser as a way of getting back at him. He is able to avenge himself years later on his tormentor while putting on display the harm that he bears on his body. Displaying his hurt, he is able to extract the submission of others. They laugh at his stories while the Church and other clergy, as well as the media, fulminate at his obscenity. He gets back exactly the responses he wants. In his stories, Duterte confesses the abuse he suffered during confession while confessing to his abuse and murder of others. Laughter and death are thus always entangled with one another. The former provides an escape from repression but can serve as a sign of submission to a force that comes before us, while the latter can strike fear in oneself but can also be transformed into a weapon for striking others.

SKETCHES III. DUTERTE'S HOBBESIAN WORLD

I am not an expert on human rights, but reading reports about the UN rapporteur's criticisms of Duterte for his statements justifying the assassination of "corrupt journalists" strikes me as a case of mistranslation. Human rights refers to the inherent dignity of all human beings and their inalienable right to freedom. Furthermore, as the UN declaration says, human rights must be protected by the rule of law, "if man is not to be compelled to have recourse, as a last resort, to rebellion against tyranny and oppression."

This idea of universal human rights does not, it seems to me, exist in the local-regional world of Duterte. In that world, human rights are abstract impositions by the West that infringe on the sovereignty of nations. They essentially amount to a form of imperialism: the West dictating to the non-West the norms of proper conduct. So it's not entirely surprising that Duterte, when asked about the UN condemnation of his statements about the killing of journalists, responded with "Fuck you." His response was a more graphic expression of a position found among other nations—China, the Gulf States, Russia, and so on—that have their own ideas of what and who counts as "human," and what are "rights."

Of course, human rights are problematic even in Western countries. In the US, they are daily violated in the structural violence and unrelenting war against racial and sexual minorities, women, the poor, the disabled, and so on. Racism, poverty, and gross inequality deprive entire populations of their inalienable rights to dignity and freedom. Indeed, capitalism, to the extent that it treats workers not as humans but as means to an end that is wholly inhuman—profit accumulation—arguably leads to violations of human rights.

Hence, the contradiction: the UN rapporteurs lecturing the Philippine president about human rights from a location that historically is responsible for their daily violation in its complicity with the "war on terror," neo-liberalism, and drone warfare, to give a few examples.

But what would happen if we did away with the normative force of human rights? One implication of Duterte's defiance of the UN is that in place of human rights, he believes in a more elementary notion of justice: revenge. It goes something like this: if you hurt me, I have the right to return the injury. Not only will I respond in kind; I will do so with interest, just like a gift. If you are a journalist who insulted my mother, then my son, then continue to defame me even after I have done you favors, I am entitled to respond with interest. I have the right to kill you. This is, of course, the story of Duterte's relationship with the murdered broadcaster and anticommunist vigilante Jun Pala, who had many enemies in Davao back in the early 1990s.

For Duterte and others like him, justice means revenge. It is about the right to seek satisfaction for an injury, real or imagined, that someone has caused you or those close to you. It entails the restoration of your honor and reputation when these have been damaged (for example, with questions about your health or your manhood). Publicly exposed and endangered, one's honor and reputation must be protected, calling for violence as a necessary resort—the exercise of a righteous force that enables me to punish you to the point of taking away your life in order to restore mine. Such a scenario is possible only when the rule of law has either broken down or is thought to be ineffectual. Every citizen can then become a law unto him- or herself, authorized to kill suspected criminals without due process. Revolutionary and counterrevolutionary justice as class warfare are both steeped in the ethos of vengeance, as the aggrieved class seeks vengeance on its oppressors.

It is this Hobbesian world, the world of perpetual civil war, that was the Davao of the 1990s—with its Alsa Masa death squads, NPA sparrow units, private armies, rogue military protecting miners and loggers, drug lords, and corrupt journalists—that shaped Duterte and that he brings with him to every press conference. It's a world where human rights are translated into highly particularized notions of honor and revenge where my freedom depends on my right to take yours away.

But what about those who do not share the same notion of honor and the desire for revenge? They are left vulnerable and unsafe. Human rights, as contradictory and hegemonic as they are, remain our best hope for protecting each other from this parochial world of revenge and the spiraling fear and violence it brings forth. Doing so requires that we claim those rights and insist on their protection not by a strongman or a tatay, a father, but by the laws that we ourselves agree to abide by, however imperfect and uneven their enforcement might be. Otherwise, it's back to Hobbes. Or forward to Stalin.

—*Philippine Daily Inquirer*, June 13, 2016

SKETCHES III. DUTERTE'S SENSE OF TIME

What's the difference between Duterte and his predecessors? For one thing, Duterte's sense of historical time differs from other presidents'. He doesn't see history as moving along a continuum of progress. Instead, what he sees is the stubborn repetition of the same crimes, the same tragedies, the same dangers. He never speaks of his vision for a better world, only about the recurring nightmares of this dystopic one—an endless chain of rapes, murders, terrorism, theft, and so on, all brought about by drugs.

Listen to his speeches. They consist of rambling, unfinished sentences held together by a ramshackle syntax looping back to the same murderous obsessions and dark fears. They are difficult to get through, not for their complexity but for their spectacular incoherence. He communicates by failing to communicate in any but the most fractured and elliptical way, stuttering between languages, slipping into jokes, non sequiturs, ad hominems, threats, and a steady stream of invective that provides affective juice to a semantically impoverished discourse. Hyperbole, paranoia, and self-pitying intimations of his own mortality go hand in glove with murderous rants and promises to kill and kill and kill. . . . And his supporters lap it up.

For Duterte, then, historical time is like the time he ascribes to the lives of addicts, enemies he is fond of dehumanizing. Earlier presidents might frame history in mythical terms—paradise, then the fall, where confusion and darkness reigned, followed inevitably by a time of awakening and hope. Duterte will have none of this, for he traffics only in vengeful nihilsm.

His version of historical time is one of unending trauma, where experience outstrips expression. Unable to conceptualize social problems in relation to their social context, he descends into the compulsive repetition of their symptoms. And like the addicts he imagines and despises, he violently reacts to any criticism, especially from human rights advocates, by threatening to violate their human rights.

This is what is novel about Duterte: the past and the future for him are marked by the same thing—the traumatic experiences which he has never resolved but merely displaces onto his audiences: the abuse he suffered as a child at the hands of an American Jesuit, the verbal and physical beatings from his mother, the violence he dealt with as mayor of Davao confronting death squads from the left and the right; the Moro insurgencies, the gangster gunfights, and so on.

By becoming president, he has imposed on us this view of history as perpetual chaos where experience itself is under constant assault, punishing the very language with which to represent it. He has nationalized trauma as the dominant basis of political discourse as he forces us to see humanity through the inhuman eyes of those he has consigned to extrajudicial hell.

Perhaps this is what makes it so difficult for critics of Duterte to develop a counter-narrative. It is not so much that the president has told a compelling story about the state of the nation. Rather, he has told many half-stories over and over again (or what some of his critics might call lies), which can't be consolidated and so pinned down, and are thus difficult to refute. It is like the man who tells the same old jokes and expects everyone to laugh like before.

We can also think about Duterte's view of history—his understanding of the past in relation to the future—by looking at the campaign slogans of past presidents. Marcos: "This Nation Can Be Great Again"; Fidel V. Ramos: "Philippines 2000"; Estrada: "*Erap para sa Mahirap*" (Erap for the poor); Gloria Macapagal Arroyo: "The Strong Republic"; Benigno "PNoy" Aquino: "*Daang Matuwid*" (the straight path) and "*Walang corrupt kung walang mahirap*" (there is no corruption if there is no poverty).

Then Duterte: "*Tapang at Malasakit*" (Courage and Compassion) and "Change Is Coming." The first slogan is not a program. It is not a vision. It is a set of moral attributes: bravery and compassion. But *tapang*—courage—against whom? Compassion for whom? The second slogan hints at drastic, even revolutionary changes, and so would seem to be more in line with the mythologies of progress espoused by earlier presidents. In the end, though, I think it is fair to say that the first trumped the second.

Duterte's sense of historical time always returns to an ever-repeating present. Hence, his signature program, the war against drugs, is bound to be, as he himself admitted, ongoing, with no end point in sight. It is nonlinear and non-redemptive. It isn't interested in any kind of temporal horizon or any of the usual bureaucratic benchmarks associated with "progress." It is indexed only to his own existence.

From Duterte's perspective, as long as he is president, there will always be a drug war because drugs will always be a problem. For every addict killed or every low- or mid-level drug lord put away, there will always be others emerging, hence making it necessary to continue the war ad infinitum. The drug war is an end in and of itself. Even in Davao the war persists to the extent that the drug economy continues to flourish. Indeed, without the drug war and the illegalization of drugs, the drug economy would not be as profitable. But that is another story.

Duterte's pessimism, then, is, unsurprisingly, the source of his debased hope. The history of his presidency is coterminous with the history of the drug war, which in turn is the source of the drug trade's immense profitability. For without a drug problem, there would be no need for a drug war, and without such a war, there would be no drug profits. Then what would be the reason for his being? There is no future except what you already have on hand.

—*Rappler*, November 10, 2019

4. THE SOVEREIGN TRICKSTER

Justice pursues the body beyond all possible pain.
—MICHELE FOUCAULT, *Discipline and Punish*

Duterte: *May Utak sa Bayag, May Bayag sa Utak*
(Duterte: Brains in the balls and balls in the brains)
—Duterte campaign bumper sticker, 2016

Provincializing Foucault and Mbembe

For the last few years, I've been teaching a course on Filipino history during the same term that I've been doing a reading seminar on Michel Foucault at my university. Not surprisingly, the two have become entangled in my mind. Whenever I try to make sense of Foucault, I tend to do so with reference to the Philippines, so that I call on the one to answer my questions about the other, much like dialing the number of a distant call center with impossible questions at all hours of the day and night. Somehow, Foucault's focus on Europe (without arguably being Eurocentric) helps me see events in the Philippines in a certain way, just as events in the Philippines permit me to reprovincialize Foucault's historical genealogies of power and knowledge. In this sense, I follow in the wake of others who have made use of Foucault to think about postcolonial conditions elsewhere. One of these is Achille Mbembe, whose writings on sub-Saharan Africa have been helpful for thinking about the postcolonial Philippines. What follows, then, is an exercise in historical translation as I move back and forth between Foucault and Mbembe in an attempt to make sense of Duterte's Philippines.

To begin with, there is Foucault's well-known idea of biopower characteristic of the modern age. Intertwined with, as much as subsuming, earlier regimes of power—what he calls the pastoral, the politico-juridical, and the disciplinary—biopower concerns control over all aspects of life as a whole. It sums up a style of governing that targets entire populations by working through each and every body. As Foucault succinctly puts it, biopower seeks to set the conditions for the "conduct of conduct," with the state acting as a kind of orchestra conductor to coordinate the movements and behavior of each individual for the sake of ensuring the survival and development of the whole population. Actualized in a wide range of institutional arrangements, from social welfare to sanitation, from tax policies to industrial regulations, from public health to policing, from education to housing, biopower is omnipresent in modern social relations. Engineering behavior while educating desire, it seeks to enlist the collaboration of each and every citizen toward the propagation of life as "more than and better than life." In the context of the postcolonial nation-state, biopower is precisely what animates the programs usually called "national development," designed as progressive and open-ended projects to ensure and improve the lives of its citizens (Foucault 1990, 2009, 2010).

But as Foucault points out, biopower also requires the continued assertion of state sovereignty. This means, among other things, that the state continues to reserve the right to determine the boundaries of national belonging. This entails deciding on those who are and can be citizens, not only legally but also culturally but also those who are not, can never be, or may no longer be considered citizens. Who is inside and who is outside the nation? Who has the right to have rights, and who are those that have no rights at all? And what to do with the latter? How are they to be othered—to be conceptualized and controlled? Are they to be treated as migrants subject to eventual inclusion? As racialized social enemies to be targeted for segregation and incarceration, condemned to bare life, exposed to death, or driven toward annihilation? Or as "abnormal" types mired in perversion and poverty bound for perpetual neglect and allowed to perish? Where biopower is about governing all facets of life, what happens to the administration of death (Foucault 2003)?

In his extended gloss on Foucault's work, Achille Mbembe has pointed out that in the context of the postcolony—whether in sub-Saharan Africa or other formerly colonized countries—the imperative of asserting sovereignty points to the persistence of what he refers to as necropower: the power to put to death, often accompanied by an "aesthetics of vulgarity"—the obscene display of violent excess that spills over and circulates between

Figure 4.1. Mideo Cruz, Duterte as a trickster figure, inspired by Duterte's tirade against the Catholic Church on All Soul's Day, 2018, calling himself "Santo Rodrigo." On the left, "Obosen," a reference to his vow to annihilate drug addicts; on the right, "Our Father," a reference to Duterte's joke about organizing a new church called "Iglesia ni Duterte."

rulers and ruled (Agamben 1995; Mbembe 1992, 2003). As the other, enabling side of biopower, necropower engages in a range of deadly measures, from permanent exile to indefinite renditions, from colonial occupation to racialized incarceration, that often include the grotesque and bloody displays of the sovereign will on the mutilated bodies of those designated as unassimilably foreign and criminal. As the murderous counterpoint to the biopolitical imperative of administering life, necropower foregrounds the sovereign will as the practice of putting to death and helps us understand the turbulent history of the present.

Such a history at this moment and for the foreseeable future is dominated by a whole series of authoritarian figures around the world. One such imposing figure is President Rodrigo Duterte. Not only does he monopolize so much of our political attention; but like his American counterpart, Donald Trump, he has also laid claim to large reservoirs of our intellectual and moral energy. How, then, can we use the critical histories of Foucault and Mbembe to understand a figure like Duterte and come to grips with the crisis brought about by his regime? Let me give a few examples.

Necropower and Barbarian Freedom

My first example has to do with the workings of necropower and its role in shoring up the idea of sovereignty, or put another way, the idea that freedom and authority stem from the right to kill. Since assuming office in July 2016, President Duterte has fallen woefully short on his promises to improve Filipino lives—from improving infrastructure to alleviating poverty, from shifting to a federalist form of government to peace talks with the Communist Party and the Moro insurgents, and much more. Instead, he has focused tenaciously on the drug war, specifically on ridding poor neighborhoods of so-called "drug personalities." Under his regime, necropower has consistently trumped biopower. One way to see his emphasis on the former over the latter is to look at a speech that he gave on August 3, 2018, in the province of Bukidnon. Making one of his frequent jokes about human rights, he addresses drug users and dealers directly in Taglish:

> You enjoy your human rights there in heaven *kasi* God promised you that *lahat ng* extrajudicial killing victims will go to heaven. '*Yan ang hiningi ko sa Diyos. Sabi naman ng Diyos,* "*Pwede, pwede.*" [laughter] *Gawain—gagawin ko ba 'yan kung walang guarantee? Kasi kaawa naman.* '*Tang ina, magdo-droga ka tapos sa impyerno ka.* If you have a [consolation?] I'm going to heaven, *sabi ko,* "*God, pagbigyan mo na lang 'yan. Ako, wala akong hingiin sa akin.* Reserve the hottest place in hell for me. And may I burn till eternity." (Republic of the Philippines 2018)

> [You enjoy your human rights in heaven because God promised you that all extrajudicial killing victims will go to heaven. That's what I asked God. And God said, "okay, okay." Would I do that without guarantee? That's because these pitiful motherfuckers, they take drugs, then they have to go to hell? If you have any [consolation?], I said, "God, do them a favor. Me, I'm not going to ask for anything for myself. Reserve the hottest place in hell for me. And may I burn till eternity."]

Enfolded in this joke is the tacit admission of having authorized the extrajudicial killings of thousands of suspected drug users (Petersen 2018). This confession, however, is displaced by another image: that of the victims going to heaven to "enjoy" the human rights they were deprived of on earth. In effect, the joke converts victims into martyrs. It is a conversion that Duterte accomplishes through a conversation with God Himself. He asks God to "pagbigyan mo na lang 'yan"—to grant them a favor—and offers to trade places with them—to "reserve the hottest place in hell for me." Duterte's joke suggests two things. First, that he reserves the right to suspend human rights by ordering extrajudicial killings. And second, that as the sovereign leader, he has privileged access to the Cosmic Sovereign Himself, a connection that we might colloquially refer to as being *malakas* (strongly connected) with Him. This divine connection is what allows the president to make deals with God. Mimicking divine power, the president aspires to wield the same awesome might. He can decide, for example, on who will be saved and who will be damned, determining the afterlife of his victims even as he usurps the very realm of the devil himself, who dwells in the "hottest place in hell."

In this and many of Duterte's other jokes, a macabre sense of humor comes with a recurring obsession with drug users. Both betray an intense fascination with death. Addiction and death are always linked in his mind. Indeed, for Duterte, the "drug personalities" he addresses are no longer human. Echoing popular belief, Duterte regards crystal meth, or shabu, as thoroughly destructive, driving users into acts of extreme violence. High on the drug, they seem as if possessed by a force beyond their control. Unable to defer their desire, they will stop at nothing to satisfy their urges. They have no qualms about raping children and killing innocent people. For this reason, they cannot be considered human, let alone claim to have any rights. Hence, when accused of committing gross human rights violations, Duterte once responded, "What crime against humanity? In the first place, I'd like to be frank with you, are they (drug users) humans?" (Lasco 2016; Ramos 2016). Against available scientific evidence, Duterte continues to claim that shabu thoroughly destroys the mental and moral faculties of its users. Their brains supposedly shrink, placing them beyond rehabilitation. Incapable of being productive members of society, they are a permanent danger to its inhabitants (PTV 2018; Salaverria 2017). Considered inhuman, drug users thus pose an existential threat to those around them. The only solution for Duterte is to exterminate them.

Why this ferocious obsession with the shabu addict, especially in impoverished areas? Why does he desire their death?

Part of the answer may have something to do with Duterte's attraction to the inhuman qualities he associates with drug addicts. Induced by drug use, their inhumanity is thought to manifest itself in their criminality. Breaking the laws and disrespecting social conventions, it is as if they recognize no other authority except their own. They seem, then, to be supremely sovereign. If they pose a danger, it is because they know no limits to their power of destruction. In addressing addicts, Duterte is at once repelled and attracted to this inhuman power and its claims to absolute sovereignty. It is as if he wants to claim that power for himself, often sounding like the criminals he seeks to pursue. For example, in one interview, in response to a question about his involvement with death squads in Davao City, he says, "Am I the death squad? That is true" (Manlupig 2015). And when asked about the death toll while he was mayor of Davao, he responds: "They said I killed 700? They miscalculated. It was 1,700" (Human Rights Watch 2017). Sounding like a gangster bragging about his prowess, he threatens to execute addicts: "All of you who are into drugs, you sons of bitches, I will really kill you. I have no patience. I have no middle ground" (Jenkins 2016).

To be inhuman is to possess a dangerous power that transcends law and life itself. It would not be too far-fetched to say that such a power, reaching beyond life, has to do with its access to death. Addicts, in Duterte's view, are driven only to satisfy their need for drugs, to the point of killing for it. Unable to check their desire, they reject normal social relations. The antisocial nature associated with the addict brings with it precisely that power that Duterte craves. He wants that power for himself.

Historically, states have executed criminals, and in so doing claim the power of death over life in the name of preserving order and defending society. Usually, the state has recourse to the law and follows a judicial process. In Duterte's case, the widespread practice of summary executions carried out by police and their paid assassins short-circuits this process. From July 2016, official police policy, referred to as "Operation Double Barrel," states explicitly that the government is committed to a "drug clearing policy" that entails the "neutralization" and "negation" of "drug personalities nationwide" (Punay 2017; Republic of the Philippines, National Police Commission 2016). Extrajudicial killings—both the policy and the practice—thus seem like the direct translation of Duterte's murderous threats (Baldwin and Marshall 2017). His rhetoric appears magical: he speaks and sure enough, one sees the effects of his words as multiple corpses nightly populate the streets. In killing them, Duterte can claim to control and channel their inhuman power. He can point to the corpses as proof that his plan is working. For example, in his remarks about an unusually large number of summary executions in August 2017, he says, *"Yung namatay daw kanina sa Bulacan, 32,* in a massive raid. *Maganda 'yun. Makapatay lang tayo ng mga* another 32 everyday then maybe we can reduce what ails this country" (the ones who died in Bulacan, 32, in a massive raid, that is beautiful. We could just kill another 32 everyday, then maybe we could reduce what ails this country) (Corrales and Salaverria 2017).

He sees in the death of alleged addicts something aesthetically pleasing. Their extermination is "good and beautiful" (maganda). Seeing the death of the inhuman addict, he imagines not only neutralizing their power but also absorbing it. With each death, he becomes more assured of his capacity to access that which is beyond life. His sovereignty is reassured by the death of those he thinks have access to another realm. Duterte thus appropriates the very excess he attributes to addicts. Indeed, his own admission of being addicted at some point to a powerful opioid, fentanyl, makes his connection to addicts as imaginative as it is real ("Duterte on Fentanyl Use" 2017; Lui 2016).[1]

The latter have what he wishes to monopolize: an inhuman and uncanny ability to overcome all limitations of the social and the political. We might say that he is addicted to the notion of addiction and the kind of antisocial and inhuman power he sees in it—a kind of power with which to transcend and dominate the human and the social. In this sense, Duterte sees the world through the lens of his enemies (Siegel 1998, 2006).

One way to understand Duterte's rise to power is to situate it within the history of Philippine state formation seen as an elaboration of a process of counterinsurgency. This means that the state is founded not only on its repression of those it deems subversive; it also depends on the active collaboration of its citizens to carry out this repression. In this sense, counterinsurgency is predicated on the simultaneous workings of bio- and necropower. The postcolonial Philippine state has been the heir of a legacy of colonial counterinsurgency dating back from the later Spanish and United States colonial period. This counterinsurgent style of governing is founded on the state's ability to confront as much as to accommodate insurgent forces that have historically challenged its authority: peasant groups, labor unions, communists, Moro secessionists, and a variety of major and minor criminals located inside and outside of official circles—often at the same time. Such insurgents are also major agents in the gray economies of smuggling, gun-running, kidnap-for-ransom, human and drug trafficking, illegal gambling, and many other forms of racketeering, allowing them to influence if not capture various parts of the state. As other scholars have pointed out, the political economy of state formation in the Philippines—and much of Southeast Asia—cannot be understood apart from the role of insurgent figures and their illicit economies in the production and operation of the state apparatus and the legal economy on both the local and national levels.[2]

In Duterte's Philippines, the drug addict currently occupies the position of the most dangerous insurgent, thanks in large part to the tendentious hyperinflation of the numbers of drug users by the president and the police (Lasco 2016).[3] It is not surprising, then, that just as Duterte has sought to co-opt the communists and the Moro rebels, he also seeks to tap into the insurgent energy of drug addicts. We can see something of this attempt to appropriate the addict's perspective in his long, improvised speeches (Republic of the Philippines 2016). Obsessed with exterminating drug users, he mirrors, if not covets, the very inhuman power he attributes to them. And the only way he can extract this power is by killing them. The "beauty and goodness" of murder is that it brings him closer to the very thing he abhors yet intensely desires.

From this perspective, addicts are not merely the "living dead" who need to be killed again and again. As insurgents who live inside society but who seek to destroy it, they come close to being what Foucault describes as "barbarians." And in coveting their power over life and death, Duterte himself becomes a kind of barbarian. What does this mean?

In his lectures entitled *Society Must Be Defended*, Foucault retraces the emergence of the figure of the barbarian in French historiography from the seventeenth to the eighteenth centuries with reference to the Germanic tribes that swept through Western Europe with the fall of the Roman Empire. What made such barbarians so compelling, according to Foucault, was their peculiar relationship to freedom. "The freedom of these [Germanic] warriors is not the freedom of tolerance and equality for all; it is a freedom that can be exercised only through domination. Far from being a freedom based upon respect, it is, in other words, a freedom based upon ferocity . . . from the Latin word *ferox*: 'proud, intrepid, haughty, cruel'" (Foucault 2003, 148–49).

The barbarian is thus the very negation of the liberal subject. Unbound to social contracts that can only limit his liberty, the barbarian sees his freedom primarily in terms of his ability to take away the freedom of others. Rather than engage in productive labor or the accumulation of property, the barbarian turns to plunder, forcing everyone else to be at his service. Contemptuous of any civilization that would tame and domesticate his rights, the barbarian's ideal government is "necessarily a military" one, "not one that is based upon the contracts and transfer of civil rights. . . . Full of arrogance, [the barbarian] has to be inhuman, precisely because he is not the man of nature and exchange; he is the man of history, the man of pillage and fires, he is the man of domination" (Foucault 2003, 197–98).

Barbarism, located within rather than outside of civilization, thus lies at the foundation of both authoritarianism *and* insurgency. Foucault's remarks on the genealogy of barbarism shed light, however partial and oblique, on Duterte's necropolitics—his fascination with the power of the inhuman to deliver death. He arrives not as an exception but as one who claims to be so—as one who will vanquish the putative enemies of the people by throwing away the cumbersome scales of Lady Justice and resorting instead to her swift and unforgiving sword. Duterte's barbarian notion of justice brings me to my second example dealing specifically with the president's endless war on drugs.

"Tokhang": Public Torture and Necro-Economy

In his 1973 Collège de France lectures gathered in the volume *The Punitive Society* (Foucault 2015) and two years later in his book *Discipline and Punish* (Foucault 1975), Foucault talks about the major forms of "punitive tactics" used in France and other places in Western Europe from the sixteenth century onward. One of these included the marking of the body of the condemned, "imposing on it a symbolic stain on his name," meant to "humiliate his character, damage his status. . . . In this system, the infraction is no longer something to be redressed . . . but rather something to be emphasized [and] . . . fixed in a sort of monument, even if it is a scar, an amputation, or something involving shame or infamy. . . . [T]he visible or social body must be a blazon of the penalties, and this blazon refers to two things: on the one hand, to the offense, of which it has to be the visible and immediately recognizable trace; . . . and on the other hand, to the power that imposed the penalty and that, with this penalty, has left the mark of its sovereignty on the tortured body. It is not just the offense that is visible on the scar or the amputation, it is the sovereign" (Foucault 2015, 7–8).

Anyone familiar with Duterte's war on drugs will immediately recognize in this punitive tactic the workings of Operation Tokhang, the process by which suspected drug users are placed on a list, visited by the police, and subsequently gunned down—their corpses left on the streets as gruesome reminders of their putative crime and as the fearsome signs of the sovereign's power. As hallmarks of the drug war, extrajudicial killings entail a conversion of sorts: the impoverished meth or, as it is more popularly known, shabu addict is converted from citizen to social enemy and hence an absolute menace to society. Beyond cure or rehabilitation, he is bereft of rights. Killing the addict is a form of public torture that marks him for definitive social exclusion. But by being killed and put on display, the corpse is recruited for another equally important task: as a medium for conveying the power of the sovereign. To put it differently, the corpse is included by being excluded. Its death signals its crime at the same time that it memorializes the power of its killers. Extrajudicial killings are thus a kind of pedagogy meant to teach the living about the consequences of addiction and the fearsome consequences of offending the king. As with all public torture, it is a vehicle for performing and intensifying the signs of the sovereign's power.[4]

Foucault makes a point of saying that, increasingly since the later nineteenth century, modern states have tended to do away with the death penalty as a punitive strategy in favor of the rehabilitation and reform of the criminal. But in places like the United States, this is patently not the case, as the death penalty continues to be practiced, and racialized imprisonment brings with it a permanent stigma and a kind of social death—the loss of voting rights, discrimination in the job market, and so on. In the Philippines, while the death penalty has been officially abolished, it continues to operate in the form of extrajudicial killings carried out by regular and private armies, death squads, vigilantes, and the police. The deaths that have resulted from Operation Tokhang, ranging from a low of seven thousand to a high of thirty thousand and counting, have a long history (Ateneo School et al. 2018; Johnson and Fernquest 2018). They were preceded by the countless executions under the colonial regimes of Spain, the US, Japan, and all other postcolonial administrations. The gruesome display of the dismembered remains of enemy bodies was standard practice—see, for example, the photographs of dead Filipino fighters during the Filipino-American war, the corpses of *Sakdalistas* in the 1930s, or those of the Huk peasants and communist insurgents, the Muslim rebels, and NPA fighters, from the 1950s to the present.

As a form of public torture and the death penalty by other means, Operation Tokhang continues the ritual of the ancient penalty of torturing and killing bodies of offenders, writing on them the nature of their guilt while staging the power of those who killed them. As I alluded to earlier, the killings are carefully planned, sustained by a technology of surveillance. Such a technology includes, for example, the making of lists of so-called drug personalities. These lists are compiled by the local government units (LGUs) that include the barangay *porok* (area) leaders and their *tanods* or village security forces appointed by the local barangay captain. The porok or block leaders compile their lists on the basis of personal knowledge, unsolicited tips, and rumors of suspected drug personalities. It is not clear how or even if these lists are vetted. Anecdotal evidence suggests that a number of those put on the list are not even involved in drugs but are simply there to fill a quota. Such lists are the basic elements for organizing policing operations directed at specific people in the community. They are, then, a kind of order of battle that allows the police, with the aid of vigilante squads, to organize the killings of specific targets ("Local Officials" 2017; "Why Intelligence Funds" 2017).

Additionally, the list of drug personalities becomes an avenue for financial gain. As Sheila Coronal and others have amply documented, the police are given substantial bonuses for each kill they produce (Coronel 2017; "'If You Are Poor'" 2017). Vigilante squads riding in tandem on motorcycles are also outsourced and paid handsomely to help the police, some of whom moonlight as assassins themselves. Billions of pesos have been set aside by Congress for the presidential and police intelligence funds that can be spent at each agency's discretion with no accountability, and one can surmise that these funds provide the financial wherewithal for the kill bonuses ("Why Intelligence Funds" 2017).

Alongside the financialization of the killings is the commodification of the corpses themselves. Cops get paid commissions by funeral parlors—some of which they themselves own—for each dead body they call in. Funeral homes have seen a boom in their business. In the absence of a city morgue, all the dead are delivered to privately owned funeral homes, where they are processed and cleaned. Each body can cost as much as 50,000 pesos (roughly US$950) to claim. To the families of the dead, the majority of whom are poor, this is a mind-boggling sum. To raise it, they must go into debt, but more commonly they hold gambling sessions during wakes, where, of course, the house gets its cut. Hence, wakes no longer follow a set time period—nine days of viewing, as was the custom. These days, burials occur whenever enough money has been raised to cover expenses.[5] In some instances, funeral parlors seek to recover the cost of processing bodies by renting out the corpses to households in order to give the latter legal

Table 4.1. Profiting from the Drug War: Menus of financial incentives for killing drug suspects

Types of police activity	Typical amounts
Extortion from drug suspects before or during arrests or while under detention	PhP 5,000–15,000 from poor victims to as much as PhP 1 million from rich victims
Theft of victims' belongings during arrests, or during entrapment operations where drug suspects are killed	This can include cash or property worth hundreds of thousands of pesos, as in the Jee Ick-Joo case; may include small amounts of cash, cell phones, jewelry, and other belongings of poor victims
Ransom demands after the abduction of so-called drug suspects, known as "tokhang for ransom"	Amounts can range from a few hundred thousand pesos to PhP 5 million, as in the Jee case
Fees or rewards paid to policemen for every person killed	PhP 5,000–20,000 for small-time drug offenders
Bonuses for police officers paid for by civilian officials	Hundreds of thousands of pesos
Commissions from funeral parlors	Up to PhP 10,000 for every dead body referred

Source: Compiled by Coronel (2017b) from interviews, news articles, and human rights reports.

cover to hold gambling sessions, inasmuch as the law allows for gambling in the case of wakes (Martin 2018). What we see, then, are the workings of necropower, understood to be neither murder nor sacrifice, accompanied by a necro-economy that profits from the accumulation and circulation of corpses. To paraphrase Marx, under capitalism, circulation squeezes money from every pore, including those of the corpse (Marx 1992). Thanks to the drug war and its lists, the dead are reanimated into labor power for the pursuit of profit.

The president himself is fond of brandishing such lists that contain the names not just of low-level dealers and addicts but also suspected local officials, such as mayors. While the poor addicts are killed, the more politically and financially well-off are rarely touched, except for a few spectacular cases, in order to set an example. For the most part, the mayors and governors, including police officials who are supposedly on the list, are left off and continue to be protected. But the fact remains that the drug lists are important instruments of intimidation. And the power of such lists comes from the fact that while their existence is widely acknowledged as a kind of public secret, their contents remain largely unknown. No one knows for sure who is on the lists, for even those who compile them—the barangay officials—could find themselves on it. Furthermore, there is no definitive way one can get oneself off them even if one is found to be innocent.

To be on the drug list is thus to be guilty regardless of one's innocence. It is to live in constant fear that one's time might be coming up. The lists thus derive their power not only from their panoptic nature—they allow the police to see you without you being able to see them—but also from the way they reorganize temporality. Put on the list, one can only be headed not for redemption or rehabilitation but for a final reckoning. The seeming arbitrariness with which these lists are put together creates a climate of suspicion in the affected communities. As the anthropologists Anna Warburg, Steffen Jensen, and Karl Hapal have pointed out in their fieldwork in the barangay of Bagong Silang in the city of Caloocan, such lists make for an "illegible terrain of violence." Triggered by police operations and vigilante attacks that litter the street with corpses, people are left with a profound sense of uncertainty as to who will be targeted next, when, and by whom. For such communities, the future holds no promise, only a continuous feeling of unease and dread. In this way, necropower is enabled by a necro-economy produced by and productive of fear as the pervasive affect and mode of control in the most afflicted barangays (Jensen and Hapal forthcoming; Warburg 2017; see also chapter 5 and conclusion of this book).

In sum, the current practice of EJKS as realized through the tactics of tokhang is not a retrograde throwback to some feudal past but part of a post-EDSA style of governing that has emerged since the overthrow of Marcos. It thrives in a setting where the legal system is profoundly politicized, where courts are backed up, and where judges as well as police are badly paid amid a largely impoverished population. And given the financial incentives that accompany the killings, one can see how EJKS work as part of a necro-economy that intensifies the necropower of the state (Montag 2013). Indeed, we can think of extrajudicial killings, as the term implies, as a kind of violent, arbitrary form of justice in a place where justice is often delayed and diverted. Setting aside the uncertain and time-consuming process of court trials and the difficult task of protecting human rights, EJKS insist on a different temporal and moral order, one where punishment is swift, visible, and unassailable. It is, of course, a justice that is steeped in injustice, one that is characteristic of the drug war and perhaps all wars.

The Drug War as Civil War

This brings me to my third example of what might be possible when thinking about the Philippines alongside Foucault: the matter of war itself. The tradition of liberal democracy in the Philippines, like that in much of the West, is fragile and daily upended. One of the most problematic aspects of liberal democracy is the notion that war and peace are two separate and distinguishable moments. Foucault has on many occasions pointed out the error of this way of thinking. War is not something that stops once peace is established. Neither is war something that happens "out there," beyond the boundaries of society. It does not end when everyone decides to enter into a social contract and give up part of their liberty to a representative king or representative body who can then make laws and adjudicate conflicts. Peace is not the natural state that succeeds war, whereby laws, guided by norms and rights, are administered beyond politics. For Foucault, there is nothing beyond the political. Invoking Clausewitz (contra Hobbes and Locke), Foucault argues that war is politics by other means, and politics is war by other means. Wherever you have power relations, you have inequalities, oppressions, and struggles that at times explode into armed uprisings and at other times manifest themselves in electoral campaigns, polemical tracts, social movements, dictatorships, coups, and the myriad varieties of insubordinations. In short, inasmuch as social relations are constituted by variegated webs of power relations alongside the resistances they call forth, they always take on a warlike nature (Foucault 2009, 2015).

For Foucault, unlike Marx, the warlike relations that pervade and infuse social relations are not simply based on class differences. Rather, class war is subsumed into a larger civil war. Whereas class war imagines society as riven by a death struggle between those who own the means of production and those whose only possession is their labor power, the concept of civil war stresses the relational, contingent nature of power relations. In civil wars, what we see are intra-class linkages and alliances. Often, these unfold as a series of factional rifts where rich and poor, middle class and working class, are allied against other similarly constructed factions reckoned less along ideological lines than on the axis of dynastic or familial affiliations. We see this, for example, in the cross-class alliances among the fiercest supporters of the president, the Diehard Duterte Supporters, or DDS—a play on the Davao Death Squads that Duterte himself allegedly authorized. The DDS are the self-proclaimed "children" of "Tatay" or Daddy Duterte and are made up of the aspirational middle class, especially overseas Filipino workers, old as well as new oligarchs, supporters and family members of previous presidents. They include working classes and lumpens from the police to slum dwellers, among whom are the great majority of victims in the drug war. Such alliances are organized hierarchically: as dispersed and mobile clusters of patron–client ties and fungible personality cults that cultivate among their members aspirations of upward mobility, as well as fears of becoming downwardly mobile. Such hopes and fears in turn tend to generate intense fantasies of patriarchal order and dreams of an authoritarian utopia with which to protect its members from real or imagined threats (Curato 2017b; Heydarian 2018).

Such threats are figured as social enemies. As Foucault points out—and so, by the way, does Marx—in civil wars, class enemies are supplanted by social enemies: those who pose an existential threat to society and who can come from any class—the monstrous dictator and his cannibalistic wife, for example, or the humanoid drug addict, the immoral female senator, the corrupt female chief justice of the Supreme Court, and so on. In this context, we can think of the People Power or so-called EDSA uprisings in 1986 and 2001 that ousted, respectively, Presidents Marcos and Estrada, as examples of civil war. So, too, with certain qualifications, were the Revolution of 1896, the Filipino-American war, and the war against Japan (Guerrero 2015; Manzanilla and Hau 2017; McCoy 1980). All of these were less class wars than civil wars pitting Filipinos against other Filipinos from different classes who either resisted, or collaborated with, the colonial rulers.

Duterte, of course, learned his political chops while serving as mayor of a highly factionalized Davao, where civil war was the norm rather than the exception. Prior to being mayor, he was a law student at San Beda College, where, as with all law schools, the hypermasculine culture of fraternities shaped Duterte's violent political outlook. Fraternities operate like gangs where neophytes are brutally initiated and members taught absolute obedience to their masters and aspire to be absolute masters themselves through a combination of coercion and mutual aid.[6] As mayor of Davao, Duterte sought to co-opt the deadliest forces unleashed by President Cory Aquino's vicious anti-communist campaign—the death squads—as well as former members of the New People's Army. Integrating these armed groups into the local police force, Duterte controlled and commanded an impressive killing machine that carried out his bidding, clearing Davao of both its lumpen criminal elements (though not its largest drug dealers and smugglers), including homeless children, political foes, and the occasional hostile journalist. Thanks to this war against crime and drugs, Davao gained a reputation, however questionable, for safety and security but one predicated on fear.[7]

Since becoming president in 2016, Duterte has sought to nationalize his style of governing. While summary killings have been the most dramatic tactic in Duterte's civil war, they are closely related to something else that I brought up at the beginning of this chapter and in chapter 3 of this book: his style of humor, especially his use of obscenities. In the last section of this chapter, I want to ask: How does humor serve as a vital weapon in the barbarian justice and the endless civil war he is engaged in?

The Sovereign Trickster

Duterte is known among his supporters as "the Punisher." But his punitive approach to governing includes telling jokes designed to disarm his audiences, often reducing them to laughter, as he names and shames his critics—often foreign and female. Those critical of Duterte have called him out on his use of obscenities and misogynistic remarks. But as far as Duterte is concerned, his sexual banter is yet another way of asserting his sovereignty. It is for him an enactment of his freedom from the constraints of responsibility and the norms of decency. Unrestrained, he takes great delight in spewing profanities. He recounts bawdy stories about masturbation, jokes about rape, publicly kissing women and admiring their anatomy, making references to vaginal odor, and much more (see chapter 3 of this book). In so doing, he has shown that he will not be bound by the norms of decency, or delicadeza, as his political opponents insist, just as he refuses to abide by the laws of due process and the protection of human rights. Duterte, to put it crudely, doesn't give a fuck and has long run out of fucks to give.[8]

For the president, then, part of his executive privilege includes the freedom to take pleasure in joking and shaming, turning these into important weapons. That he manages to hit his targets is indicated by the outrage he stirs among his opponents and the endearment he generates from his supporters. Breaking from protocols of respectability lends to Duterte a rebellious quality in the eyes of his supporters, the most ardent of whom refer to themselves as DDS (i.e., Diehard Duterte Supporters, a play on the initials of the Davao Death Squad). It confirms to them that he is unlike anyone from previous administrations. As a kind of "bad boy" who commands the room with his menacing charm, his flurry of invectives and sexual innuendos, Duterte seems excessive. It is precisely this excess that, as I alluded to earlier, makes him analogous to the drug addicts that he simultaneously despises and envies for their absolute sovereignty. By behaving irresponsibly, he places himself beyond convention and law, endowing himself with power over those who are otherwise obligated to defer to his authority. In his presence, they must observe proper behavior and attend to his authority while he himself seems to flout every rule.

Herein lies one explanation for Duterte's continuing popularity, at least if the polls are to be believed. To his supporters, his coarse language and bawdy humor resist what has been proscribed by establishment elites. They relish his irreverence, identifying with his insurgent energy to upset conventions. Indeed, not only does he escape unscathed, his aura seems to be magnified as he becomes even more emboldened with every insult and invective. His insults directed at the Catholic Church—pointing out the corruption and perversion of the clergy, for example—is often followed by hilarious retellings of the sexual abuse he suffered as a youth, literally in the hands of an American Jesuit in Davao. For, rather than paint himself as a victim, Duterte turns the story of abuse—where as a youth he was forced to submit to the priest's sexual assaults—into a vehicle for ridiculing confession, associating the ritual with masturbation ("Jesuit Priest" 2016; chapter 3 of this book). Similarly, Duterte has projected an image of himself as both a homophobe and a homophile. During the presidential campaign of 2016, he derided his opponent Mar Roxas's masculinity, implying that he was too gay to be president. However, he also surrounded himself with LGBTQ supporters. At one point in the campaign, he had a remarkable interview on the TV show of the most popular trans entertainer in the country, Vice Ganda, where he lost no time flirting with her and confided that as a young man he thought he could've been gay ("Look: Vice Ganda" 2016). Furthermore, his administration has a number of visibly queer folks who count themselves as his most ardent supporters, while a considerable number of those who serve in his social media army trolling critics are themselves gay (Carpio 2016).

Put differently, when Duterte jokes and cusses, he engages in a form of extended, recurring dissipation. He allows his desires to surface and his impulses to take over. Breaking taboos, he surrenders to what is usually forbidden—something that children are wont to do. Indeed, he performs a kind of infantile regression, lashing out at his enemies and shaming them with allusions to their sexuality. Listening to his speeches—which, when delivered in front of local audiences, usually begin with the act of throwing away his prepared speech and appearing to speak off the cuff—one is plunged into shifting linguistic registers, polemical tirades, abrupt beginnings and endings. In his speeches, he often sounds like someone who is intoxicated by his ability to act out his intoxication.

Foucault writes about what he calls the two great "illegalities" that characterized the advent of the modern period and that threatened the newly dominant bourgeoisie in Europe: depredations and dissipations (Foucault 2015, 186–200). The first was easier to police. Depredations consisting of such acts as piracy, smuggling, and various other forms of property theft require stealth, calculation, and circuits of distribution—in short, an organized economy and a political rationality. For this reason, depredations were easily codified as crimes in the nineteenth century, while the bourgeoisie carved out all sorts of exceptions that would legalize their own predatory acts.

Dissipation, however, was a different matter. It was about indulging in excess and irrationality through drunkenness, intoxication, and forbidden sexual relations. It also meant engaging in "festivities," taking pleasure in games of chance, and various other activities that could not be transformed into profit. The dissipator was regarded as lazy, one who wasted time, or better yet kept time to him or herself. This hoarding and wasting of time violated the capitalist demand that one surrender to the disciplinary demands of production that meant, above all, converting the time of life into the time of profit. By refusing to give in to the tyranny of clock and calendar, dissipators came across as dangerous elements threatening the order of things. They were to be sequestered and trained—for example, in the army, in schools, in prisons, and in factories—where their bodies could be retooled from sites of pleasure into repositories of labor power (Foucault 2015).

Duterte, in taking on the role of the dissipator-in-chief, thumbs his nose at these bourgeois demands. Indulging in what Mbembe calls an "aesthetic of vulgarity," he will not be disciplined (Mbembe 1992). Instead, he becomes a sort of trickster figure who entertains by veiling his aggression with jokes and obscenities. As a trickster, Duterte plays the role of the *pusong*, a staple figure in traditional *komedya* and folktales. It is the pusong who makes fun of those in power while managing through deceit or humor to gain power himself. As the anthropologists Donn and Harriet Hart point out, the pusong is a truly pan-Philippine character, with variations of folk tales spread all over the archipelago among Christian, Moro, and indigenous peoples (Hart and Hart 1974). In their survey of the various pusong tales in both urban and rural settings, they observe that he—for the pusong is almost always a young male—is characterized by a set of overlapping traits. More popularly known as Juan Pusong or Juan Tamad, he is at once "tricky, arrogant, and mischievous in addition to being a braggart, liar, knave and arrogant and a rogue. . . . He is always lazy and indolent . . . [while being] shrewd, witty and immoral. . . . Other stories point out the pusong's criminality, deceitfulness, bravery, compassion, and possession of miraculous powers." In nearly all the tales, he succeeds in overcoming obstacles and winning rewards such as "marrying the princess (or rich girl), [gaining] wealth, [having] illicit sexual intercourse, gaining prestige, or merely the pleasure of defeating his opponent. . . . He, like other tricksters, also has his helpful companions or stooges and often appears as a . . . child in his preoccupation with the humor of elemental incongruities, scatology, and cruelty" (Hart and Hart 1974, 136–43).

It is the pusong that most likely informs other variants of the trickster figure such as the Visayan *bugoy*—the idler and vagrant—associated with the lumpen or *tambay*—who literally sees things from below. Sitting on his bum at the sari-sari store, he calls out the pretensions to respectability of those on top. In assuming, or being attributed by his followers, the role of the trickster, Duterte converts dissipation into an aspect of his authority even as he orders the arrest and prosecution of others who would dare muscle into his monopoly of dissipation such as addicts and tambays (Almendral 2018; "Metro Manila Police" 2018). His dissipatory behavior has an anticipatory effect: he is able to criticize the authority of anyone who would dare criticize his authority. He steals, as it were, the comedic resources of his opponents, preempting their playfulness while commanding the laughter of his supporters. These supporters, in turn, are drawn to Duterte's style of political engagement, emulating it as a tactic for dealing with his critics by reducing the latter to caricatures ripe for vicious attacks. From cruel stereotyping, it is a small step to declaring critics as social enemies.

Here, then, are the two aspects of Rodrigo Duterte's governing style. He is the sovereign who decides on the exception, setting aside law and putting certain groups to death. But he is also the trickster who, in disarming his critics, endears himself to his supporters as a dissipator, one whose performative excess gives expression to what is at once forbidden and desired. In the first case, he recruits the bodies of dead addicts into signs of his fearsome authority that brooks no limits. In the second case, he transforms himself into the trickster who rejoices in his irreverence and irresponsibility. He thereby conjures the illusion of evading the time of capitalist capture and actively embraces the charges of stupidity leveled by his critics—for example, by introducing his cabinet members as all class valedictorians while he was simply a c student—all the while knowing that he's the one who has outsmarted them all.

The tactical advantage that Duterte enjoys, at least for the moment, comes precisely from his ability to craft what appears to be an impossible, because split, subjectivity: one that is both the vengeful sovereign *and* the irascible trickster. In doing so, he assuages the fears of precarity and displacement among his supporters, promising them both security and laughter. Whether newly rich, aspiring middle classes, overseas contract workers, or working poor, such supporters share a common fate. They find themselves burdened daily by the pressures and humiliations brought about by the demand for discipline and conformity in the neoliberal state, whether in the Philippines or abroad. Duterte rhetorically acknowledges their fragmented lives and addresses their uncertainty. He speaks to and of the anxieties of his supporters, who find themselves unable to escape from the endless demands of capital even as they seek security from those deemed to be their social enemies. Occupying the center, the president continues to speak as if from the periphery; wielding enormous institutional and economic power, he acts as if still pitiful and impoverished. Rather than the king with two bodies—one that dies, while the other is ritually immortalized in the classic institutions of kingship—he is the king, or *datu* (i.e., chief) with multiple organs.[9] He thus darkly refers to the many illnesses that wrack his body, calling attention to his physical frailties in between explosions of murderous rage at his enemies. Conjuring the sorry state of his esophagus, spine, anus, stomach, and skin, he alternately laments and jokes about their beleaguered state.

By imaginatively exposing his body parts to public view, Duterte literalizes a politics from below, displaying what Mbembe refers to as the "banality of power." Contra Bakhtin's idea of the carnivalesque—the periodic reversal of power relations deemed to be inherently subversive—Mbembe argues that in the postcolony, "evoking those elements of the obscene, vulgar, and the grotesque" is as much the province of official as it is nonofficial culture. As in postcolonial sub-Saharan Africa, so in Duterte's Philippines:

"Obscenity and vulgarity—when regarded as more than moral categories—constitute some of the modalities of power in the postcolony." As we saw in chapter 3, the sovereign is joined to his subjects in a relationship of "conviviality" evinced in mutually reinforcing laughter alongside fear. The "real reversal" of power is effected not by the dominated but by the sovereign trickster. For it is the latter who manages to convert obscenity into "splendor," violent visions into noble acts. In these acts of inversion, he draws his followers "to join in [the] madness and clothe themselves in the flashy rags of power so as to reproduce its epistemology; and when, too, power, in its own violent quest for grandeur and prestige, makes vulgarity and wrong doing its main mode of existence. . . . One can say that the obscenity of power in the postcolony is also fed by a desire for majesty on the part of the people" (Mbembe 1992, 1–2, 29–30).

Taking debasement for splendor, the figure of the sovereign trickster—one that Duterte had crafted earlier while mayor for over two decades in Davao—sutures the wide gap between the president's failure in the realm of the biopolitical and his obsession with the necropolitical. Reigning under the conditions of the neoliberal precarity that defines the existential conditions of nearly everyone in the country and the diaspora, he sets himself apart from the earlier strongmen in the Philippines, for example, Manuel Quezon and Ferdinand Marcos. Quezon and Marcos were anxious to project a heightened sense of bourgeois masculinity in the service of a benevolent patriarchy in the way they appeared and spoke. They dressed impeccably in formal barong or tailored suits and addressed the public in stentorian sentences, meticulously crafted and ponderously pronounced. Under late colonial and Cold War liberal conditions, they could still capitalize on middle-class conventions of respectability to hide from view the more brutal practices of their government. Unlike Duterte, who boasts of the women he has had and would like to have, Quezon and Marcos were far more discrete.

With Duterte, there is neither discretion nor shame, only a kind of heedless pride in reveling in his desires. Such brazenness is understood by his followers as the explicit permission to enjoy and engage in the verbal torture and humiliation of their enemies. For them, it signals Duterte's emancipation from colonial and bourgeois conventions of civility. However, this liberation is a ruse insofar as he seeks to govern by fear. With the help of his enablers, ranging from the police to the cabinet, from a compliant Supreme Court to his army of trolls, from the legislature to the Marcoses and their legions of ardent supporters, he is able to consolidate his hold and pursue his civil war against all those who oppose him. For Duterte faces two ways, as perhaps all sovereigns do: toward life that he animates with derisive laughter, and toward death that he commands with unremitting fear.

Coda: The Minstrelsy of Trump

Is the figure of the sovereign trickster, one who dominates both laughter and death, useful for thinking about other authoritarians, actual or aspirational? One thinks, most obviously, of US President Donald Trump. He and Duterte have often been compared in terms of their rhetorical bluntness, unapologetic misogyny, and vocal disdain for the press and other critics. Perhaps this comparison is to be expected given the colonial relationship between the two countries, whereby events in the former colony have usually been framed within the terms of the former colonial power. However, Duterte's victory in July 2016 preceded Trump's by several months, and so arguably reversed this trajectory. It seems almost as if the figure of Duterte had paved the way for rendering legible the figure of Trump as a kind of sovereign trickster, thereby recasting the postcolonial relationship between the two countries. Duterte's carnivalesque authoritarianism helps to make sense of Trump's. It is not often that events in the Philippines can shed light on events in the United States—often it is the other way around. By seeing Trump through the lens of Duterte's aesthetic of vulgarity, we might try a kind of trick, as it were, by reversing the historic privilege of one to set the terms for understanding the other.

There are, of course, important differences between the two. Unlike Duterte, whose entire career has been entirely within the government as prosecutor, mayor, vice mayor, congressman, and now president, Trump rose to power along a different route. His career has been intimately linked not to public service but to the real estate, hospitality, and entertainment industries, particularly his chain of Trump Towers and the television reality show *The Apprentice*. Rather than make people laugh, he projected in that show a kind of decisive, and often dour, personality. In his campaign rallies, however, he engages in a whole range of what we might think of as tricksterisms: making fun of the disabled, hurling elaborate threats at the media, demeaning women and people of color with racist and sexist language, engaging in wild conspiracy theories, obsessively insulting political enemies and, at times, even allies who fail to do his bidding—all to the thunderous applause and laughter of his audience. Charged up by the crowd, he performs like a man deranged, gesticulating wildly and bellowing great gusts of words that often barely make sense. In other words, he behaves, as with Duterte, like a man intoxicated with his ability to seem intoxicated, beyond the control of polite conventions. Trump's excessiveness, calculated, no doubt, to incite his base, is in many ways what "entertainment" has come to mean in the United States. In this connection, it is not strange that Trump was a big fan of wrestling—staged matches preceded by incessant and interminable insults exchanged between competitors to delight the crowd (Heer 2016). Much of popular entertainment has thus come to mean the intensification of spectacle, the ramping up of sensation, and the trafficking in affect at the expense of what used to pass for rational discourse and other modes of taking pleasure.

As with Duterte, is it possible to grasp Trump's "populism" in terms of a nationally specific history of folk entertainment and widespread notions of satire? In the case of Trump, let me propose that the roots of his trickster style may very well lie in the long history of blackface minstrelsy (see, e.g., Heer 2016).[10] The scholarship on what some have referred to as the first mass entertainment medium in North America helps us to reconstruct this genealogy. As various writers have shown, the racist and sexist tropes of blackface minstrelsy are meant to assuage white working-class anxieties about and desires for black bodies: imaginatively owning them, wanting to be like and unlike Blacks at the same time (Johnson 2012; Lott 1995; Roediger 2007; Rogin 1996; Sammond 2015). Blackface minstrelsy was also an important medium for addressing immigrant, especially Jewish and Irish, fears of exclusion and the wish for assimilation. The act of putting on burnt cork provided a way for acting out the "love" for and "theft" of black labor and culture, using these as ways of simultaneously accumulating material and cultural capital on the one hand and carving out a place in the racial hierarchy on the other.

Miming the degraded yet vibrant bodies of slaves, blackface signified that one had the power to take on, yet set aside, blackness, that one was in possession of one's labor rather than merely enslaved to capital, and that one could mock and escape the effete, feminine demands of white bourgeois respectability. Small wonder that everyone from Abraham Lincoln to Mark Twain to Walt Disney loved blackface minstrelsy. It made it possible to appear at once rebellious and hilarious, mastering social death while inducing hilarity and always at the expense of those below in the social hierarchy. It masculinized whiteness and whitened masculinity through its imagined control of the abject but reusable bodies of others. Put another way, putting on Black disguise and often appearing in female drag allowed white male performers to act out the reversal of racial, gendered, and class norms, seeking, as Toni Morrison (1993) has written, to play out the popular desire to appropriate both the labor and capital as well as the productive and reproductive powers that lay in the bodies of slaves. At the same time, such performances allowed both actors and audiences to imaginatively distance themselves in the very act of owning the abject figures they ridiculed and admired. Indeed, blackface minstrelsy, in projecting and seeking to master the unresolved legacy of slavery, lay at the foundations of white identity. It continues to thrive, even and especially without the use of burnt cork. It does so through the mimicry of the cultural repertoire of Black, as well as Asian, Native American, and Latinx peoples (Bhabha 1984; Fanon 2006; Rafael 2016).[11] As one kind of North American trickster practice among those on top as well as those who aspire toward its ranks, racial minstrelsy is a resilient and enduring form of popular entertainment that arguably informs Donald Trump's public performances and political appeal. As president, he has not only reauthorized minstrelsy's violent laughter; he has also used its capacity to obscure real historical relations by inflating what W. E. B. Du Bois famously referred to as the "wages of whiteness" (Roediger 2007). Sovereign tricksterism, from this perspective, is a kind of aesthetic for shaping the contours of contemporary racism—of blackface without the burnt cork—filtered through fake news and conspiracy theories that help sustain the daily practices of authoritarian cruelties.

SKETCHES IV. COMPARING EXTRAJUDICIAL KILLINGS

These are grim days for human rights everywhere. In the United States and its former colony, the Philippines, extrajudicial killings—long practiced but often swept aside—have recently become more common.

In the US, the targeting of Black bodies has a long history, rooted in centuries of slavery and segregation within the context of white supremacy. It is further entrenched in militarized modes of policing and sustained by a vast prison-industrial complex that disproportionately incarcerates and disenfranchises people of color. Thanks to the ready availability of guns, the US now has one of the most heavily armed citizenries, engaged in a virtual civil war where minorities and immigrants are often cast in the role of social enemies.

In the Philippines, things are different. The targets of extrajudicial killings are mostly poor. If the influential and wealthy are publicly accused, they are subjected to investigation rather than execution. For the poor, there is no due process. Suspicion or rumor about illicit drug use is warrant enough to kill them. Their bodies are displayed with signs warning other dealers and addicts while announcing the work of a deadly sovereign power. Terrorizing ordinary citizens, the display of corpses is a way for the regime to claim for itself the power of their enemies and project this power to the people.

In the US, anti-racist movements such as Black Lives Matter arise to protest the killings, drawing on a long tradition of civil rights activism. Many have also linked racist violence at home with racist warfare abroad.

In the Philippines, social movements have yet to emerge in opposition to extrajudicial killings. While some senators and human rights advocates raise objections, no one wants to be seen coddling those who are killed. As of the time of this writing (2016), the communist left has remained circumspect while it pursues peace talks with Duterte. For the majority who support the president, they subscribe to a kind of populist solipsism: the dead deserve to be dead because the president says so. Regarded as subhumans, drug addicts and dealers have forfeited their rights. Due process is a waste of time, they say, since the courts are corrupt and human rights are nothing more than Western impositions that protect the guilty.

Unlike the US, victims of extrajudicial killings in the Philippines begin as racially identical with their perpetrators. But being associated with illegal drugs renders them a different race, one deserving neither human recognition nor humane treatment. They become, in the eyes of the president, the police and vigilantes, mere garbage to be cleared away. Left on display, their corpses become living signs of an ominous power capable of overcoming the power of death itself.

In the US, the response to police violence has been organized opposition. Calls are made for reform and attempts, not always successful, to hold police accountable ensue. Even if it seems like little changes, the political and ethical stakes of opposing racialized extrajudicial killings are clear. The spread of Black Lives Matter is rooted in the long history and durability of civil rights movements in response to systemic racial violence.

In the Philippines, this sort of opposition is sporadic rather than sustained. Living in apartheid-like conditions in "squatter colonies," poor people have few rights that the powerful and wealthy feel compelled to recognize. Treated as second-class citizens, they are easily racialized, set aside as less than human and casually killed by those in power.

But what about the poor? How do they feel about their own marginalization?

Many continue to support the president even as they are suspicious of the police. They are relieved when known criminals are killed but traumatized when it is someone they love. Bereft of resources, they feel their vulnerability on the most practical level. Under such conditions, they are cowed from asserting their rights. Like colonized populations, they hesitate to confront state authorities. Many opt to negotiate by bribing, complying, collaborating, or simply avoiding them. Unarmed and unorganized, they cannot afford to retaliate legally or physically against the police, and they do what they can to survive. It is as if they, along with those opposed to Duterte, are forced to weather a storm whose end is impossible to predict.

—*Rappler*, July 17, 2016

SKETCHES IV. **DEATH SQUADS**

Amid all the inconsistencies of President Duterte's foreign policies, his domestic program has remained consistent, focused on the war on drugs and his signature approach: the use of local government officials to compile lists of suspected users and dealers. Frequently, those on the lists are targeted by police and death squads (the former at times taking on the functions of the latter) for extrajudicial killings.

What is the history of death squads in the Philippines? Insofar as they usually enjoy the support and protection of the military, police, and local and national officials, what role do they play in the formation of the state and the projection of its power? To what extent do they contribute to the making of civil society by uncivil means? What follows is a very incomplete history of death squads and their related forms—militias, private armies, vigilantes, and criminal gangs.

Death squads as paramilitary formations clearly have colonial roots. As far back as the sixteenth century, the *polos y servicios* imposed by the Spaniards included forcing native peoples to fight in colonial militias to put down local rebellions and the occasional intra-imperialist war (versus Chinese pirates in the late sixteenth century, the Dutch in the seventeenth century, the British in the eighteenth century, even the Americans in the late nineteenth century). By the nineteenth century, native militias became more organized into the ruthless Guardias Civiles, the very same ones that bedeviled *ilustrados* and common people alike, chasing Ibarra and killing Elias down the Pasig River in the climactic scene of Rizal's classic novel *Noli mi tangere*.

When the Americans invaded the Philippines, the US troops were made up of volunteers recruited from their respective state militias. They were given to using the brutal tactics of "injun warfare" adopted by their officers—

all veterans of genocidal Indian wars in the American West. One could argue that American soldiers were a collection of proto-death squads, given to pursuing exterminatory violence against Filipino fighters and civilians alike. As with the Spaniards, American troops also used native auxiliaries to put down the Revolution and the various local insurgencies it spawned.

Elections were held quickly to consolidate American rule, at the same time as the colonial government was recruiting Filipinos to pursue remaining rebels. They formed the Philippine Scouts, the forerunner of the Philippine Constabulary, as the complement to the First Philippine Assembly. Colonial democracy was predicated on the outsourcing of the state's coercive power to local officials—many of whom were veterans of the Revolution—and their local followers. This is not so strange, since the armies of the First Philippine Republic were also made up of volunteers attached primarily to their local leaders rather than to a national leadership (much to the dismay of Mabini and Aguinaldo, who were powerless to curtail the pillaging and plundering of fighters). Patronage and patriotism were indissociable in the case of the Republican army and continued through the US colonial period, blurring the lines between fighters and bandits.

During World War II, guerrilla resistance spread, with lots of armed groups operating outside of and in opposition to Japanese state power. They dispensed their own brand of extrajudicial justice against collaborators and often warred against rival factions as much as they did with the Japanese. After the war, some of these armed groups, like the Huks, continued fighting against the injustices they experienced, while other guerrillas were recruited into private armies of the restored oligarchy. The transition from wartime occupation to independent republic witnessed the mushrooming of armed bands organized around local warlords, urban gangs, and assorted paramilitary units working for public officials and wealthy private families, who were usually one and the same. Such armed gangs were routinely deployed to terrorize peasant and proletarian dissidents and extract votes during elections. Independence and the expansion of the franchise coincided with the regular use of extralegal violence and the rise of a culture of impunity to secure social hierarchy. In the midst of the Cold War, the Philippines became a veritable laboratory for "low-intensity warfare" that the CIA would wage in Latin America and elsewhere.

When Marcos declared martial law, he sought to do away with such private armies by turning the entire AFP into his own big private army. But corruption and favoritism ended up dividing the military (hence, the emergence of the Reformed Armed Forces Movement, whose failed coup attempt gave birth to EDSA). Meanwhile, the armed might of the CPP-NPA grew, and by the end of Marcos's regime, they directly controlled more than 20 percent of the countryside and had an extensive network of aboveground organizations in the cities. And the Moro rebels had also grown in power so as to outstrip the AFP's ability to put them down repeatedly. Fighting a two-front war and divided within its ranks, the military's strength was severely taxed.

In the wake of EDSA, Cory Aquino at first sought to break up the paramilitary units that Marcos had set up while negotiating with the CPP-NPA. But a year after EDSA and a month after the Mendiola massacre of 1987, negotiations with the communists broke down. She then declared all-out war. In the face of a weakened military and far more formidable communist and Moro insurgencies, she and her chief of staff, Fidel V. Ramos, eventually authorized and publicly supported the rise of vigilante groups under military leadership, which quickly became anti-communist death squads. In the areas where the communists were strong, paramilitary volunteers flourished, drawn mostly from lumpen proletariats and former rebels. They were usually attached to local police and military commanders, and/or to local oligarchies, receiving funding and protection from them (and indirectly from the US, to the extent that it was providing massive aid to the AFP). The most notorious, of course, was the Alsa Masa in Davao City, which emerged in the late 1980s through the mid-1990s, at the time when Rodrigo Duterte was mayor.

Hence, the ironic history of death squads. Rooted in colonial history, their growth was spurred during the periods of transition when state power was up for grabs: from Spanish to American colonial rule; from occupation to independence; and most recently, from Marcos to Aquino, that is, from the end of authoritarian rule to the restoration of elite democracy. Where Marcos could turn to the AFP as his own death squad, the post-EDSA oligarchy needed the aid of civilian volunteers, organized with the help of the police and the military into anti-communist vigilantes. As some scholars have pointed out, such death squads were the other side, the dark side if you will, of People Power. Indeed, that is how Cory herself referred to them when she encouraged them to wage war against the communists.

People Power was originally directed at Marcos. When he was gone, it was directed at the communists and assorted criminal gangs. Under succeeding presidents, the police were tacitly empowered to carry out summary executions of suspected communist leaders and gangs, while local elites hired killers to deal with labor leaders, journalists, and rival elites. Terror and gruesome displays of violence—severed heads, for example, displayed on roadways, along with mutilated corpses—were the signature of groups like Alsa Masa in places like Davao.

Duterte made his reputation in part by negotiating with both vigilantes and communists, absorbing elements of both into his regime. If various reports are to be believed, he, or at least those around him, recruited former NPAS and other lumpen types to serve as paramilitary forces in dealing with a new enemy: drug lords and drug users. As mayor of Davao, his reputation as "the Punisher" emerged at the crossroads of democratic transition and counterinsurgency, when "People Power" was taken to mean that ordinary people would be empowered to act on behalf of the state and kill its designated enemies. In a way, contemporary death squads are the perverse doubles of NGOs as both shared a parallel history in the outsourcing of state functions.

Things have thus come full circle. Death squads encouraged by Cory as a much-needed supplement to the military's counterinsurgency war have now morphed into the death squads used by Duterte in his war against drugs. Rather than a new development, death squads, vigilantes, and paramilitary volunteers of all sorts have long been a part of the colonial and national state. As with other modern states, the Philippine state has pursued what seems like a contradictory course: it has simultaneously sought to monopolize the use of violence even as it outsources it, using uncivil means to secure civil society. The legal and the illegal constantly blur into one other, as the language of the president often sounds like the rhetoric of a gangster. Indeed, the police double as vigilantes, while convicted felons ally with government officials to silence the latter's critics. Extrajudicial killings, sold to the public as a remedy for the inefficient and corrupt legal system, normalize murder even as they foreground fear as a primary technique of governing. Public resources are used to forge private armies—a kind of PPP, or public–private partnership for producing techniques for the efficient delivery of death. Exercising a kind of biopolitical power, the state seeks to secure the life of its citizens. But it does so by way of a necropolitical power, whereby the state consigns others as social enemies destined for abjection and disposal.

A final note: there is an interesting way in which the labor of death squads resonates with the most prevalent form of labor among the country's citizens today. Those who join death squads are essentially contractual laborers. They can be hired and fired for as short or as long as their employers need them. They occupy a very precarious existence, and are liable to be killed themselves. In short, they are like so many millions of Filipinos today working on a contractual basis, whether at home or abroad.

Just as the political history of death squads is the "underside" of People Power, especially outside of Metro Manila, its political economy of violence seems to echo the normalized violence faced by workers today.

—*Rappler*, October 27, 2016

[I'm indebted for these reflections to the works of Eve Lotta Hedman, John Sidel, Alfred McCoy, Michael Cullinane, Patricio Abinales, Donna Amoroso, Benedict Anderson, Greg Bankoff, Roseanne Rutten, Rico Jose, Mila Guerrero, and many others.]

SKETCHES IV. ON DUTERTE'S MATRIX

In 2019, *Rappler* published an article on one of Duterte's conspiracy theories that showed an elaborate matrix linking various journalists, opposition politicians, and assorted other groups into a vast conspiracy to overthrow the presidency.

The response from those who were in the matrix was one of astonishment and quick dismissal. But should we be so quick to disparage the latest pronouncement from the palace? Instead, shouldn't we seriously consider the matrix as a significant governing tactic in this and other past regimes?

For starters, the matrix is another example of the logic of tokhang at work. Tactically, it is a list of enemies, and so an order of battle. It is also a conceptual tool kit designed to raise the specter of conspiracies. The matrix implies that the government, or at least the security-executive branch within it (given that the "state" is a very heterogeneous entity made up of conflicting interests), must be on permanent alert. It must govern as if it were in a constant state of emergency.

If the country is in a state of emergency, this allows the police to operate with impunity. Impunity here does not mean ignoring laws. Rather, it entails operating in a context that allows for their selective suspension in the face of exceptional situations, for example, when your life is supposedly being endangered by a drug addict. So you can ignore due process and shoot to kill. This is the substance of tokhang, where the police operate like "petty sovereigns" deciding on the exception.

This tendency to conjure a permanent state of emergency, to institutionalize and normalize it, is pretty much consistent with the governing style of all Philippine governments—colonial and postcolonial alike. We can see its

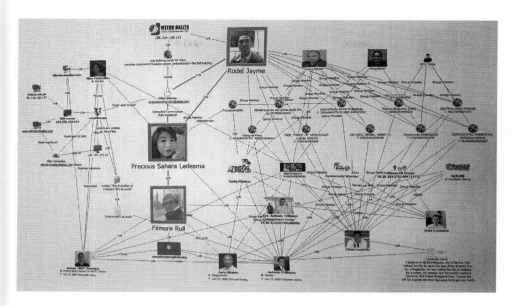

Figure IV.1. Duterte's matrix showing those he accused of a conspiracy to oust him, May 2019.

origins at least as far back as the Spanish colonial regime, reaching its apogee under Governor General Rafael Izquierdo in the 1870s (who placed all ilustrados under surveillance, opened their mail, banned books, arrested, exiled, and executed many of them), and all the way through the US colonial, Commonwealth, Japanese, and postcolonial regimes. In such contexts, conspiracies in the form of rumors, gossip, graffiti, art, clandestine movements, associations, publications, and so on all make up essential elements of power to the extent that they are regarded as threatening its exercise.

To put it differently, the national security state—which is what the modern state is—can only coalesce around its insurgent others. If insurgents did not exist, they must, therefore, be conjured. Otherwise, how else to justify extensive policing and anti-subversion laws? In the US and Europe, the insurgent figures are usually Blacks, Muslims, immigrants, people of color, queers—the list (and it is always a list) is potentially endless and open-ended.

Even the "militant" left—especially the left—has operated along the same logic, if not logistics, of policing. Recall, for example, the purges in the 1990s among the Communist Party of the Philippines, resulting in its fatal dismemberment. Even today, the CPP (and its affiliates) tends to condemn critics as engaged in counterrevolutionary conspiracies, attesting to its use of this style of governing as if it were in a permanent state of exception. NPA fighters can operate with similar impunity and decide who will live and who will die, especially in battle. Small wonder many of the fighters who surrendered in Davao back in the 1990s and early 2000s could easily move into the role of vigilante death squads.

To reiterate: In the face of insurgent conspiracies, the state, or at least its security apparatus, constitutes itself as a counterinsurgent force. Not just in the Philippines—but arguably everywhere the modern state exists as an elaborate security apparatus.

And it always starts with the most banal and basic of technologies: lists. We can then list the reasons why lists are powerful. They are:

1   open-ended. Anyone at any time can be added to it—sports figures, movie stars, journalists, and so on;
2   enumerative, so that the items on the list do not have to be vetted or their connections proven. They just simply have to be counted. Contrast this to the double-entry ledger, which at least has a minimal narrative of losses and gains and so can be audited. You can't audit a list;
3   cumulative, so that it is not a question of whether you or anyone else believes in the content of the list, only that it exists. The sheer numbers suggest that there really is a force at work out to wreck the regime. In other words, you don't have to believe that each and every person on the list is a conspirator, only that the sheer accretion of names, actual or potential, attests to the potential or real existence of a conspiracy—just like the drug list.

Seeing the matrix is like seeing a constellation of relationships whose connections seem as arbitrary as they are motivated but no less "real." It is, to use Benedict Anderson's famous term, an "imagined community" of enemies.

One last thing: the matrix and other similar lists exist not simply to say there is the threat of conspiracy and subversion. Just as important, it exists so that the palace can say: We *know* that there is a threat even if we cannot verify it. We don't have to tell you how we know it. The point is, it is no longer a secret. We've exposed it. And this knowledge allows us to control it. Thus, we know something you don't. And we can act upon it any time we want to. In whatever way we want to. This knowledge and the ability to act upon it regardless of what the world thinks is precisely what makes us powerful.

(Previously unpublished.)

SKETCHES IV. **FECAL POLITICS**

One of the things that distinguished Marcos from Duterte was the former's penchant for imprisoning his political enemies. Marcos filled army camps and prisons with thousands of activists, journalists, students, workers, clergy, and others who he suspected were plotting against him. In the camps, they were routinely tortured and at times executed. There were about 70,000 recorded incarcerations, 35,000 documented tortured prisoners, and about 3,257 extrajudicial killings during the Marcos regime. In Duterte's case, while he has incarcerated enemies like Senator Leila de Lima, he has preferred to either harass them or call for the execution of those he considers to be threats to his regime, especially, as we've seen, so-called "drug personalities." Under Duterte, then, there have been thousands of deaths—far more than those killed under Marcos—but very few political prisoners—around four hundred as of 2017, many of whom have been released. Both also sought to crush media critical of their regimes. But where Marcos confiscated or shut down newspapers, TV, and radio stations owned by his opponents, Duterte has often used the law to squeeze and harass their owners and editors with threats of jail time, while mobilizing social media trolls to demonize his critics. But so far, he has succeeded in closing down only one major media outlet, ABS-CBN, while persecuting the editors and writers of the *Philippine Daily Inquirer* and the online newspaper *Rappler*.

For these reasons, it is perhaps worth looking back to the experiences of those incarcerated under Marcos and the stories they tell of dealing with their captivity and enduring their torture. As far as I know, no similar stories have emerged under Duterte. The tales of suffering and survival among those imprisoned by Marcos and their relative absence under Duterte is a measure of the distance between the two regimes. While victims under Duterte are simply killed and silenced, many under Marcos lived to bear witness to the horrors of their captivity (Quimpo and Quimpo 2012). Their testimonies are worth revisiting if only because they provide materials for considering the fate of other political prisoners and comparing the tactics of resistance among opponents of other authoritarian rulers.

Let's start with the account of the brilliant writer/activist Pete Lacaba about the time he spent in prison during the martial law years. He vividly recalled the conditions of his cell at Camp Crame, which had no bathroom. He and his cellmates were forced to urinate kneeling down into empty biscuit cans. Each morning, a group of them were designated to empty the containers. They would walk out of the cell "carrying the foul smelling cans like the Three Kings bearing incense," and dump them outside. More problematic, however, was the matter of defecation. Access to a toilet was dependent on the moods and availability of guards, who had to be hailed by the prisoners with shouts of "Sir, etsas! Sir, etsas!" (Sir, shitting) while banging on the iron bars. If the guards failed to come, Pete and his cellmates were forced to relieve themselves on old newspapers. These were then folded and set aside to be thrown out the next day when allowed by their jailers. Once, a fellow prisoner in a fit of rage threw his fetid bundle toward the sleeping quarters of the guards. In retaliation, all the prisoners were subjected to what Pete sardonically calls "*romansa militar, alyas karinyo brutal*" (military romance, aka brutal caresses). Not until the prisoners had organized themselves and protested the lack of facilities did they finally get a toilet of their own.

In response to the internet edition of Pete's account in the listserv Plaridel, some readers wrote back about their own attempts at maintaining some sort of sanitary dignity while subjected to the routines of dehumanization in prison camps. Maria Cristina Rodriguez, for example, recycled the newspapers regularly brought by her mother while she was incarcerated at Camp Dangwa in Benguet. She consumed the paper twice, reading the news and then using it for collecting her leavings. Along with the urinal that was left in their cell, she and her fellow prisoners would deposit their remains by a canal near a volleyball court used by the soldiers. She recalls how they took particular pleasure in leaving behind their stench for the entire camp to smell, reminding their jailers of something they could not capture, much less domesticate.

Scholars have long regarded the history of prisons as integral to the rise of modernity. In the West, punitive institutions were seen to play the role of defining, separating, disciplining, and reforming individuals into modern subjects capable of internalizing the law. Such a concept was introduced to the Philippines by the United States. Colonial rule, as the historian Michael Salman has so succinctly argued, was modeled after prison reform then in vogue in the US at the beginning of the twentieth century (Salman 2009). Like prisoners, colonial subjects were to be modernized and disciplined, kept under the watchful eyes of colonial rulers and elite collaborators. Once reformed, they were to be paroled, as it were, and given their independence.

As with most other colonial institutions, the model of the reformatory prison (with the possible exception of the Iwahig penal colony in Palawan) was never fully realized. In the postwar era and through the martial law period, jails primarily became dumping grounds for so-called dangerous and subversive elements. Far from being institutions for the rehabilitation of criminals into modern subjects, prisons came to be governed by the most feudal forms of relations. In the military stockades, the lingua franca of power was torture, both mental and physical, spoken by the state through its chief interpreters, the prison guards. Held in place ("prison" comes from the Latin *prehendere*, to lay hold of), the individual was cut off from his or her society and introjected into the cavities of a system of deprivation, violence, and unceasing humiliation.

The nodal point of any system of incarceration is, of course, the prisoner's body. It is the body and its various functions that are targeted for containment for the purpose of reform or, in the most extreme cases, death. On the way toward these two possibilities, the body, especially in the case of political prisoners, is treated as the dangerous repository of secrets that must be dug out, of truths that must be laid bare, invariably by force. Guards and prisoners find themselves in the most intimate relationship as torturers and tortured, one seeking to extract hidden knowledge from the deracinated body of the other. The prisoner's body thus becomes the site on which the power of the state is performed. Its bruises, broken bones, and bloodied flesh are the signs of the torturer's ability to make the incarcerated body speak (Scarry 1987).

But as the accounts of Pete Lacaba and Maria Cristina Rodriguez show, the state's victory is never complete and always subject to challenge. That is because in prison, the incarcerated body continues to live. It thinks, thinking enough to eat, for example, and in eating reproduces itself day by day, seeking to adapt to if not transform the conditions it finds itself in. Eating whatever wretched food it is given, it knows enough to give something back to the world from which it has taken a part of itself. The body lives by taking and giving, and so always leaves behind a piece of itself. Urine and shit are not merely waste products incidental to the body; they are proof positive of the body's continued capacity to keep on living by giving back to the earth the remains of its reproductive labor. In this sense, we can think of urine and shit as that which every body gives "birth" to.

Indeed, Sigmund Freud speculated that young children often confuse the vagina with the anus. Consequently, they conflate giving birth with defecating. In addition, children subjected to the demands of toilet training realize early on a kind of power they have over their parents with regard to the giving or withholding of their feces. Thus the anus is regarded as the location for the passage of a thing that can cause either horror or pleasure when delivered at the appropriate moment. Shit in this context comes across as either gift or threat: a token of submission that the child offers to its parents by way of recognizing their authority, or a weapon with which to terrorize those on top and repel their demands (Freud 1963).

Freud's insights into fecal matter help us think about the experiences of imprisonment that often entail the return to an earlier, more elementary stage of existence. The state seeks to apprehend, in all senses of that word, the body in and through its incarceration. However, the sheer material reality of the body means that the state cannot totally comprehend its workings. The state cannot, for example, expect the prisoner to stop urinating and defecating unless it also stops feeding it, in which case the prisoner will die. Dead prisoners deprive the state of objects on which to assert its will. After all, domination requires the maintenance, however minimal, of that which is to be dominated. Even in the Nazi death camps, exterminated prisoners had to be replaced by more prisoners in a logic exactly the same as that of an assembly line. Keeping the prisoner alive, however, means acceding to some of his or her needs, such as the need to defecate. Like the child gaining leverage over the parent, the prisoner through her or his feces is able to talk back to the prison guards. In the case of Pete and his cellmates, this meant having some way to protest their conditions to the point of having a toilet built for them. In Maria Cristina's story, it meant turning shit into a weapon of revenge, releasing its smells as a way of interrupting the play and leisure of the guards.

This last consideration is extremely significant. The translation of feces from an abject source of embarrassment into a potential weapon of vengeance is perhaps the most telling instance of a kind of rebellion: the refashioning of the body from an object of captivity into an agent of its own liberation. Drawing upon its resources, the body fights back in ways difficult for the state to localize, much less contain. For it is not shit itself but its smell that disorients and disturbs. Odor can neither be conceptualized nor detained. It always escapes, only to linger on. Where shit serves as the evidence of the body surviving and living on, fecal odor is the body's ghostly emanation. It assails the mind and the senses, penetrating the borders and checkpoints of social conventions and political regimes.

The stories of Pete and Maria Cristina remind me of another group of political prisoners. In the late 1970s, incarcerated members of the Irish Republican Army (IRA) launched what came to be known as the "Dirty Protest," refusing to submit to the brutally invasive bodily searches of their British captors. As brilliantly described by the anthropologist Allen Feldman, the IRA prisoners decided to stop washing, brushing their teeth, and shaving while refusing to put on prison garb (Feldman 1991). Instead, they went about naked, wrapped only in their filthy blankets. They also refused to do their business in toilets, where they were routinely beaten up by the guards. They began to shit and urinate in their cells. Even more dramatic, they spread their shit on the walls and floors, creating an unbearable stench that made it extremely difficult for the guards to enter their cells. And they did so continuously for about five years. The fetid nature of their prisons meant that the guards risked being swallowed up into what essentially had become the extension of the prisoner's anal cavity. Fecal matter effectively created a wall protecting inmates from guards. It repelled the latter with a stench that clung to them long after they had left work. Thus was the relationship between inmates and guards reversed, as torturers were held hostage to the intractable remains of those they had tortured.

—*Bulatlat* 7, no. 15, May 20–26, 2007, https://www.bulatlat
.com/2007/05/19/fecal-politics/.

5. PHOTOGRAPHY AND THE BIOPOLITICS OF FEAR
WITNESSING THE PHILIPPINE DRUG WAR

When photographs are being used to illustrate a type of situation, rather than
to testify to a singular event, it is a sure sign that a disaster has become chronic,
that the worst is yet to come. —ARIELLA AZOULAY, *The Civil Contract of Photography*

Whatever it is I see, only my eyes are seeing it. —Elderly woman resident
of Bagong Silang, Manila

A Landscape of Death

Since becoming president of the Philippines in 2016, Rodrigo Duterte has
assiduously pursued his intention to kill as many drug addicts and pushers
as possible. He sees them as social enemies—the root rather than the symptom of the drug problem in the country and no less than existential threats
to society. No matter the occasion or audience, he brings up his eagerness
for annihilating as many of them as possible. For example, while addressing the country's most prominent business leaders in the Makati Business
Club, he offered the basic template for his policy: "It is going to be bloody.
I will use the military and the police to go out and arrest them, hunt for
them. And if they offer violent resistance . . . I will simply say kill them all
and end the problem" (chapter 4 of this book; Whaley 2016). Elsewhere, he
reiterates this wish: "My order is shoot to kill you. I don't care about human
rights, you better believe me. All those deaths happening here? Let's add to
them. Let me take care of it" (Romero 2016).

The number of dead keeps rising, whether one goes by the police esti-
mate of over seven thousand or those of various human rights groups, which
range as high as thirty thousand, most of them in the slums of the Metro Manila region (Coronel 2019a; "Investigating Duterte's Drug War" 2018; Kreu-

zer 2016). Sheila Coronel vividly describes this landscape of death: "The victims' bodies are found on sidewalks or bridges, their heads wrapped in packing tape, their hands bound with rope. Some are left lying on the streets, bathed in blood, or splayed on the shaky wooden floors of shacks in shantytowns along the river, the shoreline of Manila Bay, or further inland, in the densely packed warrens inhabited by the city's poorest and neediest" (Coronel 2017a; "'If You Are Poor'" 2017).

Such gruesome scenes of nightly killings have been amply documented by photographers and journalists, both local and foreign. From July of 2016 through much of 2018, a dedicated group of correspondents known as "night crawlers" for the late hours they kept went from one crime scene to another to take photographs and write stories about the victims and their families. Serving on the front lines of the drug war, they have witnessed the bloody toll of Duterte's necropolitics. Their photographs and stories of the dead and their families have circulated widely around the world, showing viewers the extent of the regime's brutality. In what follows, I ask about the effects of their photographic work—its possibilities as well as limits for critiquing the war it depicts. I do so with reference to the experience of the photographers themselves and of those in communities most acutely affected by the killings.

Photographs of the dead tend to have an unsettling effect. One reason may be that photographs not only preserve the past, but by bringing the past into the present of their viewing, they become inextricably part of what they show. As Roland Barthes, Judith Butler, Ariella Azoulay, and Shawn Michelle Smith, among others, have argued, photographs partake in the very events they depict. They do not simply represent events but extend and project those events across space and time, becoming veritable parts of their existence into the future (Azoulay 2008; Barthes 1981; Butler 2010; Smith 2020). For example, our modern concept of atrocity is unthinkable without visual proof. Photographs furnish evidence indispensable for proving that human rights violations and tortures exist, so that without visual documentation, it would be difficult to judge whether an atrocity actually occurred. In this way, photographs become integral parts of what they convey. Similarly, photos of extrajudicial killings provide evidence of their occurrence. But by doing so, they become part of the moment of the victims' deaths. Photographs of corpses, as I discuss below, continue to keep the corpses "alive" in the world as they keep them in circulation within our field of vision. They bring us not just to the scene of the crime but also to

Figure 5.1. Michael Aranja, 29, killed by two men riding on a motorbike, Quezon City, 2016. Photo by Daniel Berehulak/*New York Times*.

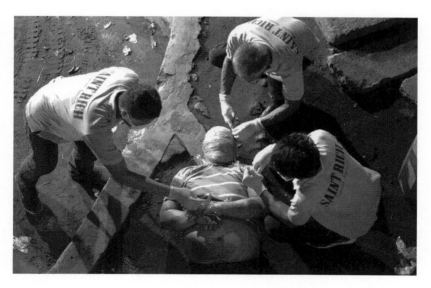

Figure 5.2. Funeral workers remove the masking tape wrapped around the head and wrists of the body of a man, who police said was a victim of drug-related vigilante execution in Manila, September 21, 2016. Photo by Ezra Acayan/Reuters.

the startling recognition of the agency of the corpse. Such agency consists of its ability to act upon the world, for example, by bringing the police and onlookers together, driving people to grieve, providing evidence of the killing, moving viewers to horror, and so on. The photographs, then, represent as much as they constitute the agency of the corpse and so become an indelible part of the death of the victim and its aftermath.

Furthermore, photographs, in soliciting our gaze, constitute a kind of "invitation to pay attention, reflect . . . examine the rationalizations for mass suffering offered by established powers" (Butler 2010, 84). They are more than voyeuristic artifacts. As Ariella Azoulay has pointed out, by pluralizing the gaze, making it possible to see through the eyes of multiple others, photographs also open up visual fields that call for an ethical response from viewers—indeed, that call upon viewers to continue the work of the photograph, interpreting it and so providing it with an afterlife: "The photograph bears the seal of the event itself . . . and anyone . . . can pull at one of its threads and trace it in such a way as to reopen the image and renegotiate what it shows, possibly even completely overturning what was seen in it before" (Azoulay 2008, 13–14).

How, then, do photographs of the drug war represent but also become an integral and inescapable part of what they convey? How do they distance us, yet draw us into the world they conjure? Absent from the scene of the crime, we are nevertheless placed amid the scene of the killings by virtue of viewing their photographs. The first and most privileged viewer, one who enjoys the best vantage point of the crime scene, is, of course, the photographer him/herself. If we look at their photographs and listen to what they have to say about them, can we see a kind of framing of the drug war that sets the terms for our own understanding of events? In other words, to what extent does the photographer's experience of taking the photograph, of framing and processing its effects, frame our own reactions? In asking about the photographer's relationship to the subjects of his or her works, can we also discern something of our own capacity for ethical response—for taking responsibility for what we are invited to see? And who exactly is this "we" that views and responds to the photographs? If we admit to a plurality of viewers and responses, can we still speak about a common "we" with a shared responsibility, a "we" held together by what Azoulay (2008) refers to as the "civil contract of photography"? Indeed, what are the limits of photographic intervention? If photographing the victims of a catastrophe, such as those in the drug war, is meant to constitute larger claims for justice, what kind of justice is at stake, for whom, and for what ends? Just as photography can succeed in provoking critiques of power, can it also fail? What would this photographic failure look like, and what would be its effects?

Photography and Trauma

Let us start by looking at the experience of photojournalists as they come into the crime scene. In various interviews, they often speak of being overwhelmed by what appears before them. What they see often outstrips what they can possibly know, much less talk about. Experience and expression are torn apart, the latter exceeding the former. Carlo Gabuco says, "There's always a moment of disbelief whenever we go to a crime scene and see the victim for the first time, see how they suffered at the hands of their killers" (Katz 2017). From Alyx Ayn Arumpac: "Recently, I've been having mini breakdowns. And I'm wondering, why am I always crying? But then I have to realize as well, actually that this is bigger than me. This is not about me" (Katz 2017). And Dondi Tawatao remarks, "You really don't think about what those images might do to you. It was only later [around] November that I felt ill. At one point, all my dreams were about crime scenes. I was about to check myself into a hospital because I was having coughing fits. . . . We lost something here in the drug war. I am still grappling with what it was we lost" (Katz 2017).

Faced with the scene of the crime, photojournalists speak of being struck with "disbelief" and "confusion." They apprehend more than they can comprehend and so don't exactly know what to think about what they are experiencing. This radical gap between what one experiences and one's ability to narrate it is usually referred to as trauma. A chasm opens up between what happened and one's ability to make sense of it, as in accidents. This failure to conceptualize what one sees and feels results in being struck "numb" or "ill" for days on end. One replays the experience rather than finding a way to frame it and set it aside. Trauma, by making speech difficult, if not impossible, compels the repetition of the event rather than its representation. In a traumatized state, one is unable to distance oneself from what one has gone through, and so finds oneself divided against one's self. Unable to judge, much less think rationally, one is contaminated by the scene one sees and is forced to relive its violence again and again (Freud 1990; Laplanche and Pontalis 1988; Siegel 1998, 2006, 2011). A nagging sense of loss persists, made worse by the fact that one is uncertain as to what exactly was lost.[1]

Arising from a crisis of experience, trauma disables photojournalists from doing what they are supposed to do: cover the event by rendering it into the true account of what actually happened. This disability, however, is only temporary. Subsequent interviews with photojournalists show a pattern for dealing with trauma and recovering what was lost. In a society where therapeutic practices are largely absent or inaccessible to all but the wealthiest, dealing with trauma comes in different ways. For the night crawlers, they speak about fostering a strong sense of camaraderie. Unlike other professional journalists who may compete to out-scoop one another for a story, those covering the drug war talk about deep horizontal ties analogous to those of veteran soldiers who have fought through many battles, feeling as if they were part of a mutually supportive "tribe" (Coronel 2017a).

But while important, the traumatized self seems to require more than such friendships to recover. This entails reconceiving one's self not simply as a passive observer but more importantly as an active witness to the events one covers. The act of witnessing converts the photographers' work into testimonies of injustice, turning photography into a civic act (Azoulay 2008; Linfield 2010; Möller 2017; Smith 2020).

Seeing photographs as claims for justice and acts of citizenship, however, requires the supplementary work of mourning. Photographers in their accounts invariably turn to the survivors of victims and join them in the labor of mourning their loss. Several forge relations with them beyond the time of the photographed event, bringing them food, helping them with housing, even sending their children to school. Witnessing as a cure for trauma is then retrospectively associated with friendship and grieving in the interest of seeking justice in the face of extrajudicial killings. Trauma, witnessing, and mourning are thus related moments in the emergence of the photographer from his or her initial state of confusion and paralysis. In the context of Duterte's narco- and necro-obsessions (see chapter 4 of this volume), such moments assume considerable significance. It is to these processes that I now want to turn.

Facing Death

When asked why they do what they do, photojournalists invariably respond with some variation of their responsibility to report what they see on behalf of those who have no voice and who remain blind to events. Ezra Acayan, for example, asserts that the photographer "must stand on the side of truth. No man should be killed without due process" (Evangelista 2018). From this and similar remarks, it seems that photojournalists are driven by a categorical imperative to do what is right for those who have been wronged. As moral agents, they act as advocates for the victims and their families. Doing so entails turning their photographs into instruments for claiming the rights of victims. This requires assuming the position of witnesses.

Becoming a witness, however, does not happen automatically. It comes in the wake of their initial shock at arriving at the scene of the crime. First, they need to interview other witnesses at the scene. This is because, as Jess Aznar tells *Vice News*, journalists are forbidden from accompanying the police during operations. "We only get to cover the event after the fact: when there's a dead body. After the gun fights" (McClure 2017). To get the story, they need to interview other people in the area who may have witnessed the killing. In short, journalists and photographers can only become witnesses by talking with other witnesses, situating them twice or thrice removed from their narratives. Unlike their stories, however, their cameras are able to capture images of the *first* and *last* witness to the death of the victim: the body of the victim itself.

Some of the most arresting and oft-reproduced images of the drug war are those of corpses. Bathed in the light of street lamps and police cars, corpses appear as the most dramatic manifestations of the drug war. They testify to the violence of the regime as they represent the fulfillment of Duterte's most cherished wish of annihilating addicts. Indeed, this is the point of wrapping many of them up in packing tape and leaving cardboard signs saying *"Pusher ako, huwag tularan"* (I am a pusher, do not imitate me).

Displayed in public, they are meant by the police to be discovered by the people and the media. The corpses become texts testifying to the power of the police acting as "petty sovereigns" (Butler 2010), not only to get rid of those it considers socially dead but also to extract their capacity to access a realm beyond the living. Thus is the corpse indentured to serve as a sign for the state's ability to overcome and appropriate the power of criminality for itself. Bound, packaged, and labeled with signs, the victims' displayed

Figure 5.3. Unidentified man with his head wrapped in packing tape, 2016.
Photo by Daniel Berehulak/*New York Times*.

Figure 5.4. Unidentified man killed by vigilantes, with a sign saying "I'm a drug pusher,"
September 2016. Photo by Noel Celis/Agence France Presse.

remains are reduced to instruments with which to enact and transmit sovereign power. It is a familiar tactic, as old as public crucifixions, hangings, and the display of decapitated heads on spikes along roadways from classical antiquity to the early modern period. The body of the addict is the figure which, as Giorgio Agamben might say, can be killed but whose death would amount neither to murder nor to sacrifice (Agamben 1995; Siegel 1998). The exposure of the corpse to public view is a way of including what has been excluded by the state. It marks not just the boundary that separates the social from the antisocial. The corpse, from the perspective of the state, is a concentrated point from which radiates sovereign power. It is thus used as a stage to perform the basis of the president's authority—which is perhaps akin to the power of all other leaders of modern states: the power to kill, from which comes the sovereign's power to keep others alive.

But is this the only way the corpse can serve as a witness? Is it simply a prop for announcing the terrible power of the state? Or does it also function in ways that can undercut the state's claim to instill fear? Do photographs of corpses also bring out a different and more unsettling power? The images and accounts of photojournalists indicate a different relationship to the dead. The strange agency of the corpse—that is, its capacity to testify to its demise and act upon the world despite having escaped from it—is evident in various interviews. Take, for example, two stories told by one of the best-known photojournalists in the country, Raffy Lerma. In one story, he talks about the first time he encountered a corpse, its head wrapped in packing tape, on the second night of his shift. "I remember this as something that had a real impact on me." Once the police arrived, they cut the tape just as Lerma was focusing on its face with his zoom lens. The camera suddenly brought up the excruciating sight of the corpse's face. "I saw the expression on his face. He was staring at me, his mouth was open. I was terrified. Really terrified because it was like I felt his last moments. How he died, like he was gasping for air, the feeling you get when you're being buried alive, that at first you lose all light, then all air. I felt that, so for a time, I didn't take any more photos like that, or if it's an extrajudicial killing, I don't focus my camera on the faces" (Coronel 2017a).

The sight of the corpse simultaneously invites and repels the gaze of the photographer. At once living and dead, it is as much a compelling object as an impossible subject of photographic interest. It appears as something that is on its way to disappearing. As the materialization of death's arrival, the body of the victim is the something becoming nothing that nonetheless continues to be in the world. Decaying and decomposing, the corpse exceeds life, yet continues to live after a fashion. It exercises an uncanny power as it occupies the radically undecidable border between the living and the dead. As such, it is the embodiment of the inhuman in two senses: as the recipient of a deadly force and as an envoy of what remains outside of the social. It is precisely this uncanny power that confronts Lerma. Seeing the face of the corpse emerging from the packing tape, he is gripped with terror. He sees on its face its "last moments." Seeing the corpse's face, he is seized by its uncanny difference from his own. Traumatized, he turns away from the corpse and vows not to take any more photos of their faces.

Why should seeing the face of the corpse be so traumatizing?

Usually, when we look at the face of an other, we expect to see something similar to our own, a sort of mirror that reflects our shared humanity. As James T. Siegel shows in his commentary on the philosopher Georg Simmel, the face is often regarded in Westernized cultures as the locus of expression, concealing and revealing the soul, understood as the energy and rationality of the person. Hence it is capable of conveying so much with so little, showing anger, for example, with the knitting of the brow or joy with the turn of the lips. The most important parts of the face that enable it to convey a sense of intersubjective humanity are the eyes. Hence the cliché that the eyes are the windows to the soul just as they are the organs for taking in appearances and indicating the workings of the mind (Simmel 1901; Siegel 2011).

Simmel distinguishes between the eyes on a human face and those found on painted portraits common in Western art. The latter function like mechanical eyes. They see only what Simmel calls "pure appearances," making no distinction between, for example, the leg of a chair and that of a child. The mechanical eye "merely sees appearances: '[it] penetrates, it withdraws, it circles a room, it wanders, it reaches as though behind the wanted object and pulls it toward itself'" (Simmel 1901, 11). The power to take in appearances without regard to distinctions or interpretations is, of course, inherent in the camera. It is a kind of technological eye that surpasses the human eye in its ability to zoom in and out, focus and unfocus on details and panoramas, capture subtle gradations of light and dark. But despite the fact that it can do so much more than what the human eye can, the camera's eye cannot synthesize or understand what it sees. It cannot edit and delete parts to form wholes and so cannot judge the images it takes. It registers images promiscuously but divorces these from interpretation and meaning.

The human eye, as Siegel stresses, moves in the opposite direction. To see is invariably to interpret and make sense. Hence, the human eye must censor and repress, include and exclude, framing images to highlight some while leaving out others. We can only see selectively, blocking out certain images in favor of others in order to comprehend what we apprehend. Doing so allows us to see distinctions and the limits of form, that is, to see the aesthetic qualities of images. And by grasping the forms of what appears before us, we are able to judge them. It is this faculty of judgment that allows us to become moral agents, telling apart what is beautiful and good from what is not. Blindness is thus the price of insight. Our vision is humanized insofar as it is founded on the ability to take on and seize hold of the autonomous and inhuman power of the camera's mechanical eye. Rather than succumb to the amoral power of the mechanical eye, however, we find ways to tame it and put it under our control, thereby aestheticizing what we see. It is the rigorous domestication of the camera's powerful vision and the aestheticization of its images that is precisely the work of the photographer (Siegel 2011, 12–18).

But in Lerma's story above, we see how his encounter with the corpse places this aestheticizing ability in crisis. He sees the face of the corpse, drawing close to it with the mechanical eye of his camera. But what appears is not a mirror reflection of him. The camera instead reveals a sight that overwhelms his own. The face of the corpse turned toward him causes him to feel that he is dying. It is as if he becomes a corpse himself. He experiences not a confirmation of his humanity, as he might by looking at the face of someone living but precisely its negation. "I felt his last moments. How he died." He finds himself in the place of the victim being strangled and buried alive, "losing all light, then all air." The corpse is the best and last witness to its death, but the sight of its face conveyed by the camera is such that it conjures in Lerma the fantasy of his own death. To see the agency of the corpse is thus to feel oneself on the verge of losing agency altogether.

The camera as an inhuman machine, for registering pure appearances *cannot not* see the corpse. It exposes the photographer to what he can no longer distinguish from himself. Not only does he become like the corpse, he also becomes like his camera. In both cases, he begins to feel as if he were losing what made him human. He is doubly captive: to the inhuman power of his camera as it records the arrival of death in the body of the corpse, and to the inhuman power of the corpse that shows him his own death. The only way he can break out of this double bind is to turn away from both. "I didn't take any more photos like that, or if it's an extrajudicial killing, I don't focus my camera on the faces" of the corpse. One can take photos of the corpse's body but not its face insofar as it threatens to expose one's own death. Doing so allows him to regain control of the mechanical eye and distance himself from the contaminating effects of the corpse's look.

Lerma subsumes the eye of the camera into his own eye while distancing himself from the powerful because impossible agency of the corpse. In this way, he would seem to regain his humanity from these two inhuman forces. But such a move is not sufficient to secure one's place as a witness. Something else is required that entails identifying with the sorrow of the victims' families. This is the work of mourning. The photographer, in order to retrieve his humanity from the traumatic exposure to the dead, turns to the living survivors and joins them in their grief. Such a turn is made possible by the photographer's harnessing of the camera's mechanical power. He converts the photographic image of the corpse from a horrific reminder of the individual's death to an icon of collective suffering and sacrifice. The corpse is reframed thus, not merely as a victim of state violence or as an envoy of one's own deadly fate but as a martyr destined for memorialization and devotion.

To see the way the corpse is idealized and iconized, let us turn to Raffy Lerma's second story, describing how he took what is probably his best-known photograph of the drug war, which Duterte himself dubbed as "La Pieta," a reference to the famous Michelangelo sculpture of Mary cradling the dead Christ.

Lerma recalls arriving at the scene of the crime, where he could see from "afar that this was a picture. This was a very strong picture" (Coronel 2017a). He remembers being struck by the way the victim, a tricycle driver named Michael Siaron, was being tenderly held in the arms of his partner, Jennilyn Olayres. Enclosed by yellow police tape and surrounded by a crowd, the couple was lit up by television lights and police headlights so that "it looked staged," Lerma says. "But what is imprinted in my mind," he continues, "is Olayres screaming for help. I felt like we were vultures. She was screaming, 'Help us, we need to bring him to the hospital,' and we were there just clicking and clicking" (Coronel 2017a).

Indeed, other photojournalists and videographers often speak of being haunted by the keening and crying among the relatives of the victims. It is the sound of grieving as much as the sight of the dead that stays with them, reminding them of their responsibility to their photographic subjects. At

Figure 5.5. Jennilyn Olayres cradling her partner, Michael Siaron, July 2016, the most iconic photo of the drug war, popularly known as "La Pieta." Photo by Raffy Lerma/*Philippine Daily Inquirer*.

the same time, they find themselves driven to carry out their task to find what Lerma refers to as "those strong pictures . . . those photos that would really make an impact." Confronted by the cries for help, the photojournalist instead keeps working. He or she finds him- or herself confronted by an ethical dilemma, torn between the imperative to convey the truth of the killings on the one hand and to respond to the urgent cries for help from the families on the other. Doing one's task, one must turn away from the immediate needs of the other. One is thus caught between being responsible and being irresponsible at the same time. It is in the face of this ethical dilemma that Lerma is assailed by what we can only surmise is a sense of guilt. In the midst of the crime scene, he confesses, "As photojournalists, we have to take—and it's sad, it's sad to say—we have to take advantage of it. We just have to do our jobs and our job is to share these pictures and convey their message. . . . All of us felt so heavy. . . . But still, when we saw the photos, we thought, shit, this is strong" (Coronel 2017a).

The next day, his photo appeared in the front pages of several newspapers and was widely printed abroad. Vindicated by the results of his work,

Lerma nonetheless feels something amiss. Haunted by the cries for help that he could not respond to, he is compelled to visit the wake of Siaron four days later. At first, the family turns him away. But then he shows the father a newspaper with the photograph he took on the front page. "I was the one who took that photo," he tells the father, who then welcomes him in. Introduced to Jennilyn Olayres, he apologizes profusely. "I told her sorry for how we behaved that night. Please understand what our work is." Jennilyn remained quiet, "but she held my hand, she nodded and cried. I think she got it. She saw the public reaction to the photo. I felt my heart grow lighter" (Coronel 2017a).

In the earlier story, Lerma relates how he has a foretaste of his own death when seeing the face of the corpse. As with the experience of the sublime, he looked death in the face only to realize his time had not yet arrived. He escaped to tell the story of his fear and subsequent recovery.[2] In this second story, it is not a matter of facing the corpse. Unlike the first story, the victim here is named and given a social identity. When Lerma arrives at the scene, it is already cordoned off and spectacularly lighted, as if it were being staged. Even more important, the body of Michael Siaron was being cradled by his partner, Jennilyn Olayres. Whatever menacing potential the corpse may have had was now safely contained by both the police cordon and the arms of Jennilyn. As a scene, its aesthetic qualities as a "strong picture" were readily apparent and needed only to be recorded.

In other accounts of this story, Lerma, in fact, alludes to the scene as if it were a picture of the sculpture *Pietà* (Coronel 2017a). The man-Christ laid out on the lap of his mother is an image of "bereavement and tenderness." Its composition is remarkably simple yet effective: the figure of the victim laid out horizontally evokes suffering and abjection. It is counterposed to the vertical figure of the mother, who acts as the healer and mourner. Together, they form the sign of the cross (Berger 2013, 111). The murderous verticality of the police is thus replaced by the caring and pity of the mourner. And in the absence of the mother, there is the girlfriend, joined by the photographer and the viewer, vertically bent and agonized as she looks upon the dead with a mixture of horror and compassion.

Such elementary formal qualities recompose the corpse into the pose of a martyr. The photograph not only alludes to the dead Christ. It is also saturated by a Filipino historical consciousness shot through with Christian narratives about martyred national heroes from José Rizal to Benigno "Ninoy" Aquino (Ileto 1979). Shot from a particular angle, it appears as

Figure 5.6. Nanette Castillo grieves next to the dead body of her son Aldrin, an alleged drug user killed by unidentified assailants in Manila, October 3, 2017. Photo by Noel Celis/Agence France Presse.

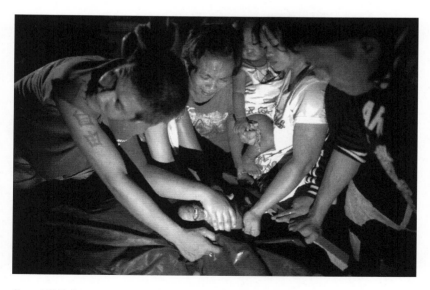

Figure 5.7. Relatives weep over the body of a man after police said he resisted arrest during a drug bust operation, Manila, August 2016. Photo by Ezra Acayan/Reuters.

Figure 5.8. Nestor Hilbano comforts his wife, Alma, after seeing their son, Richard, 32, inside a body bag in a dark alley in Tatalon, Manila. Richard was shot by the police during a drug bust operation, along with three others. Photo by Jes Aznar/Reuters.

if its abject body had been sacralized by death. Other photographs of victims similarly draw from the iconography of Christian martyrdom, showing them cradled by loved ones or mourned by family members.

Others are shown laid out with their arms spread as if they were being crucified. In nearly all cases, the images are bathed in the harsh light of police and television lights and set against the deep black of the night in ways that bring out their chiaroscuro quality. The effect is to frame the victims and their survivors in a kind of sacred space surrounded by darkness while embraced by a halo of light reminiscent of Renaissance paintings.

In the Abrahamic tradition, martyrs are, of course, synonymous with witnesses. The word *martyr*, from the Greek *martus*, signifies a witness who testifies to a fact of which he has knowledge from personal observation (Carson 2002). Martyrs are commemorated precisely as models of fidelity and courage. Depictions of martyrs are integral to the design of churches, starting with the crucified Christ in all His bloody glory. Other grisly images of martyrdom are common, from decapitation to burning at the stake.

Figure 5.9. A drug suspect killed after allegedly firing back at police during an encounter at Camarin, Caloocan City, on September 16, 2016. Photo by Carlo Gabuco/*Rappler*.

Figure 5.10. Unidentified men killed in a police encounter, 2016. Photo by Daniel Berahulak/*New York Times*.

But these images of death, meant to inspire the faithful, are all artfully rendered. Whatever horrible death the particular martyr may have suffered is softened and shaped by colors and lines that lend them a specific identity, distinguishing them from other angels and saints. To be devoted to such martyrs is to emulate the power of their witnessing.

By composing, wittingly or unwittingly, the photographs of corpses as if they were martyred, surrounding or supplementing these with photos of their grieving survivors, photojournalists set up a kind of sacred tableau that tames the trauma induced by the crime scene. It turns the nightly occurrence of violence into a narrative of injustice meant to indict the powerful. Such photographs make legible death as sacrifice, and the families' suffering as mourning designed to commemorate the dead. We get a sense of the conversion of the uncanny force of death into a narrative about martyrdom in the texts that accompany the photographs, either as captions or as more extended narratives (Evangelista and Gabuco 2016–18). Such texts focus on the singularity of the victim, beginning with his name, age, and occupation, recounting his relationship to his family and community. "I try to rebuild the person. I take the corpse and reimagine the man," the journalist Patricia Evangelista says (Coronel 2017a).

Laid out in the casket, a framed picture of the person as living is usually placed on top while the corpse is made up to look like an image of itself while still alive. In this way, funeral wakes seek to recuperate a semblance of the dead's dignity denied to him by his killers. Rather than trigger terror, the corpse on display stirs memories among the living, allowing them to tell stories apart from the murder. Narratives redeem their humanity brought out by the ritual and journalistic memorialization of the victimization. And by joining the family in mourning the dead, photojournalists become related to the relations of the dead. As Vincent Go told another interviewer, "For the government, they are just statistics, they're just numbers. But [we want] to give faces to these numbers; we want to know who these people are" (Stein 2017a). In giving them faces, photographs restore the dead in the image of the living, defying Duterte's calls for their torture and defacement. In place of trauma, there is pity. "Love is always, among other things, pity," John Berger writes. "This is the love of the vertical figure. The love of the mourner and the healer; the love of the survivor for the dead" (Berger 2013, 117).

Seeing by Not Seeing

Attempts at rehumanizing the dead and the living, including the ranks of the photojournalists, are not, however, definitive. Photographic advocacy, while compelling the world's attention, has had different effects within the country. Indeed, as of this writing, photojournalistic coverage seems to be at a standstill. The flood of images has not, so far, mitigated the deadly progress of the drug war. In fact, President Duterte has repeatedly signaled his intention to intensify his campaign, especially on poor drug users, even as his popularity and approval ratings remain sky high (Duterte 2018; Ranada 2019a; "War on Drugs" 2019). Why should this be the case? What might account for the limits of photographic intervention in the drug war?

Alongside their capacity to arouse shock and sympathy, images of injury and death, under certain conditions, tend to solicit other kinds of responses. Let me cite an example. In December 2016, the priests of Baclaran Church, one of the largest parishes in Metro Manila, set up an exhibit of the photos of the killings with the collaboration of the photographers themselves. They blew up the images and transferred them onto plastic tarps held up by steel frames. Arranged along the passageway to the church's doors, the exhibit was meant as a moral rebuke to the regime. The priests expected viewers to be scandalized by the scenes of violence and blame the state ("Graphic Exhibit" 2016). However, when my partner and I visited the church, we noticed that it was not uncommon for people to simply walk by the photographs en route to Mass, barely looking around. A few younger couples sat on benches, seemingly oblivious to some of the most gruesome images of corpses alongside them. Others glanced at the photographs briefly, at times remarking something to the effect that "they probably were addicts and deserved to die." Another viewer seemed to think that such exhibits aided the war on drugs, seeing them from the perspective of the police. "*Para matakot ang mga durugista*" (so that drug addicts would be frightened), he was quoted as saying.

For this viewer and others like him, photos of the dead seemed to confirm that the drug war was succeeding ("Look: Baclaran Church" 2016; "War on Drugs" 2019). Rather than identify with the victims and the families, a number of the people we saw, most of whom came from the same neighborhoods where many of the killings had occurred, seemed unmoved. It was almost as if they regarded the images of death as stereotypical and thus unsurprising. They seemed immune to the violent images, as the corpses on display did not appear to impinge on their own lives. Or if they did, they kept it firmly to themselves. Hence, there was no compunction to mourn as the photographs failed to stir moral outrage. Rather than furnish a new civic space of belonging through grieving, images of the drug war seemed to spur civil indifference.

Why these reactions? There is no way of definitively accounting for people's responses to such photographs. Let me hypothesize one possibility: that the quotidian catastrophe of the killings has reshaped the way people see death and organize life. We get a sense of this, for example, in a recent ethnographic study by the anthropologists Steffen Jensen and Anna Braemer Warburg set in the barangay of Bagong Silang, a dense urban neighborhood in Metro Manila. Situating the drug war within a history of postwar counterinsurgency and militarized policing, they argue that it has converted the affected neighborhoods into "illegible terrains of violence." This has to do with the way police and vigilantes target their victims. Local officials are required by the police to collect lists of names of suspected as well as known users and dealers. As we saw in the previous chapter, there is considerable arbitrariness in compiling such lists, and there is no vetting of names. Indeed, some on the lists have nothing to do with drugs. Just as no one knows for sure who will be on the list, there is no way to get your name off it. And once on the list, one is then liable to be targeted by the police or paid vigilantes. Nearly all those who have been killed are described in police reports by the same word: *nanlaban*, that is, they resisted. And since there have been few, largely inconclusive, investigations of these deaths, one can assume that nanlaban is simply a shorthand way for the police to cover up summary executions as "self-defense." Hence, residents have come to distrust not just the police but also their neighbors, who, they worry, will give their names to the cops regardless of whether or not they are into drugs. What emerges, not surprisingly, is a mode of governing by fear (Coronel, Padilla, and Mora 2019; Evangelista and Gabuco 2016–18; "Local Officials" 2017; Ou and Almendral 2017; Warburg and Jensen 2018).

The drug lists are in effect a kill list. They are productive of fear as an essential principle in reorganizing both social relations and the individual's sensorium. This biopolitics of fear is illustrated by one of the informants of Warburg and Jensen, a neighborhood watch leader in charge of gathering names of suspected users and dealers. When asked about the lists, she says, "We need to make them fear for them to stop using drugs. It is effective, this fear of being killed." From another local official, we see how death as the unavoidable by-product of list-making can only lead to order: "When the ones on the list of the President are all killed, drugs will be stopped. Naturally! . . . Everyone wants peace, whether you are a drug user or whether you are a big-time. Peace is also for them. What is hard is how can you give them peace if they continue to be drug users? What kind of peace will you give to them? It must be death" (Warburg and Jensen 2018, 10–11).

The fear that is meant to strike so-called drug personalities ends up governing the conduct of the rest of the residents, regardless of whether they have any involvement in drugs. Everyone is radically implicated and compelled to alter their ways of being and seeing. As Warburg and Jensen note, "It is not uncommon to hear of wrongful accusations between neighbors. This has, of course, increased vigilance and mistrust in the community and changed relations even between the closest of neighbors. As Flores, another longtime resident, explains: 'Now, almost no one gets out of their house when darkness comes. We used to go outside our house and talk, listen and tell stories even late at night, but we can't do that now, because we are afraid. We don't know who can be trusted anymore.'" Other residents have similarly reorganized their behavior, acting more guarded toward their neighbors. An elderly woman known for her gregariousness in the past "has become careful and withdrawn. . . . Most of the time she sits in front of her small house observing life in the street. Here, she sees people buying and selling drugs, but she keeps quiet due to fear of being involved. 'I am afraid. They might make up stories about me. . . . You have to take care. . . . Whatever it is I see, only my eyes are seeing it'" (Warburg and Jensen 2018, 11–12).

Fear emerges from as much as it induces a perennial state of emergency. It regulates sociality, compelling distance and circumspection in neighborhoods where people are forced to live in extremely close quarters with little ventilation. Under such crowded conditions, permeated by acute uncertainty and suspicion, a kind of dissociative looking arises. To say, as the elderly woman does, that "Whatever it is I see, only my eyes are seeing it" is to suggest that the "I" is split between one who sees and another who is unable or unwilling to register what appears in front of one. Like most of the residents of Bagong Silang—and perhaps like most of those visiting Baclaran Church—the speaker dwells constantly on the verge of catastrophe. By instilling fear, the drug war forces people to live on the threshold of death. Every night, gunshots are heard, corpses appear, the keening and crying of survivors pierce the night. Police and photographers converge around the scenes of violence, creating a momentary spectacle. The bodies are then taken away, leaving pools of blood in their wake. The next day, schoolchildren casually walk by the spots where people had been murdered the night before, while young boys play basketball across the alley from where one of their own was gunned down. Life seems to go on, with the expectation that death hovers close by (Evangelista and Gabuco 2016–18; Jones and Sarbil 2019).

Where people live on the edge of catastrophe—where that edge defines the very space of civic life—is it any wonder that they see images by not seeing them, by dissociating what they apprehend from what they comprehend? Whether this dissociative experience amounts to trauma, it remains difficult to overcome. Among the photographers, as we saw, trauma triggered by the scene of the killings is translated into witnessing and mourning. The work of mourning begins by way of aestheticizing the sights and sites of injury and violation. Such aestheticizing allows photographers and those in their position to forge an ethical stance, as photographs become documents for determining truth and seeking justice. But for the people of Bagong Silang and those in Baclaran Church who live under an unremitting regime of fear and conditions of precarity, things are different. Colluding with the police, neighborhood watch leaders see fear and the dissociation it produces as indispensable elements for establishing "peace" and security. The point is, therefore, not to overcome fear but to allow it to overcome you. For this reason, the conversion of trauma into witnessing among the residents is blocked. Surviving in constant proximity to death, they seek to bracket the images of war. Always vulnerable to sudden violation, they remain vigilant, cultivating indifference to views of violence and suppressing the horror that may arise when encountering the traces of the dead. To see whereby "only my eyes are seeing it" is thus a way of inoculating oneself against the expected but no less sudden arrival of death.

This is perhaps why, in the case of exhibit at the church, the photographs did not seem to visibly shock, much less stir outrage among the people as the priests and photographers had hoped. Perhaps they did but in ways difficult to determine, much less express. The priests expected parishioners to wake up and rise in indignation. Instead, they seemed insulated, seeing by not seeing; or if they were horrified, they chose not to speak for fear that they would have no one to address. Some even identified with the forces of the state and less with the fate of the victims and their families. While they may have seen the state as a source of terror, they also saw its agents, the police, as sites of address and a source of order amid a state of emergency. Indeed, at the height of the drug war, when these photographs began to appear, polls showed Duterte's approval rating higher than ever (Ranada 2017, 2019a). The appearance of the photographs undoubtedly had a critical effect, especially on those who already opposed the regime's human rights abuses. But they did not seem to decisively alter the views of the majority, as they continued to support the president who promised to spread more fear—and with it, more security. The kill lists make one the condition for, as well as the outcome of, the other: no fear, no security, and vice versa.

What about the families of victims? How did they respond to the photographs? Again, responses were far from uniform. As Raffy Lerma's account indicates, some shared in the notion of photographic mourning. Seeing the images of the dead aestheticized in martyr-like poses allowed grief to be shared by a wider public. However, as we can derive from Lerma's guilt and from what other photojournalists have told me, others came to suspect the motives of the photographers. Some resented the unwarranted exposure of the violated bodies of their family members in the news. They objected, for example, to having the photos of their relatives identified as "addicts" and "criminals" in tabloids or the evening news, no doubt feeling humiliated by these judgments. The display of such images thus redoubled the violation of the dead while reflecting badly on the family of the survivors. Instead, they preferred to show the carefully composed and framed portraits of their dead while they were still alive, placing these on top of the caskets. Rather than images of state violence, they chose understandably to display the dignified appearance of their loved ones.

The point is that reactions to the photographs were varied. As in the exhibit in the church, these ranged from indifference to guarded but silent assent, from outrage at the photographers and the media to muted criticisms of the police. Various human rights organizations have sought to mobilize the families of victims, hoping that their loss would stir outrage among others in the community. Perhaps the most dramatic show of defiance came in the wake of the well-publicized killing of seventeen-year-old Kian de los Santos on August 16, 2017, in Caloocan. Coming in the midst of an especially bloody drug operation dubbed "one time, big time" that laid to waste at least thirty-two people in a couple of days, Kian was taken to be a drug runner by the police, who dragged him along dark alleys and executed him in a filthy pigsty. Planting a gun and a couple of satchels of shabu on him, the police claimed he had resisted and so gunned him down. However, subsequent CCTV footage along with witness testimonies showed that he was dragged in his boxer shorts, where he could not possibly have kept a gun, and was heard pleading for mercy, saying that he had an exam the next day. Additionally, his friends and family claimed that there was no way Kian could have been involved in drugs, that he supported Duterte's drug war, and that he aspired to be a police officer himself.

The grainy CCTV video images did what the photographs of corpses tried to do: they sparked anger and provoked hundreds to march in protest, holding nightly vigils in the local cathedral led by the clergy, human rights advocates, opposition politicians, and members of left-wing civil society groups. Duterte himself met with the parents of Kian in the palace and vowed to punish the erring cops. However, he also insisted that his murder was an "isolated" case and that cops were otherwise justified in defending themselves if they felt threatened. Some thirteen policemen were investigated and three were charged and found guilty of murder and sentenced to life in prison a little over a year later, in November 2018. There was an attempt to pass a law declaring August 16 a day of remembrance for victims of the drug war, and a plaque memorializing the death of Kian along with all the other victims of the war was placed in the San Roque Cathedral in Caloocan (Gavilan 2018; Stein 2017). But neither the outrage nor the protests could be sustained. Kian's parents ended up posing with Duterte, giving the usual fist salute. Most people accepted the government's line that Kian's murder, as unfortunate as it was, was to be expected in a war, and that justice had been done with the punishment of the three cops. No other cops have ever been prosecuted. As with the photographs, so with the CCTV videos: the shock of seeing the images of Kian being led to the slaughter initially triggered anger among the family and human rights advocates, only to be replaced by fear and resignation rather than any sort of reform. After a brief pause, the police resumed their murderous work and Duterte's popularity has remained high (Talambog 2020).

Such shows of defiance in the face of Kian's killing were rare and short-lived. Polls have shown that there is a general preference for rehabilitating rather than executing drug users ("War on Drugs" 2019). Nonetheless, such responses have not translated into a sustained critique of the president. As of this writing, the killings have continued unabated, moving beyond Metro Manila. One difference, however, is that circulation of the photographs of the dead, published widely between July 2016 and January 2018, have leveled off. They now rarely appear in the local or international media, though they are still archived in the social media accounts of photographers. With the exception of a few, most of the photojournalists—a number of whom have won prestigious international awards in recognition of their work even as they continue to help out the families of victims—have themselves moved on to other subjects of interest.

It would seem, then, that rather than read into the photographs instances of gross injustice, viewers from the most affected areas tend to see them by not seeing them, for if they looked, they would only see what the police themselves wanted to show them: the fearsome power of the state delivering a kind of justice as cruel as it was inescapable. Why should this be the case? Why would Duterte's popularity increase with the photographic revelations of the killings among the very poor who were most intimately affected by the war? What else is at stake in seeing images of the dead? Could it have something to do with the sense that, far from being unjust, the killings, produced by and productive of fear, are in a way also seen to be just? Could Duterte's populist appeal in part lie in his ability to tap into the popular wish for a kind of swift justice, especially in a context where the criminal justice system is notoriously corrupt and dysfunctional? While photographers appealed to viewers to mourn the dead and demand their rights, could other images of the dead—for example, as returning spirits—conjure a different and more direct notion of justice fed by the desire for vengeance?

Dreams, or Phantasms of Revenge

With so many deaths happening on a nightly basis, we might expect there to be a proliferation of ghosts as well as ghost stories. This is the case with the families of victims. In some accounts, they talk about expecting the spirit of the dead to come back, usually three days after their deaths. They look forward to its return with great anticipation. Families want the spirit to reassure them that they are in a good state someplace else. There is, for instance, the story of Ericardo, who was killed in Pasay in the early part of 2017, as told by his sister Jhoy to the journalist Aurora Almendral (Almendral and Dean 2017):

> During his wake, Jhoy waited for the feeling that Ericardo's ghost was with them. She posted on Facebook asking if anyone had had contact

with him. No one had. "I was so annoyed with him," she said. "It had been six days and he still hadn't made himself felt."

It wasn't until the day before his funeral that she felt him at the convenience store near the intersection where he worked, the last place he was seen alive, climbing onto the back of someone's motorcycle. That night, Ericardo visited Jhoy in a dream.

"He was smiling," she said. When she consulted the local *spiritista*, she told her that Ericardo did not want the family to suffer. . . . It gave her comfort to know that Ericardo was not an angry spirit, lingering in this world, unable to accept his own death and demanding vengeance. "It was just like him," Jhoy said. "He was always so easy-going."

Almendral continues: "Still there is one more dream Jhoy craves. 'I want to dream about the night he was killed,' she said. 'I want to stab the person who stabbed him. So I can finally defend him,' even if just in her dreams. A dream of vengeance may be the nearest thing to justice Jhoy and others can hope for. Few of the killers are ever caught."

Here, the dead returns not to ask for something but to fulfill the wishes of the living. In other contexts, spirits usually return to possess the living, causing them to fall ill. Curers are asked to speak with these spirits and give them a voice. Hence, spirits come across as disembodied desires. They come precisely in search of a body to allow them to speak and fulfill their wishes. Once heard through the medium, the spirit leaves and the person possessed is cured of their illness (Cannell 1999; Siegel 2000). But in the context of the drug war, spirits come by way of dreams to reassure those they have left behind. The living thus look upon spirit returns as benevolent rather than malevolent. Spirits come back to grant a simple wish: that of relieving the living of their worry as to the former's state in the afterlife. Spirit visitations are conventionalized in dreams and announced by local spiritistas. In this way, their arrivals are drained of anything uncanny. Unlike the sight of corpses that trigger trauma, the visit of spirits, like that of a family member working abroad, generates expectations of comfort. Such returns help complete the work of mourning and give the living the sense that the dead are truly dead, located in another and better place apart from the living.

But while spirit returns may alleviate the grief of the living, they leave the latter with another kind of desire. As Jhoy's account shows, she wants to have another dream—not one about Ericardo but about his killer. She wants to see the last thing Ericardo saw: his own death at the hands of the murderer. "I want to dream about the night he was killed," she says. "I want to stab the person who stabbed him. So I can finally defend him." Here, the living is left with a sense of lack. She wants what the dead no longer cares for: revenge. Her dream, she hopes, would let her become a witness to her brother's death. In this way, her dream acts as a kind of camera, allowing her to see the corpse as it registers the image of its killer and the moment of its death. Like photojournalists who see their task as one of witnessing, Jhoy sees her dreaming as a way of seeking the truth about her brother's demise.

But unlike photojournalists, Jhoy's dream images are not a matter of documenting the killings for some future reckoning. They do not entail building an archive for the adjudication of guilt. They are, rather, about seeking vengeance in order to "defend him," that is, to respond to the killing of her brother in kind. In seeking justice by means of revenge, Jhoy is perhaps closer to Duterte, echoing his deadly wish to kill those who have killed others. She understands her dream not as a practice of truth-telling, as with photojournalists. Rather, it is about finding a target. In recounting her dream of vengeance, Jhoy confirms the affective pull of extrajudicial killings as a form of justice (Rafael 2005). Like Duterte promising to kill addicts, stabbing her brother's killer is how she conceives of her obligation and satisfaction. Justice by way of revenge constitutes a kind of moral economy: she returns with interest the curse of death that she received from her brother's killer (Mauss 2000; Siegel 2013). In dreams of revenge alongside spirit returns, she imagines regaining and restoring what she lost. In her world, where the poor have neither the means nor the energy to go through the legal system, dreams convey the wish for direct justice as the return of that which one receives but did not deserve. Phantasms of revenge thus allow Jhoy and perhaps others like her to carry out the work of mourning distinct from those of photographers and journalists.

Dream images here differ decisively from photographs. Unlike photographs, they can neither be exhibited publicly nor archived for a future reckoning. Resistant to display and collection, Jhoy's dreams remain hers alone and so exist outside of what Azoulay calls "the civil contract of photography" (Azoulay 2008). Instead, they stimulate the wish for vengeance and cannily reaffirm rather than elude the regime's retaliatory logic. Similarly, her brother's spirit escapes the pull of, even as it emerges from, the violence of the state. Yet it returns only to his sister and other members of his family. Coming from elsewhere, the dream pictures afforded by the dead's return remain unseen and unseeable by us, even as they generate a wish for revenge that is yet to be fulfilled. Only she sees them and holds the wish in reserve.

For this reason, the return of the spirit, like all returns, leaves Jhoy unsettled, saddled with a sense of something left undone. This experience of loss, felt like all sudden losses to be deeply unjust, leads her to wish for restitution that in the end only someone greater than she is could provide. This is perhaps why Duterte continues to be popular even among the very communities most victimized by the drug war ("Duterte's Net Satisfaction" 2018; Philippine Human Rights Information Center 2017–18; Ranada 2019a). In his vow to annihilate "drug personalities," he promises to fulfill the desire for swift justice among those who, like Jhoy, exist on the cusp of disaster. For, while her dream may not amount to much, it is not nothing. It amounts to something perhaps impossible to calculate, something that a camera cannot register and that neither you nor I can consume, much less appropriate. But as a kind of intangible reserve, her dream for vengeance is still something that the regime can extract and exploit. As such, vengeance becomes a language shared by Duterte and people like Jhoy. Thanks to the kill list, the nightly harvest of corpses articulates a grammar of fear that governs the relationship between the two. Justice in this context requires the death of the social enemy. As with the residents of Bagong Silang, the nightly killings show that someone is in charge, that authority works because there is fear, and therefore order. Thus is security mystified. Summary executions seem to deliver justice in the way that Jhoy and others like her can only dream of. For this reason, the killings continue beyond what photographers can convey and outside of what we can see.

In the conclusion, we will return to this question of fear and security in the context of communities of intimacy.

CONCLUSION. Intimacy and the Autoimmune Community

There is no way to conclude this book, if to conclude we mean, as the word's origin in the Latin *concludere* suggests, to "shut up, to enclose." Events are still unfolding in ways that are impossible to predict, much less to sum up. As of this writing, the COVID-19 pandemic continues to hold the planet in its grip. Autocrats like Duterte, Bolsinaro, Trump—or his avatars— cannot, as much as they wish to, simply order it away. In the case of the Philippines, there have been over 2,000,000 cases and over 30,000 deaths as of September 2021—numbers that rival those killed in Duterte's drug war. Indeed, Duterte has used the same draconian approach toward the virus as he has with drugs: impose a massive lockdown and imprison those caught violating quarantine, while providing only the barest minimum to alleviate people's needs. Indeed, the president has been widely criticized for his in- competent, even indifferent approach not only to the lockdown but also to the roll-out of the vaccine. At one point when asked about the pandemic, he could only reply "*Matagal pa 'to. Sabihin ko sa 'yo, marami pang mamamatay dito* (This is far from over. Let me tell you, many more will die here)" (Molo 2021). Hospital beds have been as difficult to come by as winning the lot- tery while reports of people dying in hospital parking lots abound.

Meanwhile, there has been no letup in extrajudicial killings. Despera- tion clings to the air and there is a general feeling of abandonment. Unem- ployment, not surprisingly, has shot up to over 50 percent. In the early days of the pandemic lockdown in 2020, public transportation was at a standstill as only those with private cars could get around. Jeepney drivers and their families have been driven out of their homes and forced to sleep in their ve- hicles while workers stood masked on the streets holding cardboard signs asking for food rather than money. While some businesses have reopened, many smaller operations have shut down permanently.

It is fair to say that no one feels happy or secure amid the pandemic, and criticism has been growing regarding the way Duterte has handled it. A number of his critics have vociferously called for his resignation, citing not only his gross mishandling of the pandemic but also his inability to face down growing Chinese incursions in the West Philippine Sea (Bello 2021; Molo 2021). With the dramatic contraction of the economy signaled by the precipitous fall in remittances sent by overseas Filipino workers, the usual neoliberal solutions have proven inadequate. For most, life feels more precarious than ever. "The economic cost of trying to contain the virus is leaving large scars to household and corporate balance sheets, which will weigh heavily on demand for many months to come," as two economists put it (Jiao and Yap 2020).

During the early months of the lockdown, Duterte went into a state of "perpetual isolation," as his spokesperson put it, holed up at his home in Davao. He has been given more than usual to talking about his illnesses and the possibility of his dying. Some of his supporters, in a pathetic gesture to protect his legacy, tried to form what they called a "revolutionary government" in August 2020, asking the military to take over and for Congress to give the president the power to name his own successor. That move was quickly shut down by the military themselves and disavowed by Duterte (Abad 2020). It seems that any changes in the constitution that would allow Duterte to perpetuate himself or his family and friends in power is not going to happen anytime in the near future. Instead, Duterte has chosen to use the courts and the legislature to further his grip on power. Recently, his allies in Congress rushed through an Anti-Terrorism Law that conflates dissent and activism into potential acts of terror. Further narrowing human rights, the new law promises to have a chilling effect on criticisms of the regime. True to form, Duterte has instructed the military "that if they find themselves in an armed encounter with the communist rebels, kill them, make sure you really kill them, and finish them off if they are alive" (Talabong 2021). Along with the red-tagging and assassination of human rights lawyers, union leaders and other activists, as well as the continued harassment of journalists and attempts to close media outlets critical of the president—successful in the case of ABS-CBN—the Anti-Terrorism Law takes advantage of the pandemic to tighten the president's autocratic hold (Buan 2021; McCarthy 2020; Quezon 2021; Talabong 2021).

Yet recent surveys indicate that Duterte's popularity has not suffered significantly. He remains, pardon the pun, bullet proof. His job approval rating remains high—as much as 91 percent, according to a poll at the close of 2020—even as the majority of the people have become increasingly pessimistic about the state of the country. Much of the blame has been laid at the feet of his officials, especially those running the Department of Health. The fatal incompetence and massive corruption of his own officials have insulated rather than implicated Duterte from any sense of popular disfavor (Elemia 2020; Tuquero 2020). And in a cruel gesture of historical revisionism, Congress recently approved September 11, Ferdinand Marcos's birthday, as a paid public holiday for his home province of Ilocos. In the midst of the pandemic, the government has chosen to honor a plunderer, murderer, and torturer ("Bill Declaring Marcos' Birthday" 2020). Once again, the politics of life has given way to the politics of death.

Fear and Security

We began this book with the question of Duterte's popularity, and it is a question that remains unanswered and perhaps unanswerable. How is it that a mass murderer registers such highly positive ratings, however skeptical one might be about the methods used in these surveys? Why does his genocidal approach and governance by fear meet with widespread approval? And why do the sources of opposition to his authoritarian rule remain remarkably weak and largely ineffective? Or is it the case that by focusing on Duterte, we've missed out on something much more fundamental, namely the historical persistence of structures of power that envelop and enable the survival of sprawling urban communities where his support is most evident? How does the authoritarian imaginary circulate and reinforce existing notions of community? What can we learn from looking at these largely impoverished communities that have experienced the most devastating effects of the drug war, yet where expressions of confidence in Duterte remain high? Indeed, is there something about the construction of community that preceded and will continue beyond Duterte's regime—something about the logic and logistics of living together—that also creates the conditions for cultivating violence and spreading death?

In chapter 5, we noted the paradoxical workings of a biopolitics of fear—the way in which the shock of the killings triggered what we might think of as trauma but how trauma generated the desire for security. Both fear and security found their locus in the figure of Duterte, the tatay or father who issued deadly warnings, promising to protect "good citizens" from the threats of "bad drug personalities." The drug war thus was seen to shore up community in and through the sovereign violence of patriarchy.

"People are very aware of the killings, but at the same time, they feel that Duterte's eliminated the criminals," the noted political scientist and Duterte critic Walden Bello has remarked. "The thugs, the street-corner boys, are no longer there. Women can walk the streets safely. I don't know if their lives are actually better than before, but perception is that they are. They're pro-Duterte because they feel he's cleaned up the place" (Bernstein 2020).

From their longitudinal ethnographic study of Bagong Silang, a large barangay in the city of Caloocan, the anthropologists Steffen Jensen and Karl Hapal (forthcoming) relate the following story told by residents that further illuminates the relationship between community and violence, situating the latter as a constitutive element of the former:

> Kuya Jerry had been killed in a drug bust. He was the cousin of an old informant. Ten police officers had chased him. In the end, he tried to escape by climbing a light pole to get across a wall. He had been shot in the leg in the process before being killed. The police claimed it was self-defense but a neighbor, also an old informant, had seen the incident. "In the leg . . . from below . . . ?" he asked rhetorically. However, everyone knew that Kuya Jerry was on drugs and sometimes sold smaller quantities to support his habit. Asked about the incident, his sister told us, "No, we know who it was and why. We are no longer afraid. We consider it a closed deal." In this way, the family told us that violence had been predictable. They obviously did not agree with the methods, however, ". . . it was no surprise that Jerry died," as the mother continued with grief in her voice.

Here, Jerry's execution under the usual pretext that he fought back (nanlaban) is met with a mixture of skepticism and resignation. Recognizing the excessive violence of the police, Jerry's relatives and neighbors nonetheless cling to a narrative that sees his death as necessary and unavoidable. He was a drug user, he knew the risks he faced, and so his death was simply a matter of time. "We consider it a closed deal," his sister says and in so doing reframes his death as the price for restoring order in the community. Fear as the condition of possibility for living together in a time of war is similarly echoed in the accounts of other residents of Bagong Silang as relayed by another anthropologist, Anna Warburg:

Many people would insist that it was much safer now. Inday, one of our oldest informants, assured us, "Things are much changed now. Before there were too many drug *adik* and we couldn't move at night. There was this fear. Now it is much better. We can walk up and down and feel safe. . . ." The insistence on it being safer, even in the midst of violence, is what allows people to go on living normal lives. Yes, it is violent. People die. But it is those people, the *adik* and the pusher, not me and my family. . . . [I]t works on the premise that some people around here deserve to die. (Warburg and Jensen 2018, 81)

Seen from the ground up, extrajudicial killings are regarded by residents as disconcerting yet reassuring. They have the effect of cleansing the community of "adiks" who are seen as the sources of disorder and fear. The drug war, by contrast, introduces a different kind of fear, one that seeks to restore safety through violence directed at addicts. There is, then, something clarifying about the violence of the war insofar as it seeks to separate the deserving population from those who are undeserving, making the former's life dependent on the latter's death. It thus seeks to re-create a sense of community predicated on the exclusion of the accursed other whose disposability defines the limits of one's security.

How so? Is the dialectic of fear and security an effect of the drug war, or is that what the drug war builds upon? How does violence come to structure, though not wholly determine, the making of community? What does it take to live in close proximity and comity with one's neighbors? And do the practices of making community also bring with them the very means for its undoing?

Intimacy and Autoimmunity

In his classic work on nationalism, Benedict Anderson remarked on the paradoxical nature of the nation as an "imagined community," at once limited and sovereign. It is built on the circulation of novels and newspapers as well as legal fictions of equality and inclusion that transcend local identifications, yet held together by contested symbols that seek to suppress and manage social differences. In this sense, we can think of the nationalist imaginary as constitutive of a community amid anonymity. Members of the nation will never meet each other face to face, Anderson says, but through language, print media, and various other institutions, come to share a confidence in their existence within a common polity moving inexorably toward an open-ended future (Anderson 2006). Or do they?

The recent global rise of authoritarianism seems to suggest otherwise. Nationalist discourses have been used to create seemingly unbridgeable divisions, sharpening differences within the nation. The authoritarian imaginary instead views the nation as a site of perpetual struggles between the forces of good and evil, understood as those who are insiders versus outsiders, lawful and deserving citizens versus poor, racialized criminals, between those who are gendered and sexualized as "normal" and those who are perverse and therefore "abnormal." For this reason, the authoritarian vision of the nation, as we saw in chapter 4, sees it as a site of unfinished civil wars. It deploys violence in all its forms as a way of governing an irreducibly pluralized population. As we've seen in the case of Duterte, the figure of the "drug personality" sums up all that threatens the integrity of the nation, requiring the exercise of extreme measures. Under Duterte, the necropolitical undergirds the biopolitical, as death becomes a means of governing life. But how is this possible? How do people come to accept the grim terms of this authoritarian imaginary? To answer this, we need to turn to the material and symbolic conditions for making community, especially in places where the drug war has been most intensely waged.

Let's start with the organization of space in these communities. In impoverished barangays, living spaces are organized into highly compact and crowded residences — slums that warehouse people into a surplus and highly disposable population. From the outside, slums are usually seen by the respectable middle and upper classes as sites of disorder, places that are *magulo*, or dangerous, and thus in need of policing. As products of the violence inherent in the history of displacement and the conditions of precarity, slums exist as kinds of penal colonies, constraining residents to forge bonds of protection and mutual aid. In their ethnographic study of Bagong Silang, which I have relied upon in this and the previous chapter, Jensen, Hapal, and Warburg (drawing in turn from the work of Curato 2016 and Kusaka 2017b) point out that the spatial and economic realities of the barangay require the formation of what they've termed a "community of intimacy" (Jensen and Hapal forthcoming; Warburg 2017). Given the flimsy housing materials and the tight pathways that serve as the only public spaces in Bagong Silang, residents are forced to live in close proximity, within the hearing and seeing of everything that happens to their neighbors. Privacy is at a premium, so everything is exposed to public knowledge. Additionally, gossip, or *tsismis*, and

Figure C.1. Narrow passageways serve as the only public spaces in slums and compel residents to live in communities of intimacy. Market 3 in Manila. Photo by Jes Aznar.

rumor pass as information to fill in the gaps of knowledge about others and to keep everyone on guard about what others think of them. As Jensen and Hapal put it, intimacy is both "compelled and compelling." According to one of their informants, "We have no choice. We live here and they [our neighbors] live here as well. We just need to get along with them" (Jensen and Hapal forthcoming).

The practice of "getting along" is commonly referred to in Tagalog as *pa-kikisama*, from the root word *sama*, together. It is a form of "affective rela-tionality" that entails generosity, friendliness, and hospitality, sustained by networks of reciprocal obligations. Pakikisama is thus less a "value" than it is a highly contingent and shifting set of practices that allow people to seek companionship and protection while enjoining mutual aid under con-ditions of scarcity and the constant threat of displacement. For this reason, pakikisama is never settled but must always be performed through such acts as ritual drinking and gambling—especially among men—sharing la-bor and resources, extending loans, contributing emotional and material support to important events such as illnesses, weddings, births, and funer-als, among other things. The obligation to make pakikisama, however, re-quires that one be in a position to do so. Those with more resources usually have small businesses, both legal and illegal. They also enjoy the patronage of local politicians and the police by serving in the local barangay justice system as tanods, or security agents. Most of these are older men and some women, that is, thirty-five and above in a population where the majority of people are between the ages of eighteen and twenty-five. Their ability to make pakikisama is a function of their ability to engage in *diskarte*, the highly admired skill of improvising and making do that allows one to find the resources with which to help those in need, pay off loans, bribe the police, and provide for one's family and friends, thereby enlarging one's influence and garnering respect from others.

The intimacy of community thus creates inequality and hierarchy. It privileges those who are adept at performing pakikisama and making diskarte. These are predominantly older men who have managed to accumulate resources and cultivate the skills needed for forging connections and patronage among those in authority. For this reason, as Jensen and Hapal point out, intimacy is predicated on a patriarchal gerontocracy. As exemplars of pakikisama and diskarte, older men, by virtue of their membership in the barangay justice system, also feel entitled to enforce order, disciplining younger men and uppity women who they see as falling short of the demands of intimacy. Discipline in this case includes violent measures to keep those below in line and contain their potential for disrupting community. Generosity and mutual aid come with the violent imperative to secure the boundaries of intimacy exercised by a "patriarchy of the street" (Bourgois 2003). Such violence also serves to divide the spaces of community between those who belong and those who don't by virtue of their failure to participate in pakikisama. The violence of intimacy constitutes a policing power that secures the line between those who are part of and those who are apart from community, between those who contribute to the bonds of friendship and hospitality and those who are potential threats to their functioning.

That intimacy faces two ways is not surprising. It holds the private up for public regard even as it demarcates an inside that must be kept safe from the outside. It is sustained by amity that is grounded in hostility and fosters conditional hospitality that sets rules and relies on the enforcement of the inhospitable. The drug war is built precisely upon the contradictory structures of the community of intimacy, exposing its doubleness as both a "resource and a risk" (Jensen and Hapal forthcoming). Beginning with compiling drug lists required to conduct police operations, intimate knowledge of one's neighbors along with the workings of gossip and rumor allow for the targeting of suspects by the police. The collaboration of mostly older male barangay officials with the police and vigilantes weaponizes community into the site for counterinsurgency as suspected enemies—those who are disruptive and fail to perform pakikisama—are identified for execution. The drug war thus did not determine the violence inherent in community; it amplified and transformed it by exploiting existing hierarchies and inequalities. It generated a fear beyond the everyday fear of living precariously under threat of constant displacement. It presented this other fear as a kind of regenerative violence necessary for the removal of the undeserving who endanger community. In other words, the drug war is a violent event that intensified the violence already inherent in the structuring of the community of intimacy. It exposed something about the material and symbolic constitution of community itself: its autoimmunity.

Autoimmunity is usually defined in biological terms as the condition of becoming immune to one's own self, as if one harbored foreign bodies that threatened one's health. In response, the "immune system that is meant to protect the body's organs produces antibodies that attack normal body tissues. Autoimmune is when your body attacks itself. It sees part of your body as a disease and tries to combat it" (American Academy of Allergy, Asthma, and Immunology 2020). If we think of community as a living body, we see in our examples above how its existence is dependent on the very things that endanger it: the acts of conviviality, reciprocity, conditional generosity—in a word, intimacy (Derrida 2003). "Compelled and compelling" (Jensen and Hapal forthcoming), intimacy is the condition of possibility for life under conditions of neoliberal precarity. Yet, as we saw, it also opens life to the risk of exclusion, displacement, and death. It immunizes individuals from the ever-present threats of abandonment and alienation precisely by exposing them to the quotidian violence of gendered and class hierarchies. The autoimmune community thus creates the criminal and therefore disposable other in the very process of guarding its boundaries. Thus do intimacy and impunity go together. Extrajudicial killings from this perspective are less about a violation of human rights than the affirmation of a moral calculus. They confirm that the targeted victim does not belong here, that it is not me, and its death means it no longer poses a threat to my safety. The autoimmunity of community thereby echoes Duterte's genocidal logic. During a briefing on the spread of COVID-19, for example, the president circles back to his usual obsession:

"If you die, that's because I am angry with drugs. That's what I am saying. If you bring me to court or send me to jail, fine, I have no problem. If I serve my country by going to jail, gladly."

While he is open to facing charges, Duterte said he should not be accused of committing "crimes against humanity." "*Kailan pa naging humanity itong p***** i** mga drug na ito* (Since when did these sons of b*****s become part of humanity)?" the President said.

"And how much has been reduced in the use of shabu? I really do not know until now. But we are still in the thick of the fight against shabu," Duterte said.

The President again justified his controversial war on drugs, saying the health and the welfare of the people are "really the paramount concern." He advised parents to supervise and check on their children so they would not be addicted to drugs. (Romero 2020)

To save the nation, it is necessary to kill its enemies, those bodies rendered inhuman and foreign within the body politic. Duterte thus folds the discourse of the imagined community built on notions of sacrifice and mutual caring into the vernacular language of intimacy, promising unremitting vengeance on those antibodies that menace the community. Small wonder, then, that despite mixed feelings regarding the killings, the drug war as such continues to enjoy widespread approval, especially among the poor. If the drug war is a war against the poor, as many of its critics have insisted, "it is a war," as Jensen and Hapal point out, "where the poor, willingly or unwillingly, have been made complicit. While the onslaught may have emerged from the outside, it reverberated through the resettlement site, widening and recasting existing conflictual fault lines in quite devastating ways" (Jensen and Hapal forthcoming).

Securing life by exposing one to death, the autoimmune community thus has the ironic effect of immunizing Duterte and those who support him from the critics of the drug war. The thousands of deaths and their traumatizing effects can be rationalized as the price one pays for assuring security. The terms of intimacy, pakikisama, and the means with which to practice it, the skills of diskarte, are plunged into crisis by the drug war. Mutual trust is replaced by suspicion, while the predictability of violence is supplanted by its sudden, arbitrary explosions. But from the perspective of those who suffer its effects, such violence has a clear source and can be traced back to a singular father-sovereign. Delusional, menacing, and vulgar, he speaks in the familiar accent of intimacy, reveling in the obscenity of death as the transformative cure for what sickens society. In this way, the authoritarian imaginary infects as much as it is infected by the practices of making community.

Seen from below, authoritarianism is woven into, even as it is profoundly disruptive of, intimacy. Is there some way of opposing it and offering a non-authoritarian alternative? As this book goes to press, there have been all sorts of speculation from critics of Duterte about who or what might replace him. These range from the current reformist vice president, Leni Robredo, to the son of the former dictator, Bongbong Marcos. Pundits have placed their bets on a range of political figures: Sarah Duterte, the president's daughter, who is currently mayor of Davao City; Senator Manny Pacquiao, the boxing champion turned conservative Christian; and Isko Moreno, the former movie star now serving as mayor of Manila, who seems to enjoy the support of some of the wealthiest oligarchs in the country. Meanwhile, the gerontocracy of the Communist Party of the Philippines continues to hold on to its Stalinist policies and wage what has been a futile "protracted people's war" for well over half a century, even as the military pursues its brutal counterinsurgency war against communist-tagged sympathizers such as peasant organizers, labor union leaders, human rights lawyers, and the like. Human rights advocates continue to call attention to killings, but these have had little effect on the administration and now barely register on the world stage. The Catholic Church, meanwhile, has vigorously opposed the drug war but finds itself outflanked by Duterte's attacks on clerical immorality and corruption. Within Congress and the Senate, there have been a handful of principled voices that have steadfastly criticized Duterte's policies, but they, too, have been overwhelmed by the majority's unstinting support of his rule and, in the case of Senator Leila de Lima, imprisoned indefinitely. Finally, his fiercest critics on and off social media admit that the sources of opposition, while determined, remain fairly weak. Without a social movement or political machinery to back them up, many of these oppositional figures have few prospects for challenging his rule and possible successors.

Their weakness, I suspect, stems from the fact that they are unable to account for, much less challenge, the autoimmune construction of community on which authoritarianism flourishes. Some even contribute unwittingly to its propagation by seeking to return to conventional notions of morality, decency, and patronage. Others invoke liberal democratic notions such as human rights and the rule of law without any sense of the vast cognitive and linguistic distance that separates such concepts from the vernacular practices of communities of intimacy. The paradox, which is also the tragedy, of the imagined community of the nation is that it is predicated on colonial legacies of policing as counterinsurgency; on class, gender, and sexual hierarchies as a precondition for comradeship and solidarity; on socioeconomic inequality to underwrite order but also to spur disorder that then calls for discipline; and on violence, both institutional and extrajudicial, as ways of regulating and enforcing a social order that is always in the process of being undone. The drug war is but one event in a series of other wars that are both symptom and cure for the illnesses that bedevil even as they constitute the nation. With Duterte's scheduled exit in 2022, the drug war and its authoritarian appeal will not end but will most likely continue by other means and through other figures, given the immunizing effects of the autoimmune community.

"An Infinite Amount of Hope but Not for Us"

Where, then, lies hope? How to deal with the autoimmune structuring of communities of intimacy? By eradicating the predatory police? Getting rid of pakikisama and diskarte and the inevitable corruption and violence they inspire? Doing away with patriarchy and patronage? Transforming residents from impoverished slum dwellers into middle-class homeowners with gainful jobs and happy families? Waging a social revolution that would require not only a change in the political regime but also radical transformations in the redistribution of wealth, the culture of impunity, the gendered, generational, and sexual structures of authority, the basis of community solidarity, and so much more—knowing that such periodic attempts in the past have met with a long history of failure?

It is perhaps fitting that I end this book on a deeply pessimistic note. Pessimism in this case is not a luxury but a way of coming to grips with reality and embracing rather than spurning tragedy. For this reason, it is not an admission of defeat. Pessimism can never be absolute. How can it be when it is based on the inconclusiveness, which is to say, on the persistent openness to and contingency of historical possibilities? In this sense, we can think of pessimism not as the opposite of hope but in fact its oblique affirmation, particularly with regard to the condition of the autoimmune community. "Autoimmunity is not an absolute ill or evil," Jacques Derrida writes. "It enables an exposure to the other, to what and to who comes—which means that it must remain incalculable. Without autoimmunity, with absolute immunity, nothing would ever happen or arrive; we would no longer wait, await, or expect, no longer expect one another, or expect any event" (Derrida 2003, 152).

With Duterte, we see the figure of the sovereign trickster, one whose seeming immunity derives from the autoimmune community, where intimacy enables impunity while crumbling in its wake. It is a figure that is at once murderous and suicidal, revolutionary and counterrevolutionary, populist and dictatorial. Yet this sovereign immunity cannot last, even if it will not be the last. Dependent on the autoimmunity of community, it remains open and vulnerable. To what, to whom, when, and under what conditions, we will perhaps never fully know. This not knowing and not being able to calculate, much less program change, is precisely what Nietzsche calls the "pessimism of strength . . . this pessimism of the future" that can harbor hope and bring about another kind of event that is always yet to come. Whereas optimism sees historical tragedy as a source of moral lessons that points inevitably to happy outcomes, pessimism opens up a road to other futures in all their uncertain volatility. It is less a balm than a hammer with which to unmake and remake the world.[1]

From another time and another place, Kafka comes to mind. In a story recounted by Walter Benjamin, Kafka was asked by his friend Max Brod what he thought about the decline of Europe and the human race. Kafka responded: "We are nihilistic thoughts, suicidal thoughts that come into God's head." Max Brod then said, "This reminded me at first of the Gnostic view of life: God as the evil demiurge, the world as his Fall." "Oh no," said Kafka, "our world is only a bad mood of God, a bad day of his." "Then there is hope outside this manifestation of the world that we know," Brod ventured. Kafka smiled. "Oh, plenty of hope, an infinite amount of hope—but not for us" (Benjamin 1968, 61).

So it seems we continue to be a bad mood of God's. And Duterte one of His more nihilistic thoughts. But only for now, and only for us.

Postscript

Can intimacy be separated from impunity? Is there a cure for the autoimmunity that haunts community?

One possibility is the community pantry. As this book goes to press, there has been the sudden, unexpected mushrooming of so-called community pantries throughout the country ("Community Pantries Sprouting All Over" 2021) Started by an ordinary citizen, Ana Patricia Non, in the felicitously named Maginahawa Street (i.e., comfort street) in a barangay in Quezon City in mid-April, community pantries have spread to many parts of the archipelago. With the slogan "*Magbigay ayon sa kakayahan, kumuha batay sa pangangailangan*" (Give what you can, take what you need), the pantries are based on generosity and mutual aid. People in the neighborhood are encouraged to take what they need—items such as rice, vegetables, canned goods, bread, noodles, face masks and the like—and donate whatever they can, from cash to other goods. Informal and de-centralized, the emergence of community pantries amid the hardships of the pandemic seems at once spontaneous and a cause for hope. As Non put it, "Free to come and go *lang po kayo*" (People are free to come and go in the pantry), "*Kung ano 'yung sobra 'nyo sa bahay, puwede 'nyo pong iwan; kung ano 'yung kailangan 'nyo, wala kayong bigas, puwede po kayong kumuha*" (Whatever extra you have at home, you can leave; and whatever you need, rice for instance, you can take) ("Pagod na ako sa inaction" 2021) This reflects a kind of humanitarianism often referred to in Tagalog as "bayanihan," a civic spirit built on the vernacular notions of pakikisama with diskarte. It points to the more benevolent aspect of intimacy that thrives precisely amid anonymity and thereby escapes impunity. Non stressed the collective nature of community pantries, eschewing credit for starting her own: "*Ako lang po 'yung nag set up ng community pantry, pero community effort naman po ito. Hindi ko po kinukuha 'yung full credit, katulong ko po 'yung buong community ng hawa*" (I only set up the community pantry, but this is a community effort. I don't get full credit, the whole Maginhawa community helped me). "*Normal sa mga tao na magtulungan*" (It's normal for people to be helpful) ("Pagod na ako sa inaction" 2021).

Other organizers of community pantries have echoed this collective ethos and anonymous generosity. A business owner in Paniqui, Tarlac province, for example, while filling a cart with eggs, canned goods, bananas, sugar, sweet potatoes, instant noodles, rice and vegetables said, "We are all affected [by this pandemic] but some of us are still well-off. Life is full of 'give-and-take' and that's literally what is happening. Some people will donate food and others will [benefit from the] bounty" ("From Boracay to Ora, Pantries Keep on Giving" 2021).

A spirit of reciprocal generosity has thus characterized the workings of community pantries. Poor people patiently line up to get what they need with little evidence of hoarding, while returning to render whatever little they have—chicharon, malungay leaves, packs of noodles. Others have contributed cash, including those with relatives working overseas, while still others give their time, volunteering to repackage goods and keep order and maintain safety protocols among the crowd. The "bayanihan" ethos generated by the pantries is contagious: "'Pag may isang gumawa ng mabuti, lahat gagaya" (When one person does a good deed, everyone else follows), as one volunteer remarked ("Pagod na ako sa inaction" 2021). Pantries fill the enormous needs opened up by the pandemic and the government's failure to provide services for the starving or the unemployed. They attract a variety of people, ranging from Muslim construction workers to scavengers, single mothers, manicurists, former housekeepers, and stroke victims ("Community Pantries Offer Reprieve" 2021).

The remarkable popularity of community pantries has inevitably attracted the attention of the government. Egged on by pro-Duterte internet trolls as well as by members of the National Task Force to End Local Communist Armed Conflict (NTF-ELCAC), the pantries have been red-tagged, its volunteers accused of being recruiters for the NPA, or New People's Army, the armed wing of the Communist Party. That officials could read insurgent possibilities into the pantries is an indication of its populist nature that operates outside of the authoritarian populism characteristic of the Duterte regime. As a truly grassroots movement, it eludes control from those on top while tapping into the support of local government officials who see them as a way of easing pressure from people's demands for aid. Again from Non: "The [community pantries] have no hidden agenda. Their only goal is to get food . . . and to refill the pantry" ("Community Pantries Offer Reprieve 2021). If the community pantries offer hope, it is not one based on the dialectic of security and fear, as evinced in the ruthless drug war but on a kind of democratic populism. It thrives on generosity without conditions, on reciprocity with neither the shame (hiya) of failure nor interest in matching and surpassing what one receives. "Kung buong community ang tutulong masu-sustain siya, hindi imposible. . . . Hangga't may nangangailangan, hangga't may nagbibigay rin," Non says. (If the whole community works together, it will be sustained. It's not impossible. It will work as long as there are people in need and there are those willing to give) ("Pagod na ako sa inaction" 2021).

Just how long or sustainable community pantries will be is difficult to say. As of this writing, there are more than three hundred that have sprouted all over the country. Pamphlets have appeared on how start your own pantry along with guides on what to do if the police come around to profile and red-tag you. Local governments continue to be generally supportive of the pantries and have begun to enforce rules for social distancing as the pandemic continues to spread ("Quezon City Issues Community Pantry Guidelines" 2021). Meanwhile, the Duterte regime has pulled back on red-tagging participants, at least for now.

As a counterpoint to the pessimistic conclusion of this book, community pantries instantiate the community of anonymity. Each one comes to the aid of everyone, regardless of who they are, not out of fear or in the name of security but for the sake of fostering a common life. It is a community of anonymity that might just be an antidote for the autoimmune community.

NOTES

INTRODUCTION. **Prismatic Histories**

1. By "imaginary," I mean something midway between "necessary fictions" and "real abstractions" that allows one to function in daily life. To speak about an "authoritarian imaginary" is to ask how someone like Duterte imagines himself when addressing other people, what others imagine him to be doing when he addresses them, and what they imagine themselves to be when confronted with him or his image. The fictional texture of the imaginary makes it unstable and fundamentally ambiguous, open to different interpretations subject to conflict and up for control (Johnston 2018).

CHAPTER TWO. **Marcos, Duterte, and the Predicaments of Neoliberal Citizenship**

1. There are numerous accounts of EDSA and People Power. Some of the more illuminating works can be found in Abinales and Amoroso (2017); Anderson (1988); Claudio (2014); Kerkvliet and Mojares (1992); Mazanilla and Hau (2016); Stuart-Santiago (2013).

2. On Ferdinand Marcos and martial law, there are surprisingly few studies and not a single book-length work that treat the entirety of the regime. Some of the more useful ones include Abinales and Amoroso (2017); Anderson (1988); Bonner (1987); McCoy (2009b); Mojares (2016); Seagrave (1988); Thompson (1995); Wurfel (1988). For a highly compelling family memoir of the Marcos years, see Quimpo and Quimpo (2012).

3. Along similar lines, see the other short film by Mendoza, *Father TVC*, https://www .facebook.com/watch/?t=3&v=1428333113863012.

4. See Duterte's campaign ad from 2015, https://www.youtube.com/watch?v =HjEg83ATfuQ.

SKETCHES II. *Motherland* **and the Biopolitics of Reproductive Health**

1. According to World Bank data, maternal mortality rates as of 2017 are at 121 per 100,000 live births, compared to the United States at 18 and Finland at 3 per 100,000.

These numbers actually represent an improvement from 2012, when maternal mortality rates were 221 per 100,000. https://data.worldbank.org/indicator/SH.STA.MMRT ?locations=PH. See also Shahani (2015).

2. The Church has consistently opposed any form of artificial contraception. As Bishop Gilbert Garcera of the Naga City diocese put it: "The huge Philippine population could be part of God's plans for Filipinos to be caregivers to ageing nations whose populations had become stagnant. . . . Many Filipina women would make good wives for foreigners in countries that have low population" (quoted in Danguilan 2018, 38). Here, pastoralism itself becomes a kind patriarchal neoliberal strategy to procure the commodified care and racialized companionship of Filipina women to the world.

CHAPTER THREE. **Duterte's Phallus**

1. "In Davao, I used to do it personally. Just to show to the [police] that if I can do it, why can't you?" he said. "I [would] go around in Davao with a motorcycle . . . and I would just patrol the streets and looking for trouble also. I was really looking for an encounter to kill," he said. See Rauhala (2016).

2. "While a Senate inquiry was looking into his eldest son's possible involvement in drug smuggling, Duterte told reporters, 'I said before my order was: "If I have children who are into drugs, kill them so people will not have anything to say"'; Duterte said in a speech on Wednesday night in front of government workers at the presidential palace in Manila, 'So I told Pulong [Paolo's nickname]: "My order is to kill you if you are caught. And I will protect the police who kill you, if it is true,"' he said" ("Philippines: Duterte Says" 2017).

CHAPTER FOUR. **The Sovereign Trickster**

A shorter version of this chapter was published in the *Journal of Asian Studies* 78, no. 1 (February 2019). This version has been substantially revised and expanded.

1. However, in subsequent statements, he said he was only joking. But as we saw in chapter 3, jokes for Duterte are always tendentious and so contain an element of truth. Humor is an important tactic in Duterte's struggle to maintain power. His stories and jokes are always full of aggression and murderous desire.

2. For histories of Philippine state formation that emphasize the dialectics of insurgency and counterinsurgency, see Abinales and Amoroso (2017); Coronel (2017b); Kramer (2006); Lara (2014); Lara and Schoofs (2016); McCoy (2009b); Sidel (1999a).

3. The Philippine Drug Enforcement Agency puts the number of drug-addicted people at about 1.8 million, whereas Duterte claims without any proof that it is closer to between four and five million. For a summary of these contending claims, see Lasco (2016).

4. For detailed accounts of the drug war, see Ateneo Human Rights Center (2017); Baldwin, Marshall, and Mogato (2017); Curato (2017a); Eng (2017); Evangelista

and Gabuco (2016–18); Human Rights Watch (2017); "The Kill List" (2016); Symmes (2017).

5. For accounts of funerals, see Almendral and Dean (2017); "As Corpses Mount" (2017); Freeman (2017); Gavilan and Tomacruz (2017); Lamb (2016); Macaraig (2016); Morin (2017); "Philippine Police" (2017); Tomacruz and Gavilan (2017).

6. Despite their importance in Philippine politics, there is as yet no book-length study of university fraternities. But, as Patricio Abinales suggests, there is a strong connection between the workings of fraternities and gangs, especially in their hypermasculine sociality, use of ritualized violence, and fierce demands for loyalty and obedience. See his three-part series (Abinales 2015).

7. For accounts of Duterte's Davao, see "Duterte Paid Us" (2017); Heydarian (2018); Miller (2018); Paddock (2017); Ranada (2017); "The Rodrigo Duterte Interview" (2016); Tiefenthaler (2017); Villamor (2017). On Mindanao, see "You Can Die Anytime" (2009).

8. Accounts of Duterte's joking abound. See, for example, Bacungan (2017); Café (n.d.); "Cheers, Disgust" (2018); "Palace to Media" (2016); "Philippines Rodrigo Duterte" (2016); "President Duterte" (2017). See also chapter 3 of this book.

9. The reference here is Ernst Kantorowiz's classic book *The King's Two Bodies* (1957). I owe this insight into Duterte as the king with multiple organs to Tak Fujitani.

10. Tony Lucero also reminded me about the tradition of Native American trickster tales. In such tales, tricksters take the shape of animals that mediate between the sacred and the profane. They are clever in the extreme and so are capable of both good and bad deeds. Nothing could be more different from the racialized and sexualized figure of the blackface minstrel who frames blackness as a vehicle for asserting white supremacy while satirizing white feminine bourgeois conventions of respectability. Trump's tricksterism would appear to descend from the latter rather than the former.

11. Minority cultural repertoires are in turn built on the complex and critical mimicry of dominant European and Afro-Caribbean-Latin American-Asian and other forms. Indeed, it would be interesting to read blackface minstrelsy alongside colonial and postcolonial forms of mimetic critique and expropriation and the corresponding tricksterisms that accompany such acts. The writings of Bhabha (1984) and Fanon (2006), and the films of Spike Lee also come to mind. In my other works, I prefer the term "translation" (and its related figures) to delineate mimicry that gives rise to displacement and distortion, bringing with them the subversive possibilities of tricksterism, to which Duterte and Trump would appear as accidental and perverse heirs. See, for example, Rafael (2016).

CHAPTER FIVE. **Photography and the Biopolitics of Fear**

A shorter version of this chapter originally appeared in *positions: asia critique* 28, no. 4 (November 2020). This version has been substantially revised and expanded.

1. The literature on trauma is enormous and varied. Those that have been important for this essay include Freud (1990); Laplanche and Pontalis (1988), who write that

trauma "carries three ideas: the idea of a violent shock, the idea of a wound and the idea of consequences affecting the whole organization" of the organism (465). See also Baer (2002); Caruth (1996); Fassin and Rechtman (2009); Ivy (2008); Siegel (1998, 2006, 2011).

2. It is this near-death experience at the basis of the Kantian notion of the sublime that arguably informs Western aesthetics and the formation of the modern Westernized subject (i.e., both those in the West and those in formerly colonized areas where Western notions have had significant impact, e.g., the Philippines). See Hertz (1985); Siegel (2006).

CONCLUSION. **Intimacy and the Autoimmune Community**

1. Nietzsche wrote about the "pessimism of strength" as a critique of Socratic optimism on the one hand, and Schopenhauer's notion of "romantic pessimism" on the other. In *The Gay Science*, he writes, "That there still could be an altogether different kind of pessimism . . . this premonition and vision belongs to me as inseparable from me. . . . I call this pessimism of the future—for it comes! I see it coming!—Dionysian pessimism" (Nietzsche 1974, Aphorism 370). Joshua Foa Dienstag's gloss on this Dionysian pessimism is suggestive for our purposes: "The pessimism of strength involves the use of pessimism as a hammer—a philosophical technology—to destroy and to build. Pessimism is both a critique of existing moralities and an instrument in the construction of an alternative past form of morality. Far from ending in despair and resignation, Nietzsche considers the moment when 'my type of pessimism appears, the great noon . . . [the] great point of departure.' Pessimism may not be the end of the journey but all roads to the future lead through it, and it may be necessary to remain pessimistic for 'a few millennia'" (Dienstag 2001, 933).

REFERENCES

Abad, Michelle. 2020. "Looking Back: Campaigns to Set Up a Revolutionary Government in the Philippines." *Rappler*, August 27. https://rappler.com/newsbreak/iq/campaigns-set-up-revolutionary-government-philippines.

Abinales, Patricio. 2015. "UP's Gangland Wars: A Historical Note." *Rappler*, June 27. https://www.rappler.com/thought-leaders/97510-up-gangland-wars-historical-note.

Abinales, Patricio, and Donna Amoroso. 2017. *State and Society in the Philippines*, 2nd ed. Lanham, MD: Rowman and Littlefield.

"After Drawing Flak, Duterte Makes New Rape Joke." 2017. *Rappler*, July 1. https://rappler.com/nation/duterte-rape-joke-speech-diplomats-congratulate.

Agamben, Giorgio. 1995. *Homo Sacer: Sovereign Power and Bare Life*. Translated by Daniel Heller-Roazen. Stanford, CA: Stanford University Press.

Agoncillo, Teodoro. 1956. *Revolt of the Masses: The Story of Bonifacio and the Katipunan*. Quezon City: University of the Philippines Press.

Agoncillo, Teodoro. 1960. *Malolos and the Crisis of the Republic*. Quezon City: University of the Philippines Press.

Almendral, Aurora. 2017. "Duterte's Free Birth-Control Order Is Latest Skirmish with Catholic Church." *New York Times*, January 27. https://www.nytimes.com/2017/01/27/world/asia/philippines-free-contraception-duterte.html.

Almendral, Aurora. 2018. "In Duterte's Philippines, Having a Beer Can Land You in Jail." *New York Times*, July 21. https://www.nytimes.com/2018/07/21/world/asia/philippines-duterte-crackdown.html.

Almendral, Aurora. 2020. "Why the Philippines Has So Many Teen Moms." *NPR*, August 21. https://www.npr.org/sections/goatsandsoda/2020/08/21/787921856/photos-the-hidden-lives-of-teen-moms.

Almendral, Aurora, and Adam Dean. 2017. "In Philippine Drug War, Death Rituals Substitute for Justice." *National Geographic*, February 2. https://www.nationalgeographic.com/photography/proof/2017/02/philippine-drug-war/.

American Academy of Allergy, Asthma, and Immunology. 2020. "Autoimmune Disease Definition." https://www.aaaai.org/conditions-and-treatments/conditions-dictionary/autoimmune-disease.

Anderson, Benedict. 1988. "Cacique Democracy in the Philippines: Origins and Dreams." *New Left Review*, May/June, 3–31.

Anderson, Benedict. 1998. "Elections in Southeast Asia." In *The Specters of Comparison: Nationalism, Southeast Asia and the World*, 265–84. London: Verso.

Anderson, Benedict. 2006. *Imagined Communities: Reflections on the Origins and Spread of Nationalism*, rev. ed. London: Verso.

Aquino, Belinda. 1987. *Politics of Plunder: The Philippines under Marcos*. Quezon City: University of the Philippines, College of Public Administration.

Arcangel, Xianne. 2019. "DILGs to Require Villages to Monitor CCTVs 24/7." *CNN Philippines*, December 15. https://www.cnn.ph/news/2019/12/15/DILG-barangay-monitoring-CCTV-248.html.

"Are Duterte's Multi-Million-Peso Intel Funds Achieving Their Purpose?" 2017. *Rappler*, December 18. https://r3.rappler.com/move-ph/issues/budget-watch/185617-duterte-confidential-intelligence-funds-2018-budget-part-1.

Arguelles, Cleve Kevin. 2017. "Duterte's Other War: The Battle for EDSA People Power's Memory." In *A Duterte Reader: Critical Essays on Duterte's Early Presidency*, edited by Nicole Curato, 267–87. Ithaca, NY: Cornell University Press.

"As Corpses Mount, Undertakers in the Philippines Struggle to Cope with Duterte's Deadly Drug War." 2016. *South China Morning Post*, December 9. https://www.scmp.com/news/asia/southeast-asia/article/2053237/corpses-mount-undertakers-philippines-struggle-cope.

Ateneo Human Rights Center. 2017. "Summary and Extrajudicial Killings in the Philippines." https://www.ateneo.edu/sites/default/files/attached-files/Summary%20and%20Extrajudicial%20Killings%20in%20the%20Philippines%20%28AHRC%29%20-%20UPR%203rd%20Cycle.pdf.

Ateneo School of Government, De La Salle Philippines, University of the Philippines–Diliman, and the Stabile Center for Investigative Journalism. 2018. "The Drug Archive: A Data-Driven Examination of the Philippine Anti-Drug Campaign." https://drugarchive.ph/.

"At Yolanda Anniversary, Duterte Teases Robredo about Short Skirt." 2016. *Rappler*, November 9. https://www.rappler.com/nation/151751-duterte-teases-robredo-yolanda-anniversary.

Azoulay, Ariella. 2008. *The Civil Contract of Photography*. Translated by Rela Mazali and Ruvik Danieli. New York: Zone.

Bacungan, V. J. 2017. "Duterte: 3 in 5 of My Statements Are Just Nonsense." *CNN Philippines*, February 9. https://cnnphilippines.com/news/2017/02/09/duterte-statement-nonsense.html.

Baer, Ulrich. 2002. *Spectral Evidence: The Photography of Trauma*. Cambridge, MA: MIT Press.

Bakhtin, Mikhail. 1968. *Rabelais and His World*. Translated by Hélène Iswolsky. Cambridge, MA: MIT Press.

Bakhtin, Mikhail. 1981. *The Dialogic Imagination: Four Essays*. Edited by Michael Holquist. Translated by Caryl Emerson and Michael Holquist. Austin: University of Texas Press.

Baldwin, Claire, and Andrew C. Marshall. 2017. "How a Secretive Police Squad Racked Up Kills in Duterte's Drug War." *Reuters*, December 19. https://www.reuters.com /investigates/special-report/philippines-drugs-squad/.

Baldwin, Claire, Andrew C. Marshall, and Manuel Mogato. 2017. "Duterte's War: Inside the Bloody Drugs Crackdown in the Philippines." *Reuters*, June 29. https://www .reuters.com/investigates/section/philippines-drugs/.

Barthes, Roland. 1981. *Camera Lucida: Reflections on Photography*. Translated by Richard Howard. New York: Hill and Wang.

Bello, Walden. 2021. "Mr. President, the Issue Is Incompetence, the Solution Is Resignation." *Rappler*, April 21. https://www.rappler.com/voices/thought-leaders/opinion -mr-president-the-issue-is-competence-the-solution-is-resignation.

Bello, Walden, David Kinley, and Elaine Elinson. 1982. *Development Debacle: The World Bank in the Philippines*. San Francisco: Institute for Food and Development Policy.

Benjamin, Walter. 1968. *Illuminations: Essays and Reflections*. Translated by Harry Zohn. New York: Harcourt Brace Jovanovich.

Benjamin, Walter. 1969. *Charles Baudelaire: A Lyric Poet in the Era of High Capitalism*. Translated by Harry Zohn. London: Verso.

Benjamin, Walter. 2015. *On Photography*. Edited and translated by Esther Leslie. London: Reaktion.

Berger, John. 2013. "W. Eugene Smith." In *Understanding a Photograph*, edited by Geoff Dyer, 111–17. New York: Penguin,

Bernstein, Richard. 2020. "The Paradox of Rodrigo Duterte." *The Atlantic*, February 22. https://www.theatlantic.com/international/archive/2020/02/philippines-rodrigo -duterte-china/606754/.

Bhabha, Homi. 1984. "Of Mimicry and Men: The Ambivalence of Colonial Discourse." *October* 28:125–33.

"Bill Declaring Marcos' Birthday a Local Holiday Likely to Get Senate Nod, Says Sotto." 2020. *CNN Philippines*, September 3. https://www.cnnphilippines.com/news/2020 /9/3/Senate-Marcos-holiday-Ilocos-Norte-counterpart-bill.html.

Bonner, Raymond. 1987. *Waltzing with a Dictator*. New York: Times Books.

Bourgois, Philippe. 2003. *In Search of Respect: Selling Crack in El Barrio*. Cambridge: Cambridge University Press.

Brown, Wendy. 2019. *In the Ruins of Neoliberalism: The Rise of Antidemocratic Politics in the West*. New York: Columbia University Press.

Buan, Lian. 2021. "Lawyers Should Strike to Demand Supreme Courts Action Against Abusers." *Rappler*, March 9. https://www.rappler.com/nation/lawyers-should-strike -demand-supreme-court-actions-abuses?mc_cid=ab67207a18&mc_eid=2a5b5ba5fe.

Butler, Judith. 2010. *Frames of War: When Is Life Grievable?* London: Verso.

Café. n.d. "Duterte Swearing and Cursing [Video] Compilation." http://blog.pimus.net /video/sNeToSHjWxx818.

Campbell, Timothy, and Adam Sitze, eds. 2013. *Biopolitics: A Reader*. Durham, NC: Duke University Press.

Cannell, Fenella. 1999. *Power and Intimacy in the Christian Philippines*. Cambridge: Cambridge University Press.

Carpio, Audrey N. 2016. "Who's Afraid of Mocha Uson?" *Esquire Philippines*, December 2. https://www.esquiremag.ph/long-reads/profiles/mocha-uson-full-text-a1521 -20161202-lfrm4.

Carson, Thomas, ed. 2002. *The New Catholic Encyclopedia*, 2nd ed. Detroit: Gale Research, Inc.

Caruth, Cathy. 1996. *Unclaimed Experience: Trauma, Narrative and History*. Baltimore: Johns Hopkins University Press.

"Cheers, Disgust as Duterte Kisses OFW in South Korea." 2018. *Rappler*, June 3. https:// www.rappler.com/nation/duterte-ofw-south-korea-kiss-on-the-lips-video-june-3-2018.

Cixous, Hélène. 1976. "The Laugh of the Medusa." Translated by K. Cohen and P. Cohen. *Signs* 1, no. 4: 875–93.

Claudio, Lisandro. 2014. *Taming People's Power: The EDSA Revolutions and Their Contradictions*. Quezon City: Ateneo de Manila University Press.

"Community Pantries Offer Relief for COVID 19 Hardships in the Philippines." 2021. *Washington Post*, April 21. https://www.washingtonpost.com/world/asia_pacific /philippines-pantries-covid-pandemic/2021/04/21/30ad8a5c-a1ac-11eb-b314-2e993 bd83e31_story.html?fbclid=IwARobYEulrywuJxuPPv2sqD9sM5CxKNifiFhZBs45 T1a6vg7y1bKtmTL-lhg.

"Community Pantries Sprouting All Over." 2021. *Philippine Inquirer*. https://newsinfo .inquirer.net/1420782/community-pantries-sprouting-all-over.

Coronel, Sheila. 1993. *Coups, Cults and Cannibals: Chronicles of a Troubled Decade, 1982–1992*. Pasig: Anvil.

Coronel, Sheila. 2017a. "'Have We Opened the Gates of Hell with Our Images?': Reporting on the Philippines Drug War." *The Atlantic*, February 25. https://www .theatlantic.com/international/archive/2017/02/rodrigo-duterte-philippines-drugs -reporters-siaron/517650/.

Coronel, Sheila. 2017b. "Murder as Enterprise: Police Profiteering in Duterte's War against Drugs." In *A Duterte Reader: Critical Essays on Rodrigo Duterte's Early Presidency*, edited by Nicole Curato, 167–98. Ithaca, NY: Cornell University Press.

Coronel, Sheila. 2019a. "Duterte Says Safety Comes at a Price. Filipinos Should Know What That Price Is." *Rappler*, August 20. https://www.rappler.com/thought-leaders /238088-analysis-duterte-safety-has-price-filipinos-should-know?fbclid=IwAR 1vgeZcHEiHBdA_vgMS8KTEMefYhEwtgsVKHiFUYUPVFDJMWK-ngszNz48.

Coronel, Sheila. 2019b. "The Vigilante President: How Duterte's Brutal Populism Conquered the Philippines." *Foreign Affairs*, September/October. https://www.foreign affairs.com/articles/philippines/2019-08-12/vigilante-president.

Coronel, Sheila, Mariel Padilla, and David Mora. 2019. "The Uncounted Dead of Duterte's Drug War." *The Atlantic*, August 19. https://www.theatlantic.com/international /archive/2019/08/philippines-dead-rodrigo-duterte-drug-war/595978/? fbclid=IwAR 1wkk953kGJFP-B_Sd6kHYxxuPoxXMgJ2oHlZo5Jd7cUSYm9DGN7fJrfDw.

Corpuz, Onofre D. 1957. *The Bureaucracy in the Philippines*. Quezon City: Institute of Public Administration, University of the Philippines.

Corrales, Nestor. 2018. "Duterte: I'm in Perpetual Pain." *Inquirer.net*, August 22. https:// newsinfo.inquirer.net/1023947/duterte-im-in-perpetual-pain.

Corrales, Nestor. 2019. "Duterte Mocks Jim Paredes over Video Scandal." *Inquirer.net*, April 12. https://newsinfo.inquirer.net/1106051/duterte-mocks-jim-paredes-over -video-scandal#ixzz6WHtNnjGk.

Corrales, Nestor, and Leila B. Salaverria. 2017. "'That's Good,' Says Duterte on Killing of 32 Bulacan Druggies." *Inquirer.net*, August 16. https://newsinfo.inquirer.net/923267 /president-rodrigo-duterte-drug-war-bulacan-one-time-big-time-operation#ixz z4vM55yLRL.

Cullinane, Michael. 2005. *Ilustrado Politics: Filipino Elite Responses to the United States, 1898–1908*. Quezon City: Ateneo de Manila University Press.

Curato, Nicole. 2016. "Politics of Anxiety, Politics of Hope: Penal Populism and Duterte's Rise to Power." *Journal of Current Southeast Asian Studies* 3:91–109.

Curato, Nicole, ed. 2017a. *A Duterte Reader: Critical Essays on Rodrigo Duterte's Early Presidency*. Ithaca, NY: Cornell University Press.

Curato, Nicole. 2017b. "Flirting with Authoritarian Fantasies? Rodrigo Duterte and the New Terms of Philippine Populism." *Journal of Contemporary Asia* 47:142–53.

Danguilan, Marilen J. 2018. *The RH Bill Story: Contentions and Compromises*. Quezon City: Ateneo de Manila University Press.

David, Randolf. 2013. "Redemocratization in the Wake of the 1986 People Power Revolution: Errors and Dilemmas." In *Introduction to Philippines Politics: Local Politics, the State, National-Building and Democratization*, edited by Maria L. Atienza, 150–63. Quezon City: University of the Philippines Press.

Davis, Nick. 2016. "The $10B Dollar Question: Whatever Happened to the Marcos Millions?" *The Guardian*, May 7. https://www.theguardian.com/world/2016/may /07/10bn-dollar-question-marcos-millions-nick-davies.

de Llobet, Ruth. 2011. "Orphans of Empire: Bourbon Reforms, Constitutional Impasse, and the Rise of Filipino Creole Consciousness in an Age of Revolution." PhD dissertation, University of Wisconsin at Madison.

Derrida, Jacques. 2003. *Rogues: Two Essays on Reason*. Translated by Pascale Anne-Brault and Michael Nas. Stanford, CA: Stanford University Press.

De Vera, Ben O. 2019. "Where's the President? Watching Movie on Netflix, 'Coz It's Saturday, Says DOT Chief." *Inquirer.net*, May 4. https://newsinfo.inquirer.net/1113839 /wheres-the-president-watching-movie-on-netflix-coz-its-saturday-says-dot-chief #ixzz6WM1VW3X4.

Diaz, Ramona. 2017. *Motherland*. CineDiaz. http://www.motherland-film.com/.

"Dick Move: Duterte Brags about Penis in Public Speech." 2019. *Coconuts Manila*, April 7. https://coconuts.co/manila/news/dick-move-duterte-brags-penis-public -speech/.

Dienstag, Joshua Foa. 2001. "Nietzsche's Dionysian Pessimism." *American Political Science Review* 25, no. 4: 923–37.

Duterte, Rodrigo. 2018. "Full Text: State of the Union Address, July." *Rappler*, July 23. https://www.rappler.com/nation/207989-rodrigo-duterte-sona-2018-philippines -speech.

"Duterte: Am I the Death Squad? True." 2015. *Rappler*, May 25. https://rappler.com /nation/elections/rodrigo-duterte-davao-death-squad.

"Duterte Jokes about Viagra Use in Makati Business Club Speech." 2016. *Coconuts Manila*, April 28. https://coconuts.co/manila/news/duterte-jokes-about-viagra -use-speech-makati-business-club-members/.

"Duterte on Fentanyl Use: Felt Like Cloud Nine." 2017. *ABS-CBN News*, February 10. http://news.abs-cbn.com/news/02/10/17/duterte-on-fentanyl-use-felt-like-cloud-nine.

"Duterte: Outrage as Philippines Leader Describes Sexually Abusing Maid." 2018. *BBC News*, December 31. https://www.bbc.com/news/world-asia-46720227.

"Duterte Paid Us to Conduct Davao Death Squad Killings, Claims Cop." 2017. *ABS-CBN News*, February 20. http://news.abs-cbn.com/news/02/20/17/duterte-paid-us-to -conduct-davao-death-squad-killings-claims-cop.

"Duterte's Drug War." 2016. *Rappler*. https://www.rappler.com/previousarticles?filter Meta=Duterte%20drugs%20list.

"Duterte's Net Satisfaction Remains 'Very Good' in 4th Quarter—SWA Poll." 2018. *BusinessWorld*, December 28. https://www.bworldonline.com/dutertes-net-satisfaction -remains-very-good-in-4th-quarter-sws-poll/.

"Duterte Throws Vulgar Word at NDF Consultants in Profanity-Laden SONA." 2017. *GMA News*, July 24. http://www.gmanetwork.com/news/news/nation/619288 /duterte-throws-vulgar-word-at-ndf-consultants-in-profanity-laden-sona/story/.

Edwards, Brent Hayes. 2003. *The Practice of Diaspora: Literature, Translation, and the Rise of Black Internationalism*. Cambridge, MA: Harvard University Press.

Elemia, Camille. 2020. "Explainer: Duterte's High Ratings Despite Poor COVID 19 Response." *Rappler*, October 5. https://www.rappler.com/newsbreak/explainers /explainers-reasons-duterte-high-ratings-poor-covid-19-response.

Eng, Karen Frances. 2017. "A Harrowing Look at the War on Drugs in the Philippines." *TED Fellows*, November 13. https://fellowsblog.ted.com/a-harrowing-look-at-the -war-on-drugs-in-the-philippines-b79b0796d3e4.

Evangelista, Patricia. 2018. "Photographer Ezra Acayan: 'I Am a Human First before I Am a Journalist.'" *Rappler*, May 1. https://r3.rappler.com/newsbreak/videos-podcasts /199107-ezra-acayan-video-press-freedom-philippines-war-on-drugs.

Evangelista, Patricia, and Carlo Gabuco. 2016–18. "The Impunity Series." *Rappler*. https://www.rappler.com/newsbreak/investigative/168712-impunity-series-drug-war -duterte-administration.

Fanon, Frantz. 2006. *Black Skin, White Masks*, rev. ed. New York: Grove Press.

Fassin, Didier, and Richard Rechtman. 2009. *The Empire of Trauma: An Inquiry into the Condition of Victimhood*, translated by Rachel Gomme. Princeton, NJ: Princeton University Press.

Feldman, Allen. 1991. *Formations of Violence: The Narrative of the Body and Political Terror in Northern Ireland*. Chicago: University of Chicago Press.

Fernandez, Luisa, and Rosechin Olfindo. 2011. "Overview of the Philippines' Conditional Cash Transfer Program: The Pantawid Pamilyang Pilipino Program (Pantawid Pamilya)." *World Bank*. https://ideas.repec.org/p/wbk/hdnspu/62879.html.

Fernandez, Maria Carmen, Nastastasja Quijano, and Abbey Pangilinan. 2019. "Examining the Effects of Drug-Related Killings on Philippine Conditional Cash Transfers Beneficiaries in Metro Manila, 2016–2018." doi: 10.13140/RG.2.2.32082.91849/1.

https://www.researchgate.net/publication/336317469_Examining_the_effects_of
_drug-related_killings_on_Philippine_Conditional_Cash_Transfer_beneficiaries
_in_Metro_Manila_2016-2017?channel=doi&linkId=5d9ed966458515dfoae8c184
&showFulltext=true.

Foster, Ann, and Julian Go, eds. 2006. *The American Colonial State in the Philippines: Global Perspectives.* Durham, NC: Duke University Press.

Foucault, Michel. 1975. *Discipline and Punish: The Birth of the Prison.* Translated by Alan Sheridan. New York: Vintage.

Foucault, Michel. 1990. *The History of Sexuality,* vol. 1: *An Introduction.* New York: Vintage.

Foucault, Michel. 2003. *Society Must Be Defended: Lectures at the Collège de France, 1975–1976.* Translated by Graham Burchell. New York: Picador.

Foucault, Michel. 2009. *Security, Territory, Population: Lectures at the Collège de France, 1977–1978.* Translated by Graham Burchell. New York: Picador.

Foucault, Michel. 2010. *The Birth of Biopolitics: Lectures at the Collège de France, 1978–1979.* Translated by Graham Burchell. New York: Picador.

Foucault, Michel. 2015. *The Punitive Society: Lectures at the Collège de France, 1972–1973.* Translated by Graham Burchell. New York: Palgrave Macmillan.

Fradera, Josep. 1999. *Filipinas, la colonia más peculiar: La hacienda pública en la definición de la política colonial (1762–1868).* Madrid: Consejo Superior de Investigaciones Científicas.

Freeman, Joe. 2017. "In the Philippine Drug War, Too Poor for a Funeral." *Washington Post,* February 11. https://www.washingtonpost.com/world/asia_pacific/in-the
-philippine-drug-war-too-poor-for-a-funeral/2017/02/10/f4022364-ee19-11e6-a100
-fdaaf400369a_story.html?utm_term=.0727dd57fb6e.

Freud, Sigmund. 1960. *Jokes and Their Relationship to the Unconscious.* Translated by James Strachey. New York. W. W. Norton.

Freud, Sigmund. 1963. *The Sexual Enlightenment of Children.* Translated by James Strachey. New York: Collier.

Freud, Sigmund. 1990. *Beyond the Pleasure Principle.* Translated by James Strachey. New York: W. W. Norton.

Freud, Sigmund. 2010. *The Interpretation of Dreams.* Translated by James Strachey. New York: Basic Books.

"From Boracay to Oras, Pantries Keep on Giving." 2021. *Philippine Inquirer,* April 23. https://newsinfo.inquirer.net/1422677/from-boracay-to-oras-pantries-keep-on-giving.

Gavilan, Jodesz. 2018. "Timeline: Seeking Justice for Kian delos Santos." *Rappler,* November 28. https://rappler.com/newsbreak/iq/timeline-justice-trial-kian-delos-santos.

Gavilan, Jodesz, and Sofia Tomacruz. 2017. "The Cost of Dying in Duterte's Drug War." *Rappler,* December 10. https://www.rappler.com/newsbreak/in-depth/190805-cost
-dying-duterte-drug-war-philippines-funeral.

"Graphic Exhibit of Alleged Extra-Judicial Killings Held in Popular Catholic Shrine." 2016. *CNN Philippines,* December 22. https://cnnphilippines.com/news/2016/12/21
/graphic-exhibit-on-alleged-extrajudicial-killings-held-in-popular-catholic-shrine
.html.

Guerrero, Milagros C. 2015. *Luzon at War: Contradictions in Philippine Society, 1899–1902*. Pasig: Anvil.

Hart, Donn V., and Harriet Hart. 1974. "Juan Pusong, the Filipino Trickster Revisited." *Asian Studies* 12, nos. 2–3: 129–62.

Harvey, David. 2005. *Paris, Capital of Modernity*. New York: Routledge.

Hau, Caroline. 2017. *Elites and Ilustrados in Philippine Culture*. Quezon City: Ateneo de Manila University Press.

Hedman, Eve Lotta, and John Sidel. 2000. *Philippine Politics and Society in the Twentieth Century: Colonial Legacies, Post-Colonial Trajectories*. London: Routledge.

Heer, Jeet. 2016. "Divide and Conquer: How Professional Sports and Stand-Up Comedy Taught Donald Trump How to Profit from Racial Stereotypes." *New Republic*, September 16. https://newrepublic.com/article/136321/divide-conquer.

Hertz, Neil. 1985. *The End of the Line: Essays in Psychoanalysis and the Sublime*. New York: Columbia University Press.

Heydarian, Richard Javad. 2018. *The Rise of Duterte: A Populist Revolt against Elite Democracy*. Singapore: Palgrave Pivot.

Human Rights Watch. 2016. *World Report: Philippine Events, 2016*. https://www.hrw.org/world-report/2017/country-chapters/philippines.

Human Rights Watch. 2017. "License to Kill: Philippine Police Killings in Duterte's War on Drugs." https://www.hrw.org/report/2017/03/02/license-kill/philippine-police-killings-dutertes-war-drugs.

Hutchcroft, Paul, ed. 2016. *Mindanao: The Long Journey to Peace and Prosperity*. Pasig: Anvil.

"'If You Are Poor, You Are Killed': Extrajudicial Executions in the Philippines 'War on Drugs.'" 2017. *Amnesty International*, June. https://www.amnestyusa.org/reports/if-you-are-poor-you-are-killed-extrajudicial-executions-in-the-philippines-war-on-drugs/.

Ileto, Reynaldo C. 1979. *Pasyon and Revolution: Popular Movements in the Philippines, 1840–1910*. Quezon City: Ateneo de Manila University Press.

"Investigating Duterte's Drug War in the Philippines—Facts and Fiction." 2018. *Deutsche Welle*, May 9. https://www.dw.com/en/investigating-dutertes-drug-war-in-philippines-facts-and-fiction/a-43695383.

Ivy, Marilyn. 2008. "Trauma's Two Times: Japanese Wars and Postwars." *positions: asia critique* 16, no. 1: 165–88.

Jenkins, Nash. 2016. "Why Did the Philippines Just Elect a Guy Who Jokes about Rape?" *Time*, May 9. https://time.com/4324073/rodrigo-duterte-philippines-president-why-elected/.

Jensen, Steffen, and Karl Hapal. Forthcoming. *Communal Intimacy and the Violence of Politics: Understanding the War on Drugs in Bagong Silang, Philippines*. Ithaca, NY: Cornell University Press.

"Jesuit Priest Who Allegedly Molested Duterte Had Other Victims." 2016. *Rappler*, December 4. https://www.rappler.com/nation/politics/elections/2016/114929-duterte-abuse-jesuit-identified.

Jett, Jennifer. 2018. "Overlooked No More: Leticia Ramos Shahani, a Philippine Wom-

en's Rights Pioneer." *New York Times*, May 9. https://www.nytimes.com/2018/05/09
/obituaries/overlooked-leticia-ramos-shahani.html.

Jiao, Claire, and Cecilia Yap. 2020. "Philippines Plunges into Recession and Cuts GDP
Outlook." *Bloomberg*, August 5. https://www.bloomberg.com/news/articles/2020
-08-06/philippine-economy-plunges-into-recession-as-gdp-contracts-16-5.

Johnson, David T., and Jon Fernquest. 2018. "Governing through Killing: The War on
Drugs in the Philippines." *Asian Journal of Law and Society* 5, no. 2: 359–90. https://
doi.org/10.1017/als.2018.12.

Johnson, Stephen. 2012. *Burnt Cork: Traditions and Legacies of Blackface Minstrelsy*. Am-
herst: University of Massachusetts Press.

Johnston, Adrian. 2018. "Jacques Lacan." In *The Stanford Encyclopedia of Philosophy*, edited by Edward N. Zalta. https://plato.stanford.edu/entries/lacan/.

Jones, James, and Olivier Sarbil. 2019. "On the President's Orders." *Frontline*, October 8.
https://www.pbs.org/wgbh/frontline/film/on-the-presidents-orders/.

Kabiling, Genalyn. 2020. "Duterte Reveals His Barrett's Esophagus Is Worsening." *Manila Bulletin*, August 25. https://mb.com.ph/2020/08/25/duterte-reveals-his
-barretts-esophagus-is-worsening/?fbclid=IwAR2wvtL58fUgtSbRDXTXDCU
zph3N-msrfWQ6h75y9EUZKUe5aAbNb6bLLMM.

Kantorowiz, Ernst. 1957. *The King's Two Bodies: A Study in Political Medieval Theology*.
Princeton, NJ: Princeton University Press.

Katz, Andrew. 2017. "I Am Seeing My Country Die." *Time*, February 23. https://time.com
/philippines-rodrigo-duterte-drug-war-local-photographers/.

Kerkvliet, Benedict. 2002. *The Huk Rebellion: A Study of Peasant Revolt in the Philippines*,
2nd ed. Lanham, MD: Rowman and Littlefield.

Kerkvliet, Benedict, and Resil Mojares. 1992. *From Marcos to Aquino: Local Perspectives
on Political Transition in the Philippines*. Honolulu: University of Hawai'i Press.

"The Kill List." 2016. *Inquirer.net*, July 7. http://newsinfo.inquirer.net/794598/kill-list
-drugs-duterte.

Kramer, Paul. 2006. *The Blood of Government: Race, Empire, the United States, and the
Philippines*. Chapel Hill: University of North Carolina Press.

Kreuzer, Peter. 2016. "'If They Resist, Kill Them': Police Vigilantism in the Philippines."
Frankfurt: Peace Research Institute.

Kusaka, Wataru. 2017a. "Bandit Grabbed the State: Duterte's Moral Politics." *Philippine
Sociological Review* 65:49–75.

Kusaka, Wataru. 2017b. *Moral Politics in the Philippines: Inequality, Democracy and the Urban Poor*. Singapore: NUS Press.

Kusaka, Wataru. 2020. "Disaster, Discipline, Drugs and Duterte: Emergence of New
Moral Subjectivities in Post-Yolanda Leyte." In *Ethnographies of Development and Globalization in the Philippines: Emergent Socialities and the Governing of Precarity*, edited
by Koki Seki, 71–97. New York: Routledge.

Lamb, Kate. 2016. "Philippine Secret Death Squads: Officer Claims Police behind Wave
of Killings." *The Guardian*, October 3. https://www.theguardian.com/world/2016/oct
/04/philippines-secret-death-squads-police-officer-teams-behind-killings.

Laplanche, Jean, and J. B. Pontalis. 1988. *The Language of Psychoanalysis*. London: Taylor and Francis.

Lara, Francisco J., Jr. 2014. *Insurgents, Clans and States: Political Legitimacy and Resurgent Conflict in Muslim Mindanao, Philippines*. Quezon City: Ateneo de Manila University Press.

Lara, Francisco J., Jr., and Steven Schoofs, eds. 2016. *Out of the Shadows: Violent Conflict and the Real Economy of Mindanao*. Quezon City: Ateneo de Manila University Press.

Lasco, Gideon. 2016. "Just How Big Is the Drug Problem in the Philippines Anyway?" *The Conversation*, October 13. https://theconversation.com/just-how-big-is-the-drug-problem-in-the-philippines-anyway-66640.

Linfield, Suste. 2010. *The Cruel Radiance: Photography and Political Violence*. Chicago: University of Chicago Press.

"Local Officials Are Making 'Kill Lists' for Duterte's Drug War." 2017. *Vice News*, October 10. https://news.vice.com/en_us/article/j5dvn7/these-volunteers-are-making-kill-lists-for-dutertes-drug-war.

"Look: Baclaran Church Displays Posters of Drug Killings." 2016. ABS-CBN News, December 18. https://news.abs-cbn.com/news/12/18/16/look-baclaran-church-displays-posters-of-drug-killings.

"Look: Vice Ganda Meets Rodrigo Duterte and Son Baste at Victory Party." 2016. *Coconuts Manila*, June 6. https://coconuts.co/manila/lifestyle/look-vice-ganda-meet-rodrigo-duterte-and-son-baste-victory-party/.

Lott, Eric. 1995. *Love and Theft: Blackface Minstrelsy and the American Working Class*. New York: Oxford University Press.

Lui, Kevin. 2016. "Rodrigo Duterte Says His Admission of Opioid Abuse Was a Joke but Concerns Remain." *Time*, December 18. https://time.com/4605982/philippines-duterte-health-drug-fentanyl/.

Mabini, Apolinario. 2007. *La Revolución Filiipina*. Manila: National Library.

Macaraig, Ayee. 2016. "Undertaker Misery on the Frontlines of the Drug War." ABS-CBN News, December 9. http://news.abs-cbn.com/focus/12/09/16/undertaker-misery-on-frontlines-of-philippine-drug-war.

Mangosing, Francis. 2019. "Military: No Coup d'État against Duterte Administration." *Inquirer.net*, July 3. https://newsinfo.inquirer.net/1137427/military-no-coup-detat-against-the-duterte-administration.

Manlupig, Karlos. 2015. "Duterte: 'Am I the Death Squad? True.'" *Inquirer.net*, May 26. https://newsinfo.inquirer.net/693510/duterte-am-i-the-death-squad-true.

Manne, Kate. 2016. "The Logic of Misogyny." *Boston Review*, July 11. https://bostonreview.net/forum/kate-manne-logic-misogyny.

Manzanilla, J. P., and Caroline Hau, eds. 2016. *Remembering/Rethinking EDSA*. Pasig: Anvil.

Martin, M. G. 2018. "Funeral Parlor Rented Murder Victim's Body to Fake Wake Operators." *Philippines Lifestyle News*, August 9. http://philippineslifestyle.com/fake-wake-rented-murder-body/.

Marx, Karl. 1992. *Capital: A Critique of Political Economy*, vol. I. Translated by Ben Fowkes. New York: Penguin.

Mauss, Marcel. 2000. *The Gift: The Form and Reason for Exchange in Archaic Societies*. Translated by Ian Cunnison. New York: W. W. Norton.

May, Glenn Anthony. 1980. *Social Engineering in the Philippines: The Aims, Execution, and Impact of American Colonial Policy, 1900–1913*. Westport, CT: Greenwood.

May, Glenn Anthony. 1987. *A Past Recovered*. Quezon City: New Day.

Mbembe, Achille. 1992. "Provisional Notes on the Postcolony." *Africa: Journal of the International African Institute* 62, no. 1: 3–37.

Mbembe, Achille. 2001. *On the Postcolony*. Berkeley: University of California Press.

Mbembe, Achille. 2003. "Necropolitics." Translated by Libby Meintjes. *Public Culture* 15, no. 1: 11–40.

Mbembe, Achille. 2019. *Necropolitics*. Translated by Steve Corcoran. Durham, NC: Duke University Press.

McCarthy, Julie. 2020. "Why Rights Groups Worry about the Philippines' New Anti-Terrorism Law." NPR, July 21. https://www.npr.org/2020/07/21/893019057/why -rights-groups-worry-about-the-philippines-new-anti-terrorism-law.

McClure, Tess. 2017. "What's It Like Documenting the Brutal Philippine Drug War." *Vice News*, March 2. https://www.vice.com/en_us/article/78d84x/bodies-every-night -documenting-the-brutal-philippine-drug-war.

McCoy, Alfred, ed. 1980. *Southeast Asia under Japanese Occupation*. New Haven, CT: Yale University Southeast Asia Studies.

McCoy, Alfred. 1999. *Closer Than Brothers: Manhood at the Philippine Military Academy*. New Haven, CT: Yale University Press.

McCoy, Alfred, ed. 2009a. *An Anarchy of Families: State and Family in the Philippines*. Quezon City: Ateneo de Manila University Press.

McCoy, Alfred. 2009b. *Policing America's Empire: The United States, the Philippines and the Rise of the Surveillance State*. Madison: University of Wisconsin Press.

McKenna, Rebecca Tinio. 2017. *American Imperial Pastoral: The Architecture of US Colonialism in the Philippines*. Chicago: University of Chicago Press.

Mendoza, Brilliante. 2016. *Philippines Anti-Drugs TV Ad—Mother*. Presidential Communications Office, September 26. https://www.youtube.com/watch?v=kYTNCxZCbF0.

"Metro Manila Police Arrest Almost 3,000 'Tambays' for Violating Ordinances." 2018. *CNN Philippines*, June 18. http://cnnphilippines.com/news/2018/06/18/Loitering-b ystander-tambay-arrest-Metro-Manila.html.

Miller, Jonathan. 2018. *Duterte Harry: Fire and Fury in the Philippines*. London: Scribe.

Mojares, Primitivo. 2016. *The Conjugal Dictatorship of Ferdinand and Imelda Marcos*. Quezon City: Ateneo de Manila University Press.

Mojares, Resil. 1986. *The Man Who Would Be President: Serging Osmeña and Philippine Politics*. Cebu: Cacao.

Mojares, Resil. 2006. *Brains of the Nation: Pedro Paterno, T. H. Parde de Tavera, Isabelo de los Reyes and the Production of Modern Knowledge*. Quezon City: Ateneo de Manila University Press.

Möller, Frank. 2017. "Witnessing Violence through Photography." *Global Discourse* 7, nos. 2–3: 264–81. https://doi.org/10.1080/23269995.2017.1339979.

Molo, John. 2021. "Presidential Inability and Its Many Forms." *Rappler*, April 17. https://

www.rappler.com/voices/thought-leaders/opinion-presidential-inability-and-its
-many-forms?mc_cid=63e63edb38&mc_eid=076c300f82.

Montag, Walter. 2013. "Necro-Economics: Adam Smith and Death in the Life of the
Universal." In *Biopolitics: A Reader*, edited by Timothy Campbell and Adam Sitze,
193–214. Durham, NC: Duke University Press.

Morin, Roc. 2017. "The Philippine Drug War Is Flooding This Funeral Home with
Bodies." *Vice News*, May 1. https://www.vice.com/en_us/article/d7nawk/the-filipino
-drug-war-is-flooding-this-funeral-home-with-bodies.

Morrison, Toni. 1993. *Playing in the Dark: Whiteness and the Literary Imagination*. New
York: Vintage.

Motherland. 2017. *POV*, October 16. http://archive.pov.org/motherland/film
-description/.

Nietzsche, Friedrich. 1974. *The Gay Science*. New York: Random House.

Ortega, Arnisson Andre. 2018. *Neo-Liberalizing Space in the Philippines: Suburbanization,
Transnational Migration and Dispossession*. Quezon City: Ateneo de Manila University
Press.

Ou, Ed, and Aurora Almendral. 2017. "The Kill List: The Brutal Drug War in the Philippines." *NBC Left Field*.

Paddock, Richard. 2016. "Hero's Burial for Ferdinand Marcos Draws Protests from Dictator's Victims." *New York Times*, November 18. https://www.nytimes.com/2016/11/19
/world/asia/philippines-marcos-burial.html.

Paddock, Richard. 2017. "Becoming Duterte: The Making of a Philippine Strongman."
New York Times, March 21. https://www.nytimes.com/2017/03/21/world/asia/rodrigo
-duterte-philippines-president-strongman.html.

"Pagod na ako sa inaction: How a Community Pantry Arose to Fill Gaps in Government
Response." 2021. *Rappler*, April 17. https://www.rappler.com/moveph/community
-pantry-covid-19-lockdown-april-OIh6tXwmKJ8bbUEg3nnk3iC5UnoHbT_QP9Ek37
LJBeqPrJI.

"Palace to Media: Discern if Duterte Says Facts or Jokes." 2016. *Manila Bulletin*,
November 6. https://news.mb.com.ph/2016/11/06/palace-to-media-discern-if-duterte
-says-facts-or-jokes/.

Petersen, Hannah Ellis. 2018. "My Only Sin Is the Extrajudicial Killings." *The Guardian*,
September 28. https://www.theguardian.com/world/2018/sep/28/duterte-confesses
-my-only-sin-is-the-extrajudicial-killings.

Philippine Human Rights Information Center. 2017–18. "The War on the Poor: Extrajudicial Killings and Their Effects on Urban Poor Families and Communities." https://
philrights.org/the-war-on-the-poor-extrajudicial-killings-and-their-effects-on-urban
-poor-families-and-communities/.

"Philippine Police 'Dumping Bodies' of Drug War Victims." 2017. *Al Jazeera*, July 28.
https://www.aljazeera.com/news/2017/07/philippine-police-dumping-bodies-drug
-war-victims-170728034001676.html.

"Philippines: Duterte Critic Leila de Lima Faces Drugs Charges." 2017. *BBC News*, February 17. https://www.bbc.com/news/world-asia-39005919.

"Philippines: Duterte Says His Son Will Be Killed if He Is Involved in Drugs." 2017.

The Guardian, September 21. https://www.theguardian.com/world/2017/sep/21 /philippines-duterte-son-will-be-killed-if-he-is-involved-in-drugs.

"Philippines' Duterte Skipped Asean Meetings to Take 'Power Naps.'" 2018. *BBC News*, November 15. https://www.bbc.com/news/world-asia-46217876.

"Philippines Rodrigo Duterte in Quotes." 2016. *BBC News*, September 30. https://www .bbc.com/news/world-asia-36251094.

Placido, Dharel. 2019. "Duterte Threatens to Slap Tatad over Kidney Transplant Claim." *ABS-CBN News*, February 15. https://news.abs-cbn.com/news/02/15/19/duterte -threatens-to-slap-tatad-over-kidney-transplant-claim.

"President Duterte Cracks Joke about Rape amid Concern over Martial Law." 2017. *Reuters*, May 26. https://www.reuters.com/article/us-philippines-duterte/philippines -duterte-jokes-about-rape-amid-concern-over-martial-law-abuses-idUSKBN18N05D.

Presidential Communications Operations Office, Presidential News Desk. 2018a. "Speech of President Rodrigo Roa Duterte during the 49th Charter Day Celebration of Mandaue City." Speech delivered at Mandaue City Cultural and Sports Complex, August 30.

Presidential Communications Operations Office, Presidential News Desk. 2018b. "Speech of President Rodrigo Roa Duterte during the Merienda with the Former Rebels." Speech delivered at Heroes Hall, Malacañang Palace, February 7.

Presidential Communications Operations Office, Presidential News Desk. 2019a. "Speech of President Rodrigo Roa Duterte during the 31st Annual Convention of the Prosecutor's League of the Philippines." Speech delivered at the Asturias Hotel in Puerto Princesa City, Palawan, April 4.

Presidential Communications Operations Office, Presidential News Desk. 2019b. "Speech of President Rodrigo Roa Duterte during the Partido Demokratiko Pilipino- Lakas ng Bayan (PDP-Laban) Campaign Rally in Cagayan de Oro." Speech delivered at the University of Science and Technology of Southern Philippines, Cagayan de Oro City, March 24.

PTV. 2018. "Conferment of the Presidential Medal of Merit, 2018 Philippine Heritage Awards, Gawad sa Manlilikha ng Bayan (GAMABA), and National Artists Awards." *YouTube*, October 24. https://www.youtube.com/watch?v=hOOj76ocuFY&fbclid =IwAR0aQu7wmdPaZIvFA8m5U9_TMJgxlberT7hVQ9KXDL0ZB9h_11uwmH4pX0Y.

Punay, Edu. 2017. "SC Tackles Drug War: Were Rights Violated?" *Philippine Star*, November 21. https://www.philstar.com/headlines/2017/11/21/1761341/sc-tackles -drug-war-were-rights-violated.

Quezon, Manolo III. 2021. "Liquidation," *Philippine Daily Inquirer*, March 10. https:// opinion.inquirer.net/138362/liquidations?fbclid=IwAR3b1op9Lf8NG9jZ8T6OE52 GrxSeIp3eR_ZbJu120oghG_AcsmQhSGWzLyM.

Quimpo, Susan, and Nathan Quimpo, eds. 2012. *Subversive Lives: A Family Memoir of the Marcos Years*. Pasig: Anvil.

Rafael, Vicente L. 1993. *Contracting Colonialism: Translation and Christian Conversion in Tagalog Society under Early Spanish Rule*. Durham, NC: Duke University Press.

Rafael, Vicente L., ed. 1999. *Figures of Criminality in Indonesia, the Philippines and Colonial Vietnam*. Ithaca, NY: Cornell University, Southeast Asian Program.

Rafael, Vicente L. 2000. "Patronage, Pornography and Youth: Ideology and Spectatorship during the Early Marcos Years." In *White Love and Other Events in Filipino History*, 122–61. Durham, NC: Duke University Press.

Rafael, Vicente L. 2005. *The Promise of the Foreign: Nationalism and the Technics of Translation in the Spanish Philippines*. Durham, NC: Duke University Press.

Rafael, Vicente L. 2016. *Motherless Tongues: The Insurgency of Language amid Wars of Translation*. Durham, NC: Duke University Press.

Ramos, Marlon. 2016. "Junkies Are Not Humans," *Inquirer.net*, August 28. http://news info.inquirer.net/810395/junkies-are-not-humans.

Ranada, Pia. 2016a. "83% of Filipinos Trust, Approve of Duterte—Pulse Asia." *Rappler*, January 6. https://www.rappler.com/nation/157545-filipinos-trust-duterte-pulse -asia-survey-december-2016.

Ranada, Pia. 2016b. "'Migraine Everyday' and Duterte's Other Ailments. From Barrett's Esophagus to Buerger's Disease, Here Are the Health Issues That the Septuagenarian Duterte Has Spoken about in Public." *Rappler*, December 13.

Ranada, Pia. 2016c. "Viral: Video of Duterte Joking about Raped Australian Woman." *Rappler*, April 17. https://rappler.com/nation/elections/viral-video-duterte-joke -australian-woman-rape.

Ranada, Pia. 2017. "Duterte: Davao Death Squads Formed to Fight NPA 'Sparrow Units.'" *Rappler*, March 7. https://www.rappler.com/nation/163524-duterte -davao-death-squad-fight-npa-sparrow-units.

Ranada, Pia. 2019a. "Duterte's Personal Rating Bounces Back to Personal High—SWS." *Rappler*, April 10. https://www.rappler.com/nation/227887-duterte-satisfaction -ratings-sws-survey-march-2019.

Ranada, Pia. 2019b. "Malacañang Releases New Diagrams on 'Conspiracy' to Discredit Duterte." *Rappler*, May 8. https://www.rappler.com/nation/malacanang-releases -new-diagrams-conspiracy-discredit-duterte-may-8-2019#Echobox=1557292891.

Rauhala, Emily. 2016. "Duterte Keeps Admitting to Killing People: His Supporters Keep Shrugging It Off." *Washington Post*, December 14. https://www.washingtonpost .com/news/worldviews/wp/2016/12/14/duterte-keeps-admitting-to-killing-people-his -supporters-keep-shrugging-it-off/.

Republic of the Philippines. 2016. "Archive 2016—President Rodrigo Rua Duterte's Speeches." Presidential Communications Operation Office, Manila. https://pcoo.gov .ph/archive-2016-president-rodrigo-roa-dutertes-speeches/.

Republic of the Philippines. 2018. "Speech of Rodrigo Roa Duterte during the Inauguration of the Northern Mindanao Wellness and Reintegration Center." Presidential Communication and Operation Office, August 4. https://pcoo.gov.ph/presidential -speech/speech-of-president-rodrigo-roa-duterte-during-the-inauguration-of-northern -mindanao-wellness-and-reintegration-center/.

Republic of the Philippines, National Police Commission. 2016. "PNP Anti-Illegal Drugs Campaign—Project: 'Double Barrel.'" Command Memorandum Circular no. 16, July 1. https://didm.pnp.gov.ph/images/Command%20Memorandum%20Circulars /CMC%202016-16%20PNP%20ANTI-ILLEGAL%20DRUGS%20CAMPAIGN%20 PLAN%20%20PROJECT%20DOUBLE%20BARREL.pdf.

Reyes, Celia, and Audrey D. Tabuga. n.d. "Conditional Cash Transfer Program in the Philippines: Is It Reaching the Extremely Poor?" Makati: Philippine Institute for Development Studies.

Reyes, Miguel Paolo P. 2019. "The Duterte-Marcos Connection." *Vera Files*, September 29. https://verafiles.org/articles/duterte-marcos-connection.

Rine, Abigail. 2011. "Phallus/Phallocentrism." In *The Encyclopedia of Literary and Cultural Theory*, edited by Michael Ryan, Gregory Castle, Robert Eaglestone, and M. Keith Booker. Chichester, UK: Wiley-Blackwell. https://digitalcommons.georgefox.edu/cgi/viewcontent.cgi?article=1075&context=eng_fac.

Robles, Eliodoro. 1969. *The Philippines in the Nineteenth Century*. Quezon City: Malaya Books.

"The Rodrigo Duterte Interview." 2016. *Esquire Philippines*, August 25. https://www.esquiremag.ph/politics/opinion/the-rodrigo-duterte-interview-a1502-20160825-lfrm5.

Roediger, David. 2007. *The Wages of Whiteness: Race and the Making of the American Working Class*, rev. ed. London: Verso.

Rogin, Michael. 1996. *Blackface, White Noise: Jewish Immigrants in the Hollywood Melting Pot*. Berkeley: University of California Press.

Romero, Alexis. 2016. "Shoot-to-Kill Orders Out for Pol-Narcos." *Philippine Star*, August 6. https://www.philstar.com/headlines/2016/08/06/1610558/shoot-kill-order-out-narco-pols.

Romero, Alexis. 2017. "Duterte Jokes about Showing De Lima's Alleged Sex Video to Pope." *Philippine Star*, November 28. https://www.philstar.com/headlines/2017/11/28/1763401/duterte-jokes-about-showing-de-limas-alleged-sex-video-pope.

Romero, Alexis. 2020. "Hold Me Responsible for Drug War Deaths—Duterte." *Philippine Star*, October 21. https://www.philstar.com/headlines/2020/10/21/2051155/hold-me-responsible-drug-war-deaths-duterte?utm_campaign=677a3a08ff-Arangkada_News%E2%80%A6%00%00.

Rosca, Ninotchka. 2018. "Duterte: Nada in the Heart of Bluster." In *Strongman: Putin, Erdogan, Duterte, Trump, Modi*, edited by Vijay Prashad. New York: OR Books.

Salaverria, Leila B. 2017. "Duterte Insists Shabu Can Cause Brain Damage." *Inquirer.net*, May 10. https://newsinfo.inquirer.net/895885/duterte-insists-shabu-can-cause-brain-damage.

Salman, Michael, 2009. "'The Prison That Makes Men Free': The Iwahig Penal Colony and the Simulacra of the American State in the Philippines." In *Colonial Crucible: Empire and the Making of the Modern American State*, edited by Alfred McCoy and Francisco Scarrano, 116–32. Madison: University of Wisconsin Press.

Salonga, Jovita R. 2000. *Presidential Plunder: The Quest for the Marcos Ill-Gotten Wealth*. Quezon City: University of the Philippines, Center for Leadership.

Sammond, Nicholas. 2015. *Birth of an Industry: Blackface Minstrelsy and the Rise of American Animation*. Durham, NC: Duke University Press.

Scalice, Joseph Paul. 2017. "Crisis of Revolutionary Leadership: Martial Law and the Communist Parties of the Philippines, 1959–1974." PhD dissertation, University of California, Berkeley. https://escholarship.org/uc/item/2mc0496x.

Scarry, Elaine. 1987. *The Body in Pain: The Making and Unmaking of the World*. New York: Oxford University Press.

Schumacher, John. 1997. *The Propaganda Movement: The Creation of Filipino Consciousness and the Making of the Revolution*. Quezon City: Ateneo de Manila University Press.

Seagrave, Sterling. 1988. *The Marcos Dynasty: The Corruption of Ferdinand and Imelda Marcos*. New York: Ballantine.

Seki, Koki. 2015. "Capitalizing on Desire: Reconfiguring 'the Social' and the Government of Poverty in the Philippines." *Development and Change* 46, no. 6: 1253–76.

Seki, Koki, ed. 2020a. *Ethnographies of Development and Globalization in the Philippines: Emergent Socialities and the Governing of Precarity*. New York: Routledge.

Seki, Koki. 2020b. "Post-Authoritarian Sociality and Urban Governmentality: A Socialized Housing Project in the Philippines." In *Ethnographies of Development and Globalization in the Philippines: Emergent Socialities and the Governing of Precarity*, edited by Koki Seki, 17-42. New York: Routledge.

Shahani, Lila Ramos, ed. 2012. *Boses ng Pagbabago* [Voices of Change]. Manila: Human Development and Poverty Reduction Cluster.

Shahani, Lila Ramos. 2013. "Why Conditional Cash Transfers Work." *GMA News*, July 15. https://www.gmanetwork.com/news/opinion/content/317545/why-conditional-cash-transfers-work/story/.

Shahani, Lila Ramos. 2015. "Engendering Development: The Status of Women in the Philippines." *Philippine Star*, March 2. https://www.philstar.com/opinion/2015/03/02/1428959/engendering-development-status-women-philippines.

Sidel, John. 1999a. *Capital, Coercion and Crime: Bossism in the Philippines*. Stanford, CA: Stanford University Press.

Sidel, John. 1999b. "The Usual Suspects: Nardong Putik, Don Pepe Osyon and Robin Hood." In *Figures of Criminality in Indonesia, the Philippines and Colonial Vietnam*, edited by Vicente L. Rafael, 70–94. Ithaca, NY: Cornell University, Southeast Asian Program.

Siegel, James T. 1998. *A New Criminal Type in Jakarta: Counter-Revolution Today*. Durham, NC: Duke University Press.

Siegel, James T. 2000. *The Rope of God*, 2nd ed. Ann Arbor: University of Michigan Press.

Siegel, James T. 2006. *Naming the Witch*. Stanford, CA: Stanford University Press.

Siegel, James T. 2011. *Objects and Objections of Ethnography*. New York: Fordham University Press.

Siegel, James T. 2013. "False Beggars: Marcel Mauss, The Gift and Its Commentators." *Diacritics* 41, no. 2: 60–79.

Simbulan, Dante C. 2005. *The Modern Principalia: The Historical Evolution of the Philippine Ruling Oligarchy*. Quezon City: University of the Philippines Press.

Simmel, Georg. 1901. "The Aesthetic Significance of the Face [1901]," translated by Lore Ferguson. In George Simmel et al., *Essays on Sociology, Philosophy and Aesthetics*, edited by Kurt H. Wolff, 278–79. New York: Harper Torchbooks.

Smith, Shawn Michelle. 2020. *Photographic Returns: Racial Justice and the Time of Photography*. Durham, NC: Duke University Press.

Social Weather Station (sws). 2018. "Third Quarter 2018 Social Weather Survey: Hunger Rises to 13.3%." October 12. https://www.sws.org.ph/swsmain/artcldisppage /?artcsyscode=ART-20181012173619.

Sontag, Susan. 1977. *On Photography*. New York: Dell.

Sontag, Susan. 2003. *Regarding the Pain of Others*. New York: Farrar, Strauss and Giroux.

Stanley, Peter. 1974. *A Nation in the Making: The Philippines and the United States, 1899–1921*. Cambridge: Harvard University Press.

Stein, Ginny. 2017a. "Documenting the Dead: A Photographer's Mission to Record the Victims of Duterte's War on Drugs." *ABC Australia*, September 19. http://www.abc .net.au/news/2017-09-19/ documenting-the-dead-photographing-victims-dutertes-war-on-drugs/8891886.

Stein, Ginny. 2017b. "Rodrigo Duterte: Family of Kian delos Santos Seeks Justice for Son Killed in Deadly War on Drugs." *ABC Radio National*, September 5. https://www .abc.net.au/news/2017-09-06/kian-delos-santos-caught-in-crossfire-of -dutertes-war-on-drugs/8877296.

Stuart-Santiago, Angie. 2013. *EDSA Uno: A Narrative and Analysis with Notes on Dos and Tres*. Tiaong: Pulang Lupa Foundation and Stuart Santiago.

Sykes, Tom. 2018. *In the Realm of the Punisher: Travels in Duterte's Philippines*. Oxford: Signal.

Symmes, Patrick. 2017. "President Duterte's List." *New York Times*, January 10. https:// www.nytimes.com/2017/01/10/magazine/president-dutertes-list.html.

Tabuga, Aubrey D., and Celia M. Reyes. 2012. "Conditional Cash Transfer Program in the Philippines: Is It Reaching the Extremely Poor?" Makati: Philippine Institute for Development Studies. https://ideas.repec.org/p/phd/dpaper/dp_2012-42.html.

Talabong, Rambo. 2020. "3 Years after Kian's Death, Killings Continue under Duterte." *Rappler*, August 16. https://rappler.com/nation/third-death-anniversary -kian-delos-santos-killings-continue.

Talabong, Rambo. 2021. "Bloody Sunday: 9 Dead, 6 Arrested in Calabarzon Crackdown of Activists," *Rappler*, March 7. https://www.rappler.com/nation/dead-arrested-cala barzon-crackdown-progressives-march-7-2021?mc_cid=0db8c93626&mc_eid =2a5b5ba5fe.

Thompson, Mark. 1995. *The Anti-Marcos Struggle: Personalistic Rule and Democratic Tran- sition in the Philippines*. New Haven, CT: Yale University Press.

Tiefenthaler, Ainara. 2016. "Life in Duterte's Death Squad." *New York Times*, September 15. https://www.nytimes.com/video/world/asia/100000004650523/life-on-dutertes -death-squad.html.

Tomacruz, Sofia, and Jodesz Gavilan. 2017. "Police and Funeral Homes: The Business of Picking Up the Dead." *Rappler*, December 10. https://www.rappler.com/newsbreak /in-depth/190811-police-funeral-homes-business-dead-war-drugs.

Tuquero, Loreben. 2020. "As Pandemic Persists, Are Filipinos Still Satisfied with Duterte?" *Rappler*, July 6. https://rappler.com/newsbreak/in-depth/are-filipinos -still-satisfied-duterte-coronavirus-pandemic-persists.

Velarde, Rashiel B. 2018. "The Philippines' Targeting System for the Poor: Successes, Lessons and Ways Forward." World Bank Social Protection Policy Note no. 16, No-

vember. http://documents1.worldbank.org/curated/en/830621542293177821/pdf
/132110-PN-P162701-SPL-Policy-Note-16-Listahanan.pdf.

Villamor, Felipe. 2017. "Ex-Officer in the Philippines Says He Led Death Squads at
Duterte's Behest." *New York Times*, February 20. https://www.nytimes.com/2017/02
/20/world/asia/rodrigo-duterte-philippines-death squad.html.

Villamor, Felipe. 2018a. "Duterte Jokes about Rape, Again. Philippine Women Aren't
Laughing." *New York Times*, August 31. https://www.nytimes.com/2018/08/31/world
/asia/philippines-rodrigo-duterte-rape-joke.html.

Villamor, Felipe. 2018b. "'Your Concern Is Human Rights, Mine Is Human Lives,'
Duterte Says in Fiery Speech." *New York Times*, July 23. https://www.nytimes.com
/2018/07/23/world/asia/philippines-duterte-speech-muslims.html.

Warburg, Anna Braemer. 2017. "Policing in the Philippine 'War on Drugs': (In)security,
Morality and Order in Bagong Silang." MA thesis, Aarhus University, Copenhagen.

Warburg, Anna Braemer, and Steffen Jensen. 2018. "Policing the War on Drugs and the
Transformation of Urban Space in Manila." *Environment and Planning D: Society and
Space* 38, no. 3: 399–416. https://doi.org/10.1177/0263775818817299.

"War on Drugs Working, Says PNP; Touts Survey Results." 2019. *ABS-CBN News*,
February 17. https://news.abs-cbn.com/news/02/17/19/war-on-drugs-is
-working-says-pnp-touts-survey-results.

Whaley, Floyd. 2016. "Duterte's Talk of Killing Criminals Raises Fear in the Philippines."
New York Times, May 17. https://www.nytimes.com/2016/05/18/world/asia/rodrigo
-duterte-philippines.html?_r=0.

"Why Intelligence Funds Require Scrutiny." 2017. *Rappler*, December 18. https://
r3.rappler.com/move-ph/issues/budget-watch/191579-duterte-confidential
-intelligence-funds-2018-budget-part-2.

World Bank. 2017. "FAQs about the Pantawid Pamilyang Pilipino Program (4Ps)."
https://www.worldbank.org/en/country/philippines/brief/faqs-about-the-pantawid
-pamilyang-pilipino-program.

Wurfel, David. 1988. *Filipino Politics: Development and Decay*. Ithaca, NY: Cornell University Press.

"You Can Die Anytime: Death Squad Killings in Mindanao." 2009. *Human Rights
Watch*, April 6. https://www.hrw.org/report/2009/04/06/you-can-die-any-time
/death-squad-killings-mindanao#page.

Acayan, Ezra, 109
advocacy, photography as, 121–27
Agamben, Giorgio, 111
agency, of corpses, 111–20
Aguinaldo, Emilio, 8–9, 18
Almendral, Aurora, 127–30
Alsa Masa death squads, 15, 58, 91–92
Anderson, Benedict, 135–36
Anti-Terrorism Law (Philippines), 132–33
Aquino, Benigno "Ninoy," Jr., 13, 22, 26, 116
Aquino, Benigno "PNoy," 18, 27
Aquino, Cory, 77–78; economic reforms under, 26–27; leadership of, 1–2, 12–15, 22; paramilitary under, 91–92
Arroyo, Gloria Macapagal, 27
Arumpac, Alyx Ayn, 107
authoritarian regimes: authoritarian imaginary, 3–5, 147n1; benevolence and, 18–20; developmentalism and, 21; history of, 21–26; intimacy in, 140–42; necropolitics and, 64–65; phallocentrism and, 43–49; rise of, 136–42
autoimmunity: authoritarianism and, 142–43; of communities of intimacy, 139–42
Aznar, Jess, 109
Azoulay, Ariella, 105–8

Baclaran Church exhibit, 121–24
Bagong Silang, 75, 122–24, 134–35
Bakhtin, Mikhail, 52, 82
ballot stuffing, Marcos's use of, 13
Bangsa Moro Law, 14
barangay village structure: elections and, 7;

extrajudicial killings and, 72–75; justice system and, 138–42; list making and, 75; spatial organization and, 136–37; violence in, 122, 134–35
barbarian, Foucault on history of, 70–71
Barthes, Roland, 106
Bello, Walden, 134
benevolent dictatorship, Filipino dream of, 18–20
Benjamin, Walter, 23, 143
Berger, John 120
biopolitics/biopower: Duterte's use of, 16–17, 25–26, 63–65; necropolitics and, 56; neoliberal citizenship and, 26–35; photography and, 105–30; reproductive health and, 36–41
birth control, resistance to, 37–38
blackface minstrelsy: minority cultures and, 149n11; populism and, 85–86
Black Lives Matter, 87–88
Bonifacio, Andrés, 8–9
Brod, Max, 143
Brown, Wendy, 27–28
bugoy (trickster figure), 81
Butler, Judith, 106

Camera, as inhuman machine, 113–14
campaign practices: Duterte and, 61–62; in Philippines, 11–12
cash transfers (CCTs): Duterte regime and decline of, 32–35; implementation in Philippines of, 29–35; neoliberal colonization and, 29–30; reproductive health and, 39–41

Catholic Church, 37–41, 148n2; Duterte's criticism of, 49–54, 65, 141
charisma, in Duterte, 56
China, Duterte and, 6, 17, 24–25
Christian martyr iconography, photography of killings and, 116–20
citizenship, neoliberal colonization and formation of, 26–35
City of Man project, 23
civil war, Duterte's drug war as, 76–78
Cixous, Hélène, 47
class war: Duterte's drug war as, 76–78; support for Duterte and, 87–88
colonialism: benevolent dictatorship and, 18–20; death squads and, 90–93; elections and, 7–9, 16–17; extrajudicial killings and, 72–75; prisons and, 100–102
Communist Party of the Philippines (CPP), 91, 95–96, 152
community, intimacy of, 136–42
community pantry system, establishment of, 143–45
confession, Duterte's use of, 49–54
contractualization, neoliberal colonization and, 29
Coronel, Sheila, 5, 73, 104
corpses, commodification of, 73–75
counterinsurgency: CCTs as tool for, 30; Duterte and, 25–26, 69–71; elections as, 9–12
COVID-19 pandemic: authoritarians and, 131–33; Duterte and, 139–40
cronyism, Philippine practice of, 21–23
Cruz, Mideo, 65
Cultural Center (Philippines), 23
Curato, Nicole, 33, 40–41

Davao Death Squad, 22, 46, 55, 58–59, 68–71, 76–78
death: drug addiction and, 67–71; Duterte and, 54–56, 103–7; photojournalists' documentation of, 109–27
death penalty, Foucault's discussion of, 72–75
decolonization, Philippine politics and, 18–20
De Lima, Leila, 46–49, 54, 98
de los Santos, Kian, 125–27
depredation, Duterte and, 79–84
Derrida, Jacques, 142–43

Diaz, Ramona, 36
Diehard Duterte Supporters (DDS), 76–79
diskarte, Filipino concept of improvisation, 138–42
dissipation, Duterte and, 79–84
dreams of revenge, 127–30
drug addiction: Duterte's hatred of, 6, 15–16, 55–56, 67–71; Duterte's involvement in, 54–56, 69–71; statistics in Philippines for, 148n3
drug war, as civil war, 72, 76–78; and community of intimacy, 138–39; as symptom and cure, 142
Du Bois, W. E. B., 86
Duterte, Paolo, 16
Duterte, Rodrigo Roa: conspiracy theory matrix of, 94–97; COVID-19 pandemic and, 131–33, 139–40; as the datu with multiple organs, 82; death and, 54–56; early career of, 2–3; economic reforms under, 27; election of, 6; health status of, 47–48, 54–56; historical time for, 60–62; homophobia and homophilia, 79; human rights and, 57–59; Marcos and, 22–23; martial law declared by, 14; as mayor of Davao, 15–16; obsession with addicts and addiction, 67–70; paramilitary groups and, 92–93; personal appearances by, 1–2; pessimism concerning, 142–43; phallocentrism of, 42–49; political aesthetic of his rule, 5, 42; possible replacements for, 141–42; precarity and rise of, 33–35; public support for, 125–30, 132–33; sexual abuse story, 49–54; sense of time, 60; as sovereign trickster, 63–65, 78–84; Trump and, 6, 65, 84–86
Duterte, Sarah, 15–16, 54, 141
Duterte, Sebastian, 15–16
Duterte, Soledad, 1–2, 22, 54
Duterte, Vicente, 15–16
Dutertismo, 4

East Asia Co-Prosperity Sphere, 18
economics, necropolitics and, 71–75
elections: colonialism and, 7–9, 16–17; as counterinsurgency measure, 9–12; under US rule, 90
elites: elections as tool of, 7–14; overthrow of

Marcos and, 21–23; protection from violence of, 74–75
emasculation, Duterte's discussion of, 43
Evangelista, Patricia, 120
extrajudicial killings: continuation of, 131–33; Duterte's justification of, 6, 16–17, 34–35, 55–56, 66–71, 103, 138–42; financialization of, 73–75; history of, 89–93; moral calculus of, 139; necropolitics of, 25–26; Operation Tokhang and, 71–75; photographic evidence of, 105–30; public support for, 125–27, 133–35; statistics on, 98; in United States, 87–88

fecal politics, Duterte's use of, 98–102
Feldman, Allen, 102
Filipino-American War, 77
Filipino Revolutionary Government, 8–9
Film Center (Philippines), 23
First Philippine Assembly, 90
First Republic (Philippines), 9
Folk Arts Center (Philippines), 23
force, dictators' use of, 19–20
Foucault, Michel, 27–28, 63–65, 70–71; on depredation and dissipation, 79; on punishment, 71–75; on war, 76–78
franchise expansion, in Philippines, 10–12
fraternity culture, Duterte and influence of, 77–78, 149n6
Freud, Sigmund, 52, 101

Gabuco, Carlo, 107
gentrification, reorganization of space and, 28–29
gerontocracy, in Philippines, 138–42
Gini coefficient, Philippines income inequality and, 26
Go, Vincent, 120

Hamill, Jacqueline, 43–44
Hapal, Karl, 75, 134, 136–38
Hart, Donn and Harriet, 80–81
Hau, Caroline, 21–23
hierarchy, intimacy and, 138–42
history, Duterte's sense of, 60–62
housing development, neoliberal colonization and, 29–35

Huks paramilitary group, 90–91
human capital, reproductive health and, 38–41
humanitarianism (banyanihan), 144–45
human rights, Duterte and, 57–59
humor, Duterte's use of, 51–54, 78–84
hypermasculine culture, Duterte and influence of, 77–78

imagined communities, Anderson's concept of, 135–36
income inequality, increase in Philippines of, 26
inequality, intimacy and, 138–42
international relations, Duterte's dismissal of, 24
intimacy, and impunity, 138–41; 144; spatiality and creation of, 136–42; tyranny of, 3, 42, 53
Izquierdo, Rafael, 95

Jabidah Massacre, 13–14
Jensen, Steffen, 75, 122–23, 134, 136–38
joke-telling: Duterte's use of, 51–54, 78–79, 148n1; extrajudicial killings and, 66–71
José Fabella Memorial Hospital, 36

Kafka, Franz, 143
Kusaka, Wataru, 30–31

Lacaba, Pete, 99–101
land reform programs, 26–27
Landsdale, Edward, 11
Laurel, Jose P., 18
legal system, extrajudicial killings and politicization of, 74–75
Lerma, Raffy, 111–16, 125–27
liberal democracies, elections and, 7–9
lists, political power of, 96–98, 122–27
local government units, extrajudicial killings and, 72–75
Lucero, Tony, and Native American trickster, 149n10

Magsaysay, Ramon, 11
Makati Business Club, 103
Manne, Kate, 45

Maoist Communist Party, 13

Marcos, Ferdinand: colonial system and, 23–24; dictatorship of, 1, 12–15, 21–26; Duterte and, 22–23, 83, 98–102; imprisonment of enemies by, 98–99; martial law under, 90–91; neoliberalism under, 31; ouster of, 77

Marcos, Ferdinand (Bongbong), Jr., 22, 141

Marcos, Imelda, 23–25

marketplace ideology, 27–28

martial law: under Duterte, 25–26; global prevalence of, 18–20; Marcos's imposition of, 12–15

Marx, Karl, 76–77

maternal mortality (Philippines), 147n1

matrix of conspiracies, Duterte's use of, 94–97

Mbembe, Achille, 3, 42, 63–65, 80, 82–83

Mendoza, Brilliante, 34

military, Marcos and fracturing of, 14–15

misogyny, of Duterte, 45–49, 51–56, 78–79

Misuari, Nur, 13

moral education, as supplement to neoliberalism, 28–32; and disciplinary practices, 37

Moreno, Isko, 141

Moro National Liberation Front (MNLF), 13

Morrison, Toni, 86

Motherland (documentary), 36–41

mourning, photography as work of, 114–20

Muslim separatist movement (Philippines), 13–14

nanlaban (resisted), 122, 134–35

National Democratic Front, 13

National Household Targeting System for Poverty Reduction, 30

national security state, 94–97; prisons and, 100–102

National Task Force to End Local Communist Armed Conflict (NTF-ELCAC), 145

necropolitics: biopolitics and, 56; Duterte's use of, 16–17, 25–26, 34–35, 64–65; neoliberal citizenship and, 31–35; photographic evidence of, 106; public torture and, 71–75; reproductive health and, 36–41

necropolitics/necropower, barbarian freedom and, 66–71

neoliberalism: biopolitics and, 27–35; reproductive health and, 39–41

New People's Army (NPA), 13, 15, 77–78, 145

Nietzsche, Friedrich, and pessimism of strength, 143, 150n1

Non, Ana Patricia, 144

Obama, Barack, Duterte and, 6

Olayres, Jennilyn, 114–16

Operation Double Barrel, 68–71

Operation *Tokhang*, 71–75, 94–97

Opus Dei, 47

Pacquiao, Manny, 141

pakikisama (getting along), Filipino concept of, 137–42

Pala, Jun, 58

Pantatawid Pamilya Pilipino Program (4Ps), 27, 29–30

paramilitary forces: colonialism and, 10–12; death squads as, 89–93; Marcos use of, 12; public funding of, 16–17

pastoral care, reproductive health and, 37–41

patriarchy: intimacy and, 138–42; reproductive health and, 37–41

People Power uprising, 12–13, 14–16, 21–23, 76–78, 91–93

phallocentrism, of Duterte, 42–49

Phil Health, 36

Philippine Charity Sweepstake Office, 36

Philippine Constabulary, 90

Philippine Daily Inquirer, 98

Philippines: colonialism and elections in, 7–9; as counterinsurgent state, 69–71

Philippine Scouts, 10, 90

photography: as advocacy, 121–27; documentation of death and, 109–20; as mourning, 114–20; trauma and, 107–8; as witness to war on drugs, 105–30

La Pietà (Michelangelo), Duterte's association with, 114–18

Plaridel listserve, 99

police, and extrajudicial killings and vigilante squads, 32, 72–74, 87, 91, 122, 134, 139

policing as counterinsurgency, 142

politics of anxiety, 33, 40–41; drug lists as intimidation and, 74–75

poverty alleviation programs, 26–35

prisons, modern state and rise of, 99–102

protracted people's war (PPW), 13
pusong (trickster), Duterte as, 80–84
Putin, Vladimir, Duterte and, 6

Quezon, Manuel L., 18, 83

racialization: extrajudicial killings and, 87–88;
  neoliberal citizenship and, 31–35
Ramos, Fidel V., 1, 27, 91
rape, Duterte's jokes about, 43–49
Rappler online newspaper, 94, 98
Reformed Armed Forces Movement (RAM),
  14, 91
religion, reproductive health and, 37–41
reproductive health, necropolitics and, 36–41
Ressa, Maria, 54
revenge: dreams of, 127–30; justice as, 58–59
Rizal, José, 28, 116
Robredo, Leni, 141
Rodriguez, Maria Cristina, 99–101

Salman, Michael, 100
Schopenhauer, Arthur, 150n1
sexism, authoritarianism and, 45
shabu (crystal meth), Duterte's obsession with,
  67–71
Shahani, Leticia Ramos, 1–3
Shahani, Lila Ramos, 1
Siaron, Michael, 114–16
Siegel, James T., 112–13
Simmel, Georg, 112–13
Sison, Jose Maria, 13
Smith, Shawn Michelle, 106
Social Weather Station, 26
Society Must Be Defended (Foucault), 70–71
South China Sea (also West Philippine Sea),
  17, 132
sovereignty: Duterte's assertion of, 78–84;
  necropower and, 66–71; war on drugs as
  expression of, 109–11
Spanish colonialism, Philippines and, 7–9
spatiality, community of intimacy and, 136–42
spirit returns, 127–29
Stalinist Communist Party (Philippines), 12
sublime, death and, 150n2
surveillance, extrajudicial killings and, 72–75

tambay (vagrant), 81
Tapang at Malasakit (Courage and Compassion), 34, 61–62
Tatad, Kit, 47–49
Tawatao, Dondi, 107
trauma: dissociation and, 124–27; photography and, 107–8
trickster: Duterte as, 63–65, 78–84, 143; Native American tradition of, 149n10; Trump as, 84–86
Trump, Donald, 6, 65, 84–86

United Nations, Duterte's defiance of, 57–59
United States: Duterte's dismissal of, 6, 24;
  extrajudicial killings in, 87–88; invasion of
  Philippines by, 9, 89–90
urban space, neoliberal colonization of, 28–29

values formation classes, 30, 39
Vice Ganda, 79
Vice News, 109
violence: under Aquino, 14–15; Duterte's justification for, 138–42; elections and, 7–9,
  16–17; electoral counterinsurgency and,
  11–12; in Philippine elections, 12–15; photojournalism and, 107–8; as political intimidation, 75
vote buying, in Philippines, 11–12
voting rights, Philippine expansion of, 10–12

Warburg, Anna Braemer, 75, 122–23, 134–35, 136
war on drugs: as civil war, 76–78; Duterte's
  extrajudicial killings and, 6, 15–16, 139–40;
  financialization of, 73–75; images of corpses
  in, 109–20; necropower and, 66–71; neoliberalism and, 33–34; Operation *Tokhang*
  and, 71–75; photography as witness to, 105–30
weakness of opposition, 141–42
women: cash transfers to, 27, 29–30; Duterte
  and, 51–56; reproductive health and, 36–41;
  voting rights for, 10–12
World Bank, 30
World War II, Philippine guerrilla resistance
  during, 90–91

Xi Jinping, Duterte and, 6, 24–25